YOUR TODDLER
MONTH BY MONTH

YOUR
TODDLER
MONTH BY MONTH

EDITOR-IN-CHIEF
DR. TANYA BYRON BSc, MSc, PsychD
CONSULTANT CLINICAL PSYCHOLOGIST

London, New York, Munich,
Melbourne, Delhi

Editor-in-Chief Dr Tanya Byron
Text The Doris Partnership
Consultants Dr Sarah Gregory and Sarah Sutton

Senior Art Editor Helen Spencer
Senior Editor Laura Nickoll
Executive Managing Editor Adèle Hayward
Production Editor Luca Frassinetti
C.T.S. Sonia Charbonnier
Art Director Peter Luff
Publishing Director Stephanie Jackson

Produced for DK by
Emma Forge, Dawn Bates, and Corinne Roberts

Photography by Vanessa Davies
Jacket Design by Helen Spencer

First published in Great Britain in 2008
by Dorling Kindersley Limited,
80 Strand, London WC2R 0RL
A Penguin Company

2 4 6 8 10 9 7 5 3 1

A CIP catalogue record for this book is
available from the British Library.
ISBN: 978-1-4053-2211-9
Reproduced in Colourscan, Singapore
Printed and bound in Singapore by Star Standard

Discover more at
www.dk.com

Dedicated to my best friend,
Samantha Berlevy, and to her
boys, Toby and Jonnie, and to
my children, Lily and Jack.

Contents

Family life

Your independent child

3–4 years

"Enjoy the toddler years; they are a unique and precious time of bonding and discovery for both parent and child that paves the way for later childhood."

Introduction

I am in the privileged position of being both a clinical psychologist and a parent, with over 18 years experience of working with families, teenagers, and young children, and 13 years experience of being a mother. That means that, while I have every confidence in my clinical and professional ability, I can also tell you that I fully understand the insecurities, fears, hopes, and huge joys that come with parenting – as well as the endless self-questioning:

- "Is that normal behaviour?"
- "Why won't my child eat/sleep?"
- "Should I worry that my child isn't crawling/walking/talking?"
- "What should I do when my child misbehaves?"
- "Is my baby developing as he should?"
- "Will my toddler suffer if I return to work?"
- "Am I doing something wrong?"

For many parents, anxiety is never greater than during their child's transition from being a dependent baby to an energetic toddler. It is a time of enormous and rapid change for both parent and child. Your child's brain will develop faster between the ages of one and four than at any other time in his life. He will learn a wider variety of new skills than any adult – or the most willing student; and the next time his body grows and changes so quickly will be during adolescence. Although very much dependent on you, your child will start to develop a personality of his own during these years and will begin to show characteristics that will remain constant for the rest of his life. It is a time of joy, laughter, challenges, and sometimes, total exhaustion, for all of you.

DR TANYA BYRON –
consultant clinical psychologist and a mother of two.

A book for every parent

The purpose of this book is to equip parents and carers with the knowledge they need to understand what kinds of behaviour are healthy and appropriate for children at each age and stage of toddlerhood. It is not about creating the perfect child, but about celebrating his uniqueness. It focuses on child-centred parenting and puts the trust in your own abilities; enabling you and your child to be comfortable and happy with who you are.

The parents whose stories are included in this book (see Real Life boxes throughout) are people like you. They come from all walks of life. They range from parents who have one child to those who have many; they include sole parents and carers, those who are divorced and separated, long-married couples, and those who co-habit. There are families who are financially secure and those who face social and financial challenges; there are those who had no trouble conceiving, and those who turned to assisted reproduction or adoption. Our background and experiences shape who we are, and our experiences influence our parenting choices and style; but whatever the shape of a family, the needs of a young child remain the same. **All children need the following, consistently:**

■ To trust that they have comfort, food, and shelter.
■ To be given clear guidance and boundaries.
■ To know that they are loved and safe.
■ To understand that they are valued equally as a member of the family.

"Face your child's toddler years with positive enthusiasm and you both will have the time of your life!"

Helping you to be a parent

You may find the reality of juggling life and relationships with the responsibility of parenting is not always plain sailing; it can be fraught with emotional ups and downs. Memories of a less than happy childhood, tensions within adult relationships, and holding on to an ideal view of what parenthood "should" be, can all affect your relationship with your children. The plethora of well-meant advice and ever-changing insights from the media, medics, psychologists, and so-called childcare experts, only adds to the confusion.

No-one can take the guilt out of parenting. It may sometimes feel as if the two go hand in hand from the moment of birth. The aim of *Your Toddler Month by Month* is to encourage you to trust yourself to go with the flow and to provide you with enough knowledge and understanding of child development to increase your self-confidence and your level of enjoyment, which will help you care for your child more effectively. This book will help you to assess your own expectations of yourself as a parent and to understand and be conscious of your parenting style. It is designed to encourage you to feel confident about your parenting style and the choices you make.

It will give you an understanding of:

■ Your child's mind – how his brain learns and develops, according to his environment.

■ How he develops his emotional responses – and how they differ from an adult's.

■ Appropriate behaviour and the need for boundaries (yours and your child's) at every age and stage of development.

■ Your child's development milestones: physical, intellectual, emotional, social, sensory, and language skills – and how you can encourage healthy development.

■ The theories of child development that inform our modern-day understanding of childhood and of growing up.

■ The warning signs – to learn the difference between "normal" behaviour and when professional assistance may be needed.

■ Your role in your child's life – the importance of love and security and how early experiences influence the development of self-esteem.

The overall aim of this book is to encourage more child-centred parenting. That is not to say you should always give in to your child's needs. As well as feeling loved and nurtured he needs to be helped to learn to manage his emotions, to learn socially appropriate behaviour, and to grow into a responsible, assertive, and caring adult. In today's world it can feel like a tough job on occasion.

THE PASSING YEARS *The toddler years will fly by so try to cherish every moment. There will be challenges but also many, many rewards.*

Each child is unique

Conscious parenting and remaining aware of the individual needs and dreams of each of the children in your care is a rewarding challenge that will shape their life. Your child represents the future: his and yours – but mostly his. All children are unique, and whatever their genetic make-up and inherited family situation, their life belongs ultimately to them. The early years of parenting are an extraordinary rollercoaster and will zoom by all too fast. This book will answer all of your questions about the development stages that your child will pass through during the first four years – helping you to relax enough to enjoy the ride.

How the book works

The toddler years extend from approximately one to four years of age. Some children will develop faster than others, but most will have passed the same range of milestones by their fourth birthday. If you have a toddler, and perhaps more than one child, you may have a range of questions, but very little time to sit down and read! As a result, *Your Toddler Month by Month* has been written and designed to answer the questions that are relevant to your toddler at the stage he is at right now.

How the book is organized:

■ Chapter 1, *You and Your Child*, encourages you to explore your feelings about parenthood, your personal history, and your hopes and expectations for yourself and your child in the future.

■ Chapters 2–5 take a closer look at the developmental milestones and stages that each toddler will pass through in the first four years. Each chapter begins with an overview of the skills that your child is likely to develop and explains the physical, emotional, language, and learning milestones that your child will pass through during the months ahead. Many parents worry about "non problems" that are a challenging but natural part of toddler growth. Pages 64–65 provide an overview of common concerns, but my main aim has been to put your fears into the context of what is the normal range of development. Other features include explanations of brain development, learning, and play in each age range and a section for parents on managing emotions, creating a support network, and how to keep any concerns in perspective. Each chapter ends with a summary of the key points and strategies that are a useful ready-reference for day-to-day parenting.

■ Chapter 6, *Family Life*, covers general lifestyle issues, with guidance on helping children to adjust to transitions, such as separation and divorce, how to handle special needs and how to manage difficult behaviour. Whether you want to browse through the book from beginning to end,

DEVELOPMENT *Discover more about milestones, such as your toddler taking her first steps.*

or head straight for guidance on the latest toddler challenge, you will be able to find the information you need quickly and easily.

A range of approaches

Childcare "experts" have been around since the dawn of time. The development gurus of the past such as Maria Montessori and Benjamin Spock, and others, are variously in and out of fashion, but nevertheless their theories are likely to have had an impact on our lives and our upbringing at some point – either in the form of a parent's childcare manual, via a GP's approach to childcare, or through the education system. Throughout the book, the major theories are summarized and put into context, to help you to make up your own mind about the approach you most favour when making childcare and education choices.

At the end of the day, however, the most important person in your child's life is you. As a clinical psychologist and a parent, my ideas and beliefs are both scientifically based and synonymous with my own cultural background and training. Some of the ideas in the book may fit with your own ideas about parenting; others may not. The important thing is to find what sits with your own beliefs and what works for you and your child.

Every child, whatever his background, deserves to be comfortable in the knowledge that he is loved, fed, safe, and cared for; that the adults who look after him are warm and consistent in their care; and that his parents are approachable and available when he needs them – even if they can't be with him all the time.

We all want to be the best parent we can, but there is no need to aspire to being a "perfect" parent. There is no such person. This book aims to provide you with the essential information you will need to have a better understanding of your toddler, to empower you to make parenting choices that are right for your own unique situation. I hope it will help you to relax and enjoy your journey of discovery with the little person who fascinates you the most and who you couldn't live without.

YOU AND
YOUR CHILD

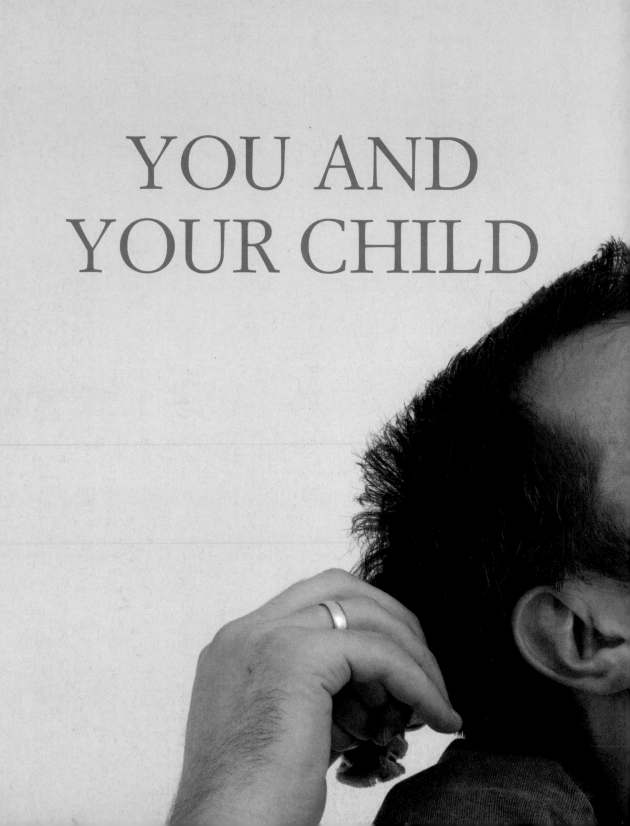

Being a parent

Your baby's first birthday will be a major milestone for all of you. Just when you think you have your routine worked out, and know what to expect, your rapidly developing baby may start to resist your attentions and show every sign of developing an independent mind. Welcome to the toddler years!

The first twelve months of parenting are always memorable and during this time you will have developed beliefs about yourself as a parent and about your baby's personality, likes, and dislikes. If you had an easy time in the first year, you may find the toddler years a bit of a shock as your baby transforms into an independent soul. If you had a more challenging time – coping with night-time waking, feeding problems, postnatal depression or other issues – you may be relieved by the new phase.

Reflecting on your experiences

Your young baby will have been completely, totally, and utterly dependent upon you for her every need and this may at times have felt overwhelming and frightening, as well as enjoyable. How you responded to this challenge, and your overall experience of the first year of parenting, will inevitably impact on your relationship and parenting style.

"It's been perfect. We are so lucky. Amy sleeps through the night and is happy to be left with my parents during the day. The last twelve months couldn't have been easier." For some fortunate parents the first year is quite calm and trouble-free. However, if your baby slept through the night and you had no significant problems, be prepared for change. It is completely normal for a "good" baby to start to become less compliant as she develops; this change shouldn't be mistaken for "bad" behaviour.

"It has been a mixture of joys and challenges, but on the whole the first year has gone well and we still find time for ourselves." If you managed to get through the tough times, and have achieved a balance between making your baby a priority and having a life yourself, this will stand you in good stead for the ups and downs that you will face in the toddler years.

"The first year was a challenge, but then my baby began to develop a real personality, and it made all that hard work worthwhile."

Caroline, aged 28

"Our daughter Lucy is the centre of our world. I know we are spoiling her, but she is only a baby." It is natural to want to spoil your newborn baby, especially if she is your first child. However, getting into a habit of being very permissive, and prioritizing your child ahead of everything else can set up problems for later years. As your baby develops into toddlerhood she will need to be given clear boundaries so that she learns how to behave and stay safe, and so that you maintain control.

There is also a danger that in becoming totally focused on your child, your sense of fulfilment may come solely from her achievements. It is important to make time for your own interests to avoid putting undue pressure on your child to fulfil all your needs and expectations. Inevitably both parent and child will suffer feelings of failure and disappointment if, at a later stage, things don't turn out as planned.

"Parents, like children, will improve their skills by learning from their mistakes. Remember that love and affection are more powerful than perfection."

"I have felt quite depressed and isolated. I can't help feeling that everyone is judging me and that other people's babies are developing faster than mine." Most parents tend to worry about what people think and will to some extent try to present an ideal picture to the outside world. In reality, no child is perfect and all parents have worries and challenges. If you feel isolated and have no-one to confide in, there is a danger that life will become a real challenge once your baby becomes a toddler and is on the move. Your mood can impact on how you bond with your baby and so social support and professional support are vital if you are feeling low (see pages 310–311). Planning and building a support network are essential to help you care for your child through the toddler years.

"We have been amazed at how fast our baby has developed. He is chatting away and can nearly walk. We want to encourage his development to give him the best chance in life." Wanting to encourage and nurture your child's development is a good thing. There is, however, a difference between nurturing and pushing. Children develop at their own rate and pressure is unhelpful. Encouragement, however, is good.

How was your first year of parenting?

The following questions will give you a starting point from which to consider the effect that your baby's first year has had on you, and how your experiences may affect your relationship with her. The answers will give you a chance to consider how you feel about yourself as a parent, how you view your baby, and how you want to approach the next stage of parenting.

Postnatal recovery Your experience of childbirth will have a direct effect on your early relationship with your child.

■ What kind of delivery did you have?

■ Were there any complications, such as a premature birth, or illness?

■ How long did it take you to recover from the birth?

■ How did you feel in the early weeks and months of parenthood?

■ Did you bond with your baby during the first three months or so?

Caring In the first year, parents (especially mothers) are intimately involved in the care of their baby. Personal "success" or otherwise, at each stage, will impact on the way you feel about yourself as a parent.

■ What were your experiences of breastfeeding? For example, did you enjoy it or find it difficult? Was it painful and problematic?

■ What were your experiences of bottle-feeding? Did you find it easy? Or was it tinged with guilt because you weren't breastfeeding?

■ Have you begun the process of weaning off the breast or bottle?

■ Was it difficult to get your baby to settle, or stop crying?

■ How were her early sleeping habits? Did she sleep through the night?

Development Interacting and playing with young children at their pace and at their level is the best way to promote development. Avoid treating them as miniature adults. It is through play and exploration that children develop their inquisitive nature and enjoy learning and developing new skills.

■ How much time do you spend playing with your baby and having fun?

■ What kinds of responses have you had from her?

■ Do you compare your baby with other babies?

■ Do you socialize with parents who have babies of the same age?

■ Do you communicate regularly with your child in baby language, or with adult words – or use both?

■ Do you find you are labelling your baby in a way that could influence your parenting style – for example, as "difficult" or "perfect"?

HOW SHE LEARNS
Watching your baby discover her world is one of the most fulfilling aspects of parenting, but let her develop new skills at her own pace.

Relationships The quality and style of your relationships with other key adults in your baby's life will affect your parenting style. Think about the basis for your relationships and whether they are, for example, co-operative, confrontational, passionate, compliant, or controlling.

■ How do you relate to your partner or significant others in your life?

■ What is your relationship like with other children in the family?

■ Do you enjoy your relationship with your parents and in-laws?

■ Are there any other significant people who are influencing or impacting on your baby's life? How do you feel about your relationship with them?

Work Most parents have concerns about combining work and parenthood. Financial pressures are such that few people have a choice, and at some point will be trying to juggle two very different parts of life.

■ Were you primarily at home or at work during your baby's first year?

■ How do you feel about the balance between your work and home life?

■ How do you feel about your choices for the year ahead?

In each situation, consider how your feelings have affected your relationship with your baby and your feelings about yourself as a parent. Is there anything you would like to change? What has struck a particular chord with you, and what might you like to approach differently in the future?

"I expected to be a natural earth-mother type. What a shock to find I was so nervous and worried about being a parent. The first few months were a real challenge and it took a while to bond with Zak." Aisha, aged 36

Your hopes

There are as many personal reasons for having children as there are for not having children. For some parents, children represent the hopes, dreams, and ideals that are unmet in their own life; they represent the chance to "put right the wrongs" of the past; for others, having a child is the natural evolution of a partnership or marriage and the desire for a family; for some, a child is an unexpected outcome of a relationship or liaison that was never going to be long-term; for others, it is a deep and powerful biological instinct. If you have been brought up as part of a large family, you may

FROM BABY TO TODDLER *You'll have been counting the days for her to take her first steps. Then, before you know it, she'll be walking, running, jumping, and climbing – and your main challenge will be to keep up with her.*

THE REWARDS *Being a parent may bring out a whole new side of you. Through your children you can rediscover a sense of fun and find new ways to relax.*

hope for the same environment for your own children, or you may see value in being an only child. Whatever the motive for becoming a parent, the vision of what it means will be influenced by your own past.

Ask yourself, honestly – what are your expectations of your child? Are you anticipating that she will be just like you? Have you already begun to look for signs of super-intelligence or natural ability? Are you imagining that your daughter might become a rock star or a brain surgeon? Your son a teacher or a top athlete? These impulses are natural, and part of the fun of watching your child develop, but learning to manage your own expectations from an early stage is very important.

Nature and nurture

Your child's development is a healthy mix of nature (the result of her genes) and nurture (your influence and her life experiences). She will eventually grow up to be uniquely herself, for better or worse. The more children you have, the greater the scope for variation and unpredictability. Each child is an individual and will develop in a way that is uniquely different from her brothers, sisters, cousins, and friends – and you.

What's your story?

Raising a child may prompt deep-seated memories of your own childhood. This meeting of past and present is completely natural and inevitable, but may mean that your child's behaviour becomes affected by something that is going on in your life rather than hers. Likewise, if you and your partner are experiencing relationship difficulties, these may sometimes be reflected in your child's behaviour. When a child has behavioural problems a clinical psychologist will begin by asking the parents about their relationship, their past, and their own experiences of being parented. The clearer you can be about the impact that your past may be having on you or your relationship, the more aware you will be when something that occurs in your child's life is actually more about you, rather than her.

Consider for a moment:

■ Was your childhood happy, sad, loving, playful, strict, liberal?

■ Would you say you were/are close to your parents?

■ Were there any traumatic events in your past such as parental separation or divorce, continual rows, bullying, accidents or illness, bereavement?

■ What was your experience of your child's birth? Were you separated from your child for longer than a few hours?

■ Have you ever lost a child or seen her suffer serious illness?

■ How do you view your relationship with your child's mother or father? Is your relationship secure, loving, passionate, full of conflict, finished?

■ What are your expectations of yourself as a parent and of your future relationship with your child and with your partner?

This is not an exhaustive list of questions, but by considering your answers you can learn how your life and experiences have had a lasting impact and will influence the way you feel about yourself as a parent, and the way in which you nurture your child.

Parents' expectations

Having appropriate expectations is an important aspect of being a contented parent. Expecting too much from your toddler at too young an age, can cause frustration and disappointment.

By what age would you expect your child to...

1. Use her first word.
2. Walk without assistance.
3. Wave goodbye without being asked to do so.
4. Look at where you point to, instead of at your finger.
5. Ask for something by pointing at it.
6. Stop putting objects into her mouth to explore them.
7. Echo your words and phrases back to you.

8. Put two words together in a meaningful way.
9. Draw a circle by copying you.
10. Show concern, and try to comfort a child who is crying.
11. Begin to "pretend play", such as "Mums and Dads" and cooking tea.
12. Be toilet trained during the day.
13. Be dry and clean during the night.
14. Be aware of differences between boys and girls.
15. Pedal a tricycle independently.
16. Learn to count to 10.
17. Understand the concept of time – for example, the difference between today and tomorrow.
18. Start to understand that you or someone else has a different point of view to her own.
19. Understand sharing.

20. Enjoy simple jokes.
21. Dress and undress unassisted.
22. Recognize her own name and try to write it down.
23. Be able to use a child-sized knife and fork.

ANSWERS *(Note: these are not a precise guide.) 1. 10–15mths, 2. 10–18mths (50 per cent by 13mths), 3. 10–12mths, 4. 12–18mths, 5. 12–18mths, 6. 15–18mths, 7. 15–24mths, 8. 18–24mths, 9. 2–3yrs, 10. 2–3yrs, 11. 2–3½yrs, 12. 2–3yrs, 13. 2–5yrs (Note the wide age variation here. A child should not be pushed too early. See page 128.) 14. 3–4yrs, 15. 3–3½yrs, 16. 3–4yrs, 17. 3–4yrs, 18. 2½–3½yrs, 19. 2½–3½yrs, 20. 3½–4½yrs, 21. 4–5yrs, 22. 5yrs, 23. 4½–5yrs.*

Your premature baby

If your baby was born prematurely, she may have spent time in a neonatal intensive care unit. Such a challenging start is bound to impact upon the early years of parenting, but it is important to try to come to terms with and handle your feelings.

Your baby was born early, so she will reach her first birthday at a slightly earlier stage of development than babies who were born at 40 weeks. For example, if she was born six weeks prematurely, she will be only 10½ months in development terms on the day you light that first birthday candle. A week can be a very long time in toddler terms and it can be helpful to remember to subtract those early birth weeks from estimated ages and stages of development, and to focus instead on enjoying and celebrating each of your child's small achievements.

Your child's developmental milestones will be the same as other children's, although they may occur at a slightly later calendar date. And the good news is that most children who are born prematurely will have "caught up" by the time they are 2–3 years old and will benefit from your encouragement to enjoy toddlerhood to the full.

NATURAL ANXIETIES

It is normal to feel anxious if your baby was born prematurely. You will have probably dealt with a whole range of challenges during the first twelve months: you may have been unable to breastfeed, and may not have been free to hold or touch your baby as you would have liked; she may have had breathing difficulties or been ill. Even though you have been told that she will "catch up", you may wonder whether she will lead a "normal" life.

During the early months you will have had to handle a whole range of difficult emotions: feeling robbed of a natural birth and precious time with your newborn; constant worries about your baby's health; and fears of loss and death.

REAL LIFE

My daughter Rachel was just 1.7kg when she was born prematurely. The first year of Rachel's life was full of mixed feelings and anxiety. Every time she cried or refused the bottle I worried that she was about to die. I was paranoid about cleanliness and warmth and found it really hard to accept that she was genuinely well and healthy. I was so terrified of losing her that I found it hard to let myself love her or show affection in case she was snatched away. Looking back, I feel as if I lost the first 12 months of her life, which makes me feel very sad and all the more determined to make up for lost time. Now, at almost two years old, Rachel is showing immense strength of character and determination. She definitely rules the household – and we feel so grateful to have her, although because of my experience I am still quite fearful of having another child.

"I can reassure you that most premature babies catch up on their development during the toddler years."

TALK ABOUT YOUR FEARS

Your thoughts and feelings about the past will influence your current feelings and actions towards your toddler, and will therefore affect the way she relates to you. It is normal to feel so grateful that your child has survived that you feel unable to reprimand or manage her behaviour as she grows older.

It can be helpful to talk about your experiences, so that you are conscious of how they are influencing the present day. Keeping in contact with other parents of premature babies can be helpful, as they will be encountering similar issues. Specialist guidance will be available from your GP or health visitor or you can consult a specialist organization (see pages 310–311).

BONDING

Some parents will find that the impact of seeing their baby so small and vulnerable during the first weeks of life will make them cautious about holding or touching their baby, even when she is older and stronger. This in turn may mean that your baby does not become used to being touched or held.

Physical closeness and cuddling are very important elements in a baby's development, and a lovely way to help reduce her anxiety, making her feel safe and nurtured. If cuddles have been absent up until now, begin to give your toddler hugs and gentle massage – but take it slowly. Every baby has different needs – she will soon show you what she enjoys and what she doesn't, so follow her lead.

AS YOUR CHILD GROWS

Health concerns may have dominated the first twelve months, but now your toddler is getting older and stronger you can start to let her play and explore. Focusing on enjoying silliness and playtime, instead of on health issues, can help reduce anxiety, too.

Try to remind yourself that even though your toddler may seem vulnerable and smaller than average during her early years, she will need

LETTING GO Try not to let anxiety connected with the past curtail your child's enjoyment of life. Keep safety in mind, but remember that toddlers will only learn through exploration.

the same clear and loving behaviour boundaries, and eating and sleeping routines, that apply to all children. This period of transition may be a challenge for you and your toddler. Other parents will help you to gain perspective concerning "normal" progress and problems.

Only 15 per cent of mothers who have a premature baby are likely to have another baby prematurely.

Your parenting style

You will want to give your children the best direction and care, but at some point you are likely to slip into a style of parenting that is convenient and instinctive, rather than developed consciously. How do you find a way of parenting that works for you and your family, and what should you avoid?

"Parenting is about finding what works best for you and your child. There is no such thing as a 'one size fits all' approach."

Your parenting style will develop from: your personal beliefs of what a good parent should be; from your own experiences of being parented; from your instinctive understanding of your child; and from personal results (that is, whether your approach works or not). As children develop, many parents become critical, and look at their children's "problems" as a marker of lack of competence, rather than as a part of the process of growing up. Mistakes and challenges are an important aspect of learning and developing competence – for children as well as parents.

All parents of all children will encounter parenting challenges. If you can be realistic about the ups and downs of raising children and realize that you cannot get everything right all of the time, you are more likely to be able to cope realistically with the challenges. The important thing is to learn what works and what doesn't for you and your child – so that she

The basic rules of parenting

There are five basic rules of parenting that should be applied whenever possible, especially when you are feeling exasperated and the least likely to want to follow them:
▶ Love your child unconditionally – love her for who she is, no matter what she does.

▶ Remember every child is unique – so avoid comparing your child with another and don't label her (see page 43).
▶ Cuddle and praise her whenever possible – you don't need to wait for a reason to be affectionate to your child.

▶ Respect her feelings at all times – treat your child as you would wish to be treated yourself.
▶ Follow the basic rules of behaviour management (see page 88) – being clear and consistent in your parenting is one of the greatest gifts you can give to your child.

feels loved, happy, and secure. If you set yourself up as a "perfect parent" you are likely to feel disappointed or that you are a failure – and your child may come to feel that she has let you down in some way.

What the psychologists say

Psychologists tend to look at two main aspects of care when looking at parenting styles: the *level of control* that parents exert, and the *degree of warmth* they show towards their children. A healthy combination of warmth and control results in assertive, or authoritative, parenting that will give your toddler clear and consistent boundaries. Guidelines need to be balanced with love and warmth so that your little one does not feel personally isolated or rejected by you, even when being disciplined.

Four styles of parenting

A = Authoritarian (high control/low warmth) *"I'm totally against all this liberal parenting nonsense. Children need to learn how to behave. A clip round the ear never did me any harm."* Parents who have an authoritarian approach to parenting tend to think that keeping children under control is the top priority and that showing them warmth when they have misbehaved is a weakness. The quote above shows an obviously unacceptable and extreme example of this attitude. Using physical punishment can set up a negative cycle between parent and child and lead to the child growing up to think that violence is an acceptable way to solve problems. Imagine how you would feel if your boss hit you every time you were late for a meeting!

Authoritarian parents will tend to tell children what to do and how to do it, without allowing the child much room for trial and error. They may give severe punishments and have expectations of their child's behaviour that are inappropriate for their child's developmental age and stage. It can be a hard pattern to break without help or guidance. At the heart of this style of parenting may be a deep-rooted anxiety based on a fear that the child may not behave, or what may happen if the parent does not retain control at all times.

If this sounds like you, both you and your child will benefit from more playtime and cuddles. Your child needs to feel secure and to know that she is loved. Research suggests that there are no advantages to

BEING REALISTIC *There are many different ways of parenting, and it is important to remember that perfect parents and perfect children simply do not exist.*

THE RIGHT BALANCE
Being authoritative is a positive trait in a parent, and, as long as it's coupled with love and warmth, your child will feel secure and know what is expected of him.

experiencing a persistently authoritarian upbringing. A lack of parental warmth can lead to a sense of being unloved. In the long term, this may lead to a person having problems with aggression, withdrawal, internalized distress, and low self-esteem.

B = Authoritative (high control/high warmth)
"We have tried to put in place behaviour guidelines and a daily routine. It doesn't always work, but when it does, it helps life run more smoothly – and everyone in our household knows what is expected." Authoritative parents are keen to keep control in their household, and tend to partner behaviour guidelines with a high level of warmth for their children. Clear rules and expectations help young children to feel safe, as they enjoy routine and knowing what to expect. Parents who are comfortable giving their children clear guidelines and showing affection will often adapt their response according to the level of need or distress of their child. These parents often show more awareness of what kinds of behaviour are appropriate for the age and stage of the child than those who fall in the other categories.

High control partnered with high warmth is the ideal combination for parents to adopt. A big challenge for all parents is maintaining a consistent approach when under pressure. The more you can achieve this, the greater will be the rewards for both you and your children. In the long term, research has shown that children of parents who use an authoritative approach tend to have fewer behavioural problems and are better able to make friends and enjoy academic success.

"The use of physical punishment should be avoided for all children and is never acceptable at any age. Smacking or using any form of punishment that leaves a mark is against the law in several countries."

C = Neglectful (low control/low warmth) *"The kids never seem to listen to me anyway so I have given up trying and leave them to sort themselves out."* A low level of parental warmth combined with few or no behaviour guidelines (low control) is hard for children because it implies that the parent has no expectations of them, as well as a lack of interest in their development. This style usually develops if the parents themselves have been severely neglected, or if a severe trauma or period of separation interferes with the forming of an early bond between parent and baby. Neglectful parents are usually depressed. Children who have been neglected in terms of both their emotional welfare and behaviour boundaries are vulnerable to developing

What's your parenting style?

Imagine the scenario You have had a stressful day and are home alone with the children. You have a terrible headache following a very tough day full of irritations and challenges, and you are now trying to get the children fed and washed single-handed, before tackling an untidy house and getting ready for tomorrow. You are tense and in no mood for bad behaviour. Your two- and three-year olds, no doubt sensing your anxiety, decide to start pummelling one another and shrieking.

Which reaction is closest to your response?

A. I shout at the children and threaten them with a slap if they don't behave.

B. I take a deep breath, separate them, and wait for the noise to subside. I then tell them that if they eat their supper nicely they can have their favourite story at bedtime.

C. I ignore them. I'm too tired to deal with it. They will exhaust themselves eventually.

D. I stop what I'm doing and go and join them. As usual I am unlikely to get them to bed before 9pm, anyway.

Imagine the scenario Your toddler is drawing a picture, which he says is of a house, but to you it looks like a mass of scribbles.

Which of the following is closest to your response?

A. I tell him that a house has walls and a roof and suggest that I show him so he can copy my picture.

B. I encourage him to describe the picture to me and reflect back to him what he is saying. He will learn to draw in his own time.

C. It looks like a load of scribbles to me. I just let him get on with it.

D. I like to see him expressing himself. I wish he wouldn't scribble on the walls, but I suppose we can always redecorate.

Answer B, the authoritative approach, is the ideal response in both scenarios, although we all have our "off" days where other approaches may creep in. An authoritative style scores highly on the control and the warmth scales and is appropriate for raising happy, well-adjusted children.

difficulties later on in life. Having a warm and positive relationship with your toddler will reap huge dividends as she gets older.

D = Permissive (low control/high warmth) *"It upsets me when I see my daughter crying. I haven't the heart to put my foot down. It's so much easier to give in to her and enjoy a cuddle."* Permissive parents may believe that they are being very loving, showing a high degree of personal warmth towards their child and worrying little about having control. The difficulty for the child in this scenario is that she doesn't know where her behaviour boundaries are and so will keep pushing and pushing until she finds them.

With little structure or discipline, and very few demands or expectations of appropriate behaviour, a child whose parents adopt this style predominantly are setting themselves up for trouble in later years. There is a risk that their children will be alienated socially because they have not learned how to regulate their own behaviour and have trouble assessing what is acceptable. Research shows that children brought up in an overly permissive environment may have a tendency towards aggression, impulsiveness, lack of responsibility, and misbehaving at school.

Of course, there may be more than one style of parenting within a household, and you may adopt different styles at different times. Your style will depend on your own experience (see page 22). The important thing is to find the right balance between warmth and control, and to keep it consistent, so that your child feels loved even in situations when you are being tough in your approach.

Real life

My husband and I both had a strict upbringing. When we had children we found it hard to agree on a parenting style. I admired my parents and respected them. I wanted to put in place strict rules and was quite controlling of the children. My husband, on the other hand, had been smacked frequently and had less respect for the authoritarian parenting style. He hated conflict and was determined to compensate for his own upbringing by being more permissive and playful. He found it a challenge to discipline the children and constantly undermined me. Inevitably the differences caused tensions in our relationship and confusion in the children. We began to discuss the problem and generated a set of routines to follow together. As part of this, we agreed that there would be an anti-smacking agreement with space for the children to be themselves.

HOW YOU PARENT *Most of the ways in which we care for and bring up our children are instinctive, but it is worth taking a step back sometimes to work out what lies behind your actions and responses.*

Being your own person

Your child's experience of the world will be shaped by you and drawn from a range of influences that will all have their roots in your past. She will naturally look to you for guidance on what is "right and wrong" – and will push the boundaries of acceptable behaviour during the learning process.

To be a parent is to tread a fine line between wanting to "do what's best" based on the knowledge and understanding of others; and wanting to do "what feels right" based on personal instinct and the bond with your child. A first-time parent is going to feel more uncertain than one who has several children, but when trouble hits it can be easy to feel overwhelmed by the conflicting and well-meaning advice that abounds.

Avoiding comparisons and choosing advice

"Lisa and I have been best friends since school, and our kids are about the same age, but she has the support of both sets of parents and her husband, whereas I am pretty much on my own when my husband is stationed overseas. I get so tired of hearing about their latest holiday and how brilliant her children are. It just makes me worry about mine even more." Families are infinitely varied in shape, size, and gender mix, but one thing seems to be universal – when there is a toddler on the loose, and when there is a problem, everyone has an opinion and a story that they would like to share. The trouble is that other people's toddlers are not yours – and no two children are exactly the same. It can be very tempting if you are feeling unconfident to compare your child's progress with that of another child of the same age. As this book will stress again and again, there are guidelines and milestones but no fixed rules when it comes to child development. Unless there are special needs (see page 292) most children will have reached a similar stage of development by the time they start school.

Swapping stories and tactics with other parents is often invaluable, but unwanted advice can be hard to take. If by nature you tend to be unsure of yourself then other people's views can make you feel put upon, and may

lead you to feel stressed or guilty, too. This would be a good time to learn
to listen objectively rather than take things personally. You may like to have
a chat with those who have overstepped the mark to explain that you
appreciate their advice and can see their method works for their child,
but that you choose to do things a different way.

Bear in mind that:
- Others who have been through it may have something useful to say.
- Some books, articles, and TV programmes offer sound advice, but not all.
- Your GP is better qualified than you to diagnose a health problem. Do,
however, always follow your instincts if you think your child is ill.
- Unless your child is in physical, emotional, or psychological danger, you
are more entitled than anyone else to decide what is right for her.

Separating your needs from those of your child

Sometimes we can become confused between which actions are being
taken for the good of our child and which are for our own good. A classic
example occurs at bedtime. There are few experiences more likely to make
your heart melt than your cuddlesome toddler snuggling in for a bedtime
story and telling you she loves you, or the sight of your otherwise "terrible"
two-year-old lying asleep with the look of an angel. Is it any wonder that
parents give in when their little one gets up for more cuddles or wants the
comfort of snoozing in their bed rather than the child's own? It is not only
toddlers who suffer from separation anxiety: parents do, too. Parents want
to know they are needed and don't want to risk being rejected or disliked
by their child, by causing them distress.

Provided you act with calmness and clarity, rather than anger or impulse,
your child will not feel rejected and will eventually learn to feel safe without
your physical presence: a vital survival skill. If, on the other hand, you give
in to her immediate impulse to satisfy your own needs, you are in danger
of delaying her development over time. Be aware of when you are acting
for your own need rather than the good of your child.

Shared parenting

Raising children together needs to be a co-operative partnership – and the
more honest you can be with yourself and with one another, the easier it
will be. Although a challenge, this is especially true when parents live

YOUR CHILD'S NEEDS
*Consistency and routine
are essential in the
early years. If you are
less than consistent,
your child will find your
weak spot and may use
it to his advantage!*

A SOLID PARTNERSHIP

Young children need a clear message so they know what is expected of them. This can only be achieved if you and your partner are in agreement.

apart. Some compromises will be necessary, for the good of your children – and your sanity! It is not always easy to achieve, but it makes parenting a great deal easier if you can manage it. Parents who disagree over parenting principles give contradictory signals to their children and reap havoc in return. Children become confused by contradictory guidelines and may either try to please both parents at once, or "play up" in frustration. No-one is the winner and the ensuing "bad" behaviour of the child is often the one thing that the parents can agree on. A self-fulfilling cycle has begun.

Discuss the following with your partner:

■ What are your beliefs about parenting?

■ Do you share the same viewpoint?

■ Have you ever discussed what matters to you, and what you would like to avoid as a parent? If not, now would be a very good time.

■ Do you have any moral, spiritual, educational, social, or cultural beliefs or boundaries that need to be built in to your parenting plans?

■ Is one of you a more dominant character than the other? If so, how will you ensure that you parent equally?

Beliefs about behaviour

Our thoughts about children's behaviour, and what makes it acceptable, vary greatly depending on personal expectations and our ideas about what is appropriate for the age group and the circumstances. As the questionnaire on page 23 shows, parents may have unrealistic or inappropriate ideas about what is the right age for a development stage. For example, two-year-old Harriet mimicking a grown-up might be seen as disrespectful by one adult, as creative and amusing by another, and as "going through a stage" by someone else. In fact, mimicry during the toddler years is developmentally appropriate for the age group and part of the learning process. The three viewpoints wouldn't differ as much if Harriet were twelve, by which time she would be expected to know what kinds of behaviour are acceptable and appropriate.

If you are sharing the parenting of your child with a partner or other adult, one of the most important aspects of satisfying and successful parenting is to mutually agree on the behaviour guidelines that you want to put in place, especially around issues such as mealtimes, bedtimes, acceptable behaviour, and so on.

If you draw up a joint plan in advance of any problems developing, you are more likely to take joint responsibility when things go wrong. In order for any guideline to work, it is important that your children understand that you and your partner will be of one mind on the key issues of the day. Undermining one another in front of the children sends a very confusing message. Throughout this book you will find age-appropriate guidelines to teach your child to behave in a socially acceptable way – without crushing the essential spirit of childhood.

You are a role model

Role models play an important part in life. Like most people, you have probably experienced the positive impact of being inspired by someone upbeat and contented. Likewise, you may know the debilitating effect of being around someone negative. Children need role models, too – and you are your child's main influence.

One of the hardest aspects of adjusting to parenthood is self-management and the awareness that you need to remain a positive role model for your child. Easier said than done on occasion – especially when your toddler is pushing all your tolerance buttons to their absolute limit.

"Your child has rights – but so do you. It is not an 'either/or' situation, but a balance of needs and actions."

Part of the problem is that some parents feel threatened by the transition from babyhood to toddlerhood and find themselves powerless in the face of childhood rages and emotional rejection. The important thing is to know yourself well enough to be able to take diversionary tactics if things show signs of getting out of hand – and to keep things in perspective. "I hate you!" does not really mean I hate you, but simply, "I would rather have things my way, right now!" If you had an emotionally charged childhood yourself, it can be all too easy to take things personally instead of recognizing it as normal toddler behaviour.

It is natural to feel exhausted or exasperated by your children from time to time, and vital to remember that child-centred parenting (see page 38) is not about making your child the most important person in the

"When you are a parent it's important to remember that you are the adult and your toddler is only a child. She needs you to stay calm."

household. You, your partner, other children, and other adults all have a role and rights. Planning ahead to make time for yourself and your relationship, to make sure you relax and have fun, is essential for keeping your energy levels high and toddler behaviour in perspective.

Revisiting your childhood

During the many years that I have worked with families, I have rarely met a parent who did not want the very best for their child, or a carer who was not motivated by the positive needs of the children in their care. But sometimes our own issues get in the way of our parenting style. There is nothing like raising a child for triggering pressure points relating to your own childhood. At the heart of many child behavioural problems there is a parental or adult issue that needs to be resolved. It helps if you recognize when you are projecting your own experiences on to your child. Whether as adults we look back at childhood with pleasure or pain, our legacy will impact on our own attitudes and experiences as parents. It is important that we understand our own issues so that we are able to manage our emotions when caring for our children.

Memory triggers

As adults, we have a great deal of information stored away in our memory. Much of it we have forgotten ever existed. Inevitably, as our children start to grow, a gesture, a smell, a response, or a situation may suddenly trigger a long-lost memory – some good, some bad. An event may trigger a long suppressed trauma, such as loss or abandonment, for some; others may be tempted to re-live life through their children, encouraging them to achieve in areas that they enjoyed as a child or wished that they had.

Memories are highly personal, and will be different for each of us. They are triggered by sensory responses: sights, sounds, smells, and so on, and may increase as your child gets older.

Some examples of memory triggers:
■ The smell of baby lotion may trigger memories of a baby sibling.
■ Sitting on a swing may remind you of falling off and grazing your knee – or of a feeling of exhilaration.
■ The sight of your child crying as you leave the room may remind you of how you felt when you were scared or alone.

■ Your child may look at you with his father's eyes and say, in true toddler style: "I hate you, Mummy." You take it personally and over-react, because his father left you.

■ You encourage your son to take up the piano because you have a memory of how it felt to sit and play with your grandfather (even though your son would rather be playing with a ball).

When clinical psychologists work with children, they focus not only on the child, but also on the child's family or personal situation. Your personal history will influence your reaction to certain situations. Thinking about the impact of key events and experiences from your past can help you to understand your present-day actions and feelings. Our experiences dictate how we see and interpret the world around us and influence how we behave.

Increased personal awareness will help you to work out what drives your behaviour and feelings – especially towards your child – and whether some of your instinctive responses are more due to ghosts from your past rather than the needs of the immediate situation. Be aware that your relationship with your partner can have a significant effect on your child's behaviour, too.

"Good enough" parenting

The term "good enough" parent was first coined by Donald Winnicott (1896–1971). He used it in a very precise way to describe why aspiring to be a "perfect" parent can have a negative long-term effect on children. "Perfect" parents, who aim to fulfil their child's every need, at whatever age and stage of life she is at, will inadvertently encourage her to remain dependent and therefore prevent her from developing as a separate individual.

The term "good enough" parent describes a more balanced approach to bringing up a child, whereby parents encourage their children to learn to cope (once they are old enough) by gradually "loosening" the ties between them and not always providing them with all the answers.

Winnicott called this choosing to "fail" so that your child learns to succeed on her own. Of course, this is not failure as we usually think of it. What he meant was that by not always providing your child with exactly what she thinks she wants, exactly when she wants it, you are teaching her healthy survival skills. By not always pre-empting your child's requirements, you are helping her to learn to think about things and to ask.

As she grows up, this approach helps your child to realize that she is an independent being who is not dependent on her parents to provide her identity or for long-term survival.

Being a child

Parenting trends and expert opinions come and go as society alters, and every generation of parents wants to do things "better". In reality, however, children's needs and wants remain unchanged. The challenge is to listen to the combined wisdom of the "experts" and decide what is right for your child.

Most parents and childcare professionals now support the idea of child-centred parenting. This means looking closely at your child's behaviour and attempting literally to see the world from her perspective. For example, kneel down and look at the room from your child's point of view and ask yourself, "How does the world look at her level?" Consider whether or not it is a comfortable, safe, and exciting view. Your new perspective will help you to understand her needs and behaviour.

The child-centred approach doesn't mean that your toddler is the most central person in your family unit and that you should give her everything she wants, on demand. It means helping her to understand what she is experiencing and gradually to develop frustration-tolerance. This approach will encourage your child to learn: with your guidance and through her own experience. This approach is at the heart of developing self-esteem.

Child-centred parenting

At the heart of child-centred parenting there are four important principles. It should:
▶ Highlight the rights of children alongside the rights of parents, but should rebuff the belief that children are the property of their parents.
▶ Be positive and reinforcing as much as possible, rather than using threats and punishment.
▶ Focus on the needs and best interests of children and recognize the significance of the parents' role.
▶ Encourage a view of the parenting role as positive, enjoyable and fulfilling whilst acknowledging that it can be challenging and difficult.

Child-centred parenting recognizes the importance of boundaries and guidelines in curbing behaviour problems. Frustration-tolerance is an important skill for children to learn so they can develop self-control and accept social boundaries.

HER VIEW OF THE WORLD *Try to put yourself in your child's shoes and see the world from her viewpoint. This will help you to understand her behaviour and why she sometimes gets frustrated.*

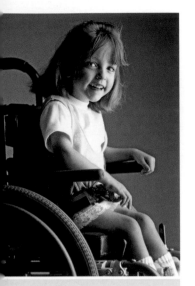

SHY TIMES *Even an outgoing child will withdraw at times. Try not to compare your child to siblings or criticize or label her because of how she responds to a situation.*

Temperament and personality

"I sometimes wonder whether our son was swapped at birth with another child! He is so full of energy and bounce, and quite unlike his brother and sister at the same age." There are times when every parent wonders, "How can I have produced a child whose character seems so different to my own?" A conservative and calm couple may be surprised by having a creative livewire of a child; an extrovert couple may find their child is born shy and cautious. How dull it would be if we were all the same! Our essential nature is known as our temperament. It is a part of what becomes our personality, and it is uniquely our own. Temperament is a behavioural style that influences the way we think and respond, and is one of the reasons that two siblings with essentially the same upbringing may respond differently to the same parenting approach.

Linked to our genes, our basic temperament is largely mapped out before birth, but may be modified by later life experiences. It is possible to see individual difference in temperamental traits in babies while still in the womb in terms of how they respond to temperature change, noise, stimuli, and in their level of activity.

If temperament is what we are born with, you may wonder what difference parenting makes. How can the style of upbringing influence personality? Whereas initial temperament remains constant, the development of a child's personality is much more complex.

Personality is influenced by:

- Our genes and temperament (hereditary factors).
- Our learned responses to our upbringing and life in general.
- How others respond to us (which affects our behaviour).
- Our broader physical and social environment.

Personality develops over many years, into our twenties and beyond, as we learn and respond initially to our parents and home environment, and later to broader social and life experiences. Your child's personality will also be influenced by how others – especially you – respond to the things she says and does.

For example, a shy child who has an anxious temperament may withdraw from new experiences. As she grows, however, she will learn to adapt and acquire a level of tolerance if her parents gently and repeatedly introduce her to new situations. While never likely to become extrovert, as a growing child she will be better able to cope than if her parents were to interpret the anxiety as distress and constantly protect her from new experiences, which would instead reinforce the anxiety.

How parents react to, and label, their child's behaviour depends not so much on the behaviour itself, as on their view of that behaviour. For example, in a family that admires individuality, a boisterous youngster may be called independent or strong-willed or "just like me" with some admiration; whereas in a family that prefers a greater level of conformity, the child may be seen as "difficult" or stubborn. Similarly, a child may be described positively as calm or content in a family that does not enjoy disruption, or passive in one that is more extrovert.

How you view and respond to your child's temperament depends on your expectations, demands, and perceptions of what your child should be like. A poor "fit" can lead to a period of tension and stress while you "get to know" your child's nature and response. It is important for you to understand your own temperament, as well as your toddler's, in order to respond to her in a positive way, regardless of expectations.

Understanding your child's temperament

Much of what we understand about children's temperament derives from a study of 233 children aged 0–8 that began in the USA in the 1950s. Known as the New York Longitudinal Study of Child Temperament, it is still going strong today. Although times have changed, young children haven't, and so the findings are highly relevant. The study has found that a child's temperament is generally made up of nine broad traits. There are no "good" or "bad" traits, and no rights or wrongs about the mix. Understanding and recognizing which apply to your family will help you to get to know, and bond with, your toddler.

How physically active is your child? A child who is constantly active may have moved and kicked a lot in the womb; in contrast with a very laid-back and calm child who may not have moved as much.

How predictable is your child? Some children are very predictable and regular in their habits. Their biological functions (eating, sleeping, and bowel movements) are very routine. These children will react well to a set regime. Others may have needed a more flexible and varied approach from birth. In time, all children need boundaries and to learn what behaviour is

LOOK AT ME! *Your child's temperament is unique to him and needs to be recognized, respected, and nurtured as a central part of his developing personality.*

Real life

My little girl is three now, and I've found that parenthood has made me want to change things about myself. When you have a child, you see all of your own traits lived out in front of you, such as being shy and hating crowds. It makes you want to try and change how you act, so that you give out a more positive message. I so much want my daughter to have higher self-esteem than I did, but she is already quite timid. I try to encourage her and give her "coping techniques" in situations she's not keen on, such as going to a party. I have promised myself that I will never tell her that she will "enjoy it once she's there", as I hated being told that when I was little. It is a taboo to say how hard it is to be a parent sometimes, but I think the difficulties should be talked about so that whatever parents go through they know it is normal and they are not alone.

acceptable, but there is no harm in being more sensitive to your child's temperament when she is small, and building up to a routine gradually.

How shy is your child? A child's immediate response to a new person or a new environment tells a story. Does your child go in boldly without seeming to hesitate or think when she meets someone new or goes somewhere different? Or is she cautious and watchful? Does your child withdraw, cling, and try to avoid newness? Many children go through a clingy period where they are anxious about being separated from their parent, in particular; but a shy child will show this trait more consistently.

Does your child take time to adjust to change? If you alter your child's routine or introduce a new carer, how long will it take her to adapt to the change? Some children are very flexible and will calm quickly, others find change difficult and take longer to adapt.

How intensely does your child react? Some children respond to situations with more energy than others, whether positively or negatively. The scale of response may vary from mild protest to full-on tantrum, or from "quiet and tense" to "calm and quiet".

How would you describe your child? Is she generally contented and smiley? Or is she more fractious, tending towards crying and fussiness? A young child is easily influenced by factors in her environment.

Is it easy to distract your child? Some toddlers are more easily distracted than others and find it difficult to focus on a task. Others appear intently focused and are not easily distracted, for example, when feeding or playing.

Can your child cope with frustration? Some children are more frustration-tolerant than others. One may stick with a task for a length of time in spite of encountering obstacles to progress, whereas another child may give up as soon as she is frustrated or distracted. For example, a very persistent child may get upset if you interrupt self-feeding attempts, whereas a less persistent one may get frustrated if you do not.

How sensitive is your child? The sensitivity referred to here is not to do with emotions (your toddler is too young for this to apply), but to the sensory system: how easily your child is affected by changes in temperature, noise, light, or texture. For example, some babies when wet will cry straight away and need changing; others seem not to notice. A very sensitive child may not like to be rocked, whereas a less sensitive child may find the rocking movement very soothing when trying to sleep.

As you come to know and recognize your child's character you will learn to react appropriately. If your child's reaction is different to what you would have expected, it is probably still healthy and normal. Differences may become more pronounced as she grows older depending on how you respond and depending on factors in her personal environment. For example, moving house might prove to be quite a challenge; or she may initially hold back from making friends at school.

Avoiding labels

Every child is a unique mix of the traits listed above, but there are three clusters of traits that the New York study (see page 41) showed were more common than others. Although it is important not to straight-jacket your young child with a rigid label, it can be useful to understand how her character may have an impact on the way you respond to her. These traits give some insight into the kind of approach that would work when setting guidelines and nurturing your child.

Easy baby "Easy" babies will tend to adjust quickly to change, be very regular in their eating and sleeping habits and bowel movements, and it may be easy to predict their response to a situation. As they have a high level of discomfort- and frustration-tolerance, these babies are generally contented and positive, and easily soothed when distressed. Parenting such a contented baby can sometimes feel too easy. A parent may feel almost unnecessary in the relationship. It is important to remember this phase will

"Avoid making unfair comparisons between children; each is unique and has their own needs."

YOUR EXPRESSIVE CHILD *A small child is emotionally transparent and his or her individuality will be evident from the earliest months of life.*

pass and your baby still needs stimulation, attention, and her unique relationship with you.

Shy baby "Shy" babies, described in the original New York study as "slow to warm up" have a cluster of traits that lead them to reject or withdraw instinctively from new people and situations. They tend to be cautious and watchful rather than approach and get involved physically. These babies do not always show their discomfort, so it can be difficult to know when they are in need of attention, reassurance, or a nappy change. They can cope with irregular routine and are not demanding.

Some parents may worry about their child's "shyness", but children may pick up on this anxiety, which can itself lead to other traits, such as clinginess. Parents need to give their child gradual but frequent opportunities to experience new situations and people. If children are given plenty of time to warm up to new situations, and are under no pressure, they will adapt and learn coping skills in time. If your child appears anxious or stressed, or over-stimulated by something new, withdraw from the situation, reassure her, and try again. If you have a tendency to withdraw from new people and prefer to avoid new experiences yourself, your reactions will reinforce the characteristics in your child. However, you have several years to overcome your own fears – so you might start to gradually challenge yourself, too. Meeting other parents is often a great place to start.

"Difficult" baby Very physically active, restless, and easily distracted babies are often wrongly labelled "difficult" or spirited because they tend to demand constant and immediate attention and are not easily settled. These are the children who tend to respond vigorously and vocally to discomfort or change and are intensely emotional. Hard to soothe and get to sleep, they do not settle into an easy routine. New situations and people are a challenge and they may react strongly to sensory and environmental changes.

"Appropriate behaviour and healthy emotional development in toddlers is the result of sensitive, loving and responsive parenting, regardless of their temperament, and how like or unlike you they seem to be."

GETTING TO KNOW HER
*Don't always assume
your child is being
deliberately awkward –
she may simply act in
a certain way because
her temperament is
different to yours.*

If treated in a caring and responsive way, most of the so-called "difficult" behaviour, such as fretting and being over-reactive to change, will calm by the age of one and can be overcome by the age of four. These toddlers often grow into active, energetic, and emotionally expressive children. The challenge is to stay positive, loving, and consistent towards your child in spite of the challenges. If a negative relationship builds up, there is a danger that behavioural challenges will develop in later life.

The way parents respond to spirited behaviour in children include: guilt and anxiety that they are doing something wrong as nothing seems to please their child; anger and blaming, as if the child is behaving this way on purpose; or a sense of rejection because of being unable to soothe or comfort her. Although understandable responses, it is important to remember that children under the age of four are not yet capable of calculated thought. Instead, you need to prepare and protect your child from upset by being aware of the sensory challenges (such as the discomfort of a wet nappy, or a light that is too bright) and environmental changes (such as a change in daily routine) that are having an impact, and be ready to respond. A consistent routine will help your child learn about predictability and will offer reassurance.

■ **Others** A further 35 per cent of children do not fit clearly into any of these three categories above, but are a unique mix of the nine characteristics described on pages 41–43.

Is birth order important?

The evidence is mixed on the effects of birth order on a child, and tends to depend on the approach of the parents. Older children who have spent lots of time in the company of adults, may find being with adults easier than being with children; whereas younger children, used to having an older sibling as a role model, may develop social skills more quickly and relate to their peers more naturally. First-born children may be encouraged to develop leadership skills and to take responsibility from a younger age than a sibling, who has to compete for resources and attention. In contrast, younger children may develop faster and be more confident because the parents are more experienced and relaxed. A single child will adjust in a similar way provided she is given opportunities to socialize and is not treated from an early age as a "little adult".

Dear Tanya...

▶ **My girlfriend seems to have changed since we had our daughter. She is the perfect mother and takes pride in making our home immaculate, but I am beginning to wonder where the fun person has gone.**

Becoming a parent is a life-changing event and a period of great personal transition. Many parents believe that they should aspire to be perfect for the sake of their child, but in reality this is neither possible, nor ideal. The pressure to lead a perfect life and to be the perfect role model invariably takes its toll, because it is unnatural. Both the child and the parents' relationship suffer in the long run. Constant worrying about the minutiae of running the household and trying to keep a step ahead of impending chaos means an end to fun, relaxation, and spontaneity.

Talk to your girlfriend and tell her how you feel. Make sure she knows how much you care. If her battle to be perfect is the main issue, reassure her that your child just needs her to be herself. Your daughter will benefit from understanding that her parents have imperfections and don't always know the answer. The "perfect" parent, who aims to fulfil their child's every need, encourages dependency. In the long term this can prevent children from "letting go" of their parents and developing as separate individuals.

▶ **My mother is insistent that I am spoiling my toddler and that I should leave her to cry herself to sleep. Is she right? I find it so hard to leave her to cry.**

Your mother may be passing on advice that was current at the time she was raising you. The childcare gurus of the day believed that a feeding routine was the route to good parenting and that it wouldn't be harmful to allow a child to cry herself to sleep.

While it is true that it does a young toddler no harm to grizzle for a few minutes while she is learning to settle herself, allowing her to become distressed will simply increase her anxiety levels and delay the settling response. A baby of this age is too young to be manipulative and there is always a reason for the distress. It would be wise to adopt a frequent checking approach (see page 202) to let her know that you are there. Remember, if it makes you feel uncomfortable to leave your child to cry she will pick up on your anxiety, so you need to find a way that works best for you.

▶ **My son of 12 months has started sucking his thumb and becomes completely hysterical if he doesn't have his favourite toy in bed with him at night. Should I be worried, and at what age should I try to wean him off these habits?**

Your son is finding ways to comfort himself when he is separated from you. He is using his thumb as a pacifier to help soothe himself to sleep, and his toy has become a source of emotional comfort that helps him to cope when you are not around. Don't think of these props as a sign of weakness or insecurity. Your son's impulse is healthy and normal and both the thumb-sucking and comfort toy are tools that will help him make the gradual transition to independence – from you and from them. He will give up both in his own time.

Areas of development

Child development is a simple term that describes the extraordinary cognitive, motor, emotional, and psychological journeys that will impact on your toddler from head to toe. Prepare to be astounded as she grows and learns month by month.

Young children are often on the move. Although their growth rate is not as rapid as during the first year of life, a toddler's average height by age two is 86.4cm (34in), and average weight gain over the course of a year is 1.5-2.5 kg (3-5lb). Their heads also grow larger to accommodate a fast-developing brain.

The large muscles of the body develop more rapidly now. These control the big movements a child makes (gross motor skills), such as sitting, walking, climbing, running, and jumping. The smaller muscle groups also become stronger. These control the way your toddler uses her limbs, hands, and feet to achieve smaller movements (fine motor skills), for more focused or precise tasks.

Toddlers gradually learn enough muscular control to make large movements, such as swinging the arms to throw and kicking with the legs.

Smaller-scale movements involving precise control of the hands and fingers will take longer to develop, but you will gradually see your toddler learn to point, draw, use a spoon, and write.

COGNITIVE SKILLS

The ability to learn and think is known as cognitive development – this affects the area of the brain responsible for reasoning and our understanding of the world. Sensory development and language skills have a major impact on cognitive development.

SENSORY SKILLS

Young children learn by taking in and understanding the world around them. The senses play a vital part in this process, through physical development and learning. Your toddler is alert to new sensations and discoveries and needs to experience as wide a range of safe sensory experiences as possible. What your toddler sees, hears, smells, feels, and tastes has an impact on her memory, and how she perceives the world. Awareness of how big or small she is, and where she fits physically, in relation to other people or things, is also important.

COMMUNICATION SKILLS

Your toddler's ability to talk makes a profound difference to the way in which she relates to her world. Language is the bridge that allows clear communication of personal needs and enables her to express her preferences and personality. There are three categories of language development:

▶ **What she says (expression):** the words themselves, the phrases, the context, and how the language is used.
▶ **How she says it (articulation):** the pronunciation and tone of those words
▶ **What she understands (reception):** what she takes in, and understands the

"Your toddler's senses are more heightened than yours, and each new experience enhances her sensitivity, increases her brain development, and her ability to interpret the world."

words to mean – including the individual words and their context.

By the time your baby has reached 12 months she will probably have developed a style of baby language that is partially recognizable and may even have said her first word, such as "dada" or "mama". "No" will not be far behind. The next three years will bring profound changes.

EMOTIONAL DEVELOPMENT

The toddler years are fairly self-centred. Your young toddler's brain is not yet developed to a level where she will be aware of the impact that her behaviour has on other people, although she will be very aware of the impact her environment has on her.

Feelings will emerge gradually:

▶ **Self-awareness** – of personal feelings, and the development of self-esteem and confidence.

▶ **Awareness of others** – development of feelings for and about other people.

▶ **Intuition** – sensitivity to mood and atmosphere.

Early emotional experiences have a profound impact on brain development. Your child's early experiences of joy, fear, excitement, love, security, and comfort have an impact on the way the brain develops and on behaviour shaping. You will play a vital role in helping her develop a healthy self-image and learn to manage her emotions. She will crave instant

rewards and gratification, will have little concept of time, and will be driven by immediate wants and needs. Over time and with guidance she will learn what is reasonable behaviour.

SOCIAL SKILLS

Your toddler's social skills will develop gradually by watching and mirroring you through play, hand-in-hand with language and emotional development. The mechanics of social behaviour can be taught when she is old enough,

PHYSICAL PLAY *Young children are naturally active and become more skilled at physical play as the large muscles of their body develop.*

through learning good manners, but social skills involve mainly intuition and feelings. Your child's innate temperament will also have an impact. By the age of four she will have started to develop personal beliefs to guide her behaviour, based on your example and her own experiences.

The importance of play

All young creatures learn through play, and children are no exception. Toddlers are naturally curious and will interpret their world using all their senses, learning all the time from their experiences. Their instinct for discovery is naturally expressed through playfulness and doesn't need to be forced.

Children are amazing. They think of the most extraordinary things and have so much to say, but to truly understand them, we need to give them our time. Playtime is your toddler's route to rehearsing life's survival skills, and is also the perfect time for you to get to know each other better. Play at this age needs a lightness of touch and should be a time of great fun and laughter. A toddler's brain has not yet developed enough to understand complex instructions and explanations (see below). Simple guidelines and easy outcomes will be enough to stimulate interest.

Playing with your toddler regularly will help you get to know her in a deeply intimate and instinctive way that will serve your relationship well for life – it is essential for her development.

Play will help your child to:
■ Develop imagination and nurture creativity.
■ Try new things and develop self-confidence.

Stages of brain development

Your child's brain develops in stages. The "lower" brain areas, which drive instinctive and emotional responses, develop first. The "higher" rational brain, which distinguishes humans from animals and reptiles, develops later. It contains the frontal lobes, which have only partially developed at the time of birth. Not until the age of three will they have matured to a point where they will help a child to manage her emotions or curb her impulses. The need for instant gratification can be overwhelming, which is why toddlers are prone to tantrums when they can't have what they want.

Varied play helps children to start to learn self-control and will develop the behaviour-regulating function of the frontal lobes of the brain.

LEARNING FROM GRANDAD *Your own parents may have more time than you to play with your toddler. This level of attention can lead to a very special bond developing between grandparents and grandchildren.*

■ Manage emotions (in a safe environment), by experiencing frustration, success, disappointment, and enjoyment.

■ Develop problem-solving skills and reasoning ability.

■ Build physical strength and competence.

■ Develop motor skills, such as co-ordination, movement, and balance.

■ Develop cognitive skills, such as planning, problem solving, memory, and testing a theory – for example, "If I hide teddy, will he still be there later?"

■ Develop social skills and eventually develop friendships.

■ Encourage language development.

Parents are often surprised when I tell them that the solution to their toddlers' behaviour problems is to increase the amount of time they play with them. Little ones of this age are very attached to their parent figure – you are likely to be their favourite playmate – and will do anything to gain attention, even if the attention is negative. The advantage of playtime is that a child does not need to "play up" to get quality attention.

Where does play stop and learning begin?

Psychologists have struggled over a formal definition of play for decades. For a child however, it is probably obvious: children play for the sheer joy of it! They love freedom of movement, fun and laughter, imagining things, making new discoveries, and the feeling of being secure in their environment. The boundary between exploration and play is indefinable, and children will generally learn new skills and information far more easily if they are enjoying the task and thinking of it as playtime.

Play is about much more than "pretending"; it is about exploring and learning new skills vital to physical and emotional health. Play teaches that communication can be fun and motivates children to learn to communicate in other ways, too. It is through play that children first come to understand that objects can represent other things (for example, an empty packing box can become a boat, a house, a car). The ability to make associations and to use imagination is at the heart of learning language.

Types of play

Different styles of play are vital to encourage gross and motor skill development (see page 48) and to encourage creative, social, mental, physical, and imaginative development:

BOOKWORM *Picture books help language development, reinforce memory, and stimulate the imagination. Your child will love to look at the same pictures again and again.*

Mental play Your toddler's cognitive skills (see page 48) develop through mental play. This includes language play, number rhymes, songs, and playing with different shapes and textures. Pre-school children have a wonderful sense of the absurd, but their understanding of word play and humour evolves over time.

Creative play This involves your child's fine motor skills (see page 48) and includes activities such as drawing, painting, sticking things, model building, and playing with modelling dough and construction toys. This kind of play works wonderfully in partnership with the skills needed for mental play (see above) to help your child understand the connections between sounds and words and pictures.

Physical play Movement helps the body and brain to develop normally. The patterns that are put in place now will have an impact on your child's development and metabolism for life. Running, jumping, walking, climbing, hopping, and play fighting are all examples of physical play. Swimming is also an appropriate form of play from an early age. Children who do not get enough exercise and stimulation through play will look for it elsewhere, by running around the house or "playing up".

Imaginative play Children aged three and upwards have fertile and boundless imaginations. They can transform themselves into a "character" in an instant, will love to dress up, and may find the boundaries between fantasy and reality hard to distinguish on occasion. Imaginative play is closely linked to role play. Your child will love to copy those around her, especially the significant adults in her life, and will also be influenced by any older siblings, and other strong characters. Like many parents, you may at some point be embarrassed to hear your own words and behaviour echoed by your young toddler! Early role play is at the root of learning important social and life skills.

Social play Through play your child will learn to co-operate and empathize with others. Play develops instinctively and spontaneously and leads to the development of essential skills that she needs for socialization and survival in later life. The good news is that playtime provides many of the things that your adult brain needs, too. All too often we forget how to relax and have fun when overwhelmed by the stresses and strains of everyday life – so give yourself a break and re-connect with your own childhood playtime as you unwind with your toddler.

GETTING STRONGER
Energetic play is physically demanding, so it's great for tiring out your lively toddler, and it will strengthen her muscles and keep her body healthy.

The stages of play

Having age-appropriate expectations is crucial. Babying a four-year-old will stop her from testing her capabilities and developing, while having expectations beyond your child's years will set her up for early anxiety and the possibility of "performance failure" and disappointment.

Play develops through a number of stages:

■ Exploratory play – using the senses of touch, taste, and smell to comprehend new experiences.

■ Relational play – using things as they are meant to be used. For example, using a fire truck to pretend to extinguish a fire.

■ Symbolic play – using an object as something else. For example, using a house brick as an oven to cook on.

All children begin by playing alone. Solitary play then transforms into parallel play (playing alongside peers) and imitative play (that may involve peers). Finally, there is co-operative play when a child learns to share toys and playtime. Newborn babies are so attached to their mother that they have no notion of being separate or having their own identity. By twelve months a unique personality will be more apparent, but your little one will not be ready to play co-operatively with other children until her brain has developed more fully and language skills have developed to a point where communication with other children becomes more effective.

12–15 months At this age your child needs guidance from you on how to play. For example, show her how a toy functions and then allow her to explore it in her own way. You may notice early signs of play activity, especially if you demonstrate things. She may watch other children, but will play alone, with no attempt to interact with another child.

16–20 months Your child will still need to be guided in her play at this age, and will constantly watch and imitate. Imaginative or "pretend" play will develop later. She will become more aware of other children and be more likely to copy their actions and play alongside them.

21–24 months By the time your child is two, there will be the first signs of role-reversal in your relationship. You will suddenly find that you are the recruit in her play and your role will have evolved into one that supports and encourages rather than leads. She will begin to understand the concept of, for example, pretending to drink from a toy cup and enjoy creating her own world and stories. As she learns to direct her play, she

"There is a time for directed play (leading your child to follow your instructions), but children must be allowed to explore and learn from experience, too."

will develop reasoning skills and a sense of
achievement. Importantly, this also sows the
early seeds of self-esteem and self-confidence.
25–30 months By this age your toddler will be
able to suggest a storyline and will look to you
to elaborate the scenario and to add new
developments. Your child will now be able to
play alongside other children. When playing
together, children will give a running
commentary and start to tell each other what to
do, but they will not yet be ready to co-operate
or plan a joint activity.

31–36 months At this age your toddler will
begin to think for herself and may begin to
experiment with the difference between fantasy
and reality, through basic imaginative play, using
props. By the age of three most children can
understand the concept of sharing, but will still
find it hard to accept it in practice.

Children are quite territorial at this age and tend to think of toys
and any other objects they are attached to as an extension of themselves
even when they do not belong to them and they are not using them.
They have a short attention span and are too egocentric to understand that
other people have needs or feelings. Egocentric does not mean selfish in
this context. Your toddler is at a stage where, when she closes her eyes, she
thinks that no-one can see her – because she can't see anyone. Her view of
the world is her whole world view. A child that is refusing to share is not
being wilfully disobedient, but is simply too young to be able to fully
understand your reasoning. Learning how to respond to others, share,
compromise, and put the needs of others before yourself are highly
sophisticated skills that take years to acquire.

37–48 months (and beyond) By the age of four your child may play
independently and adopt an imaginary role. She will understand the
difference between characters and roles and have clear ideas about a
storyline. Some (up to the age of eight) will have an imaginary playmate
and may find it difficult to tell the difference between fantasy and reality.

LEADING PLAYTIME
*Young children are
usually fascinated by
older children and very
willing to follow their
lead, which can
accelerate their
social skills.*

12–18
MONTHS

YOUR AMAZING TODDLER

12 18 24 30 36 42 48
MONTHS

ON THE MOVE YOUR BABY'S HORIZONS WILL SUDDENLY EXPAND AS SHE LEARNS HOW TO WALK AND STARTS TO VIEW HER ENVIRONMENT FROM A WHOLE NEW PERSPECTIVE

NEW ACTIVITIES AS YOUR TODDLER'S HAND-EYE CO-ORDINATION DEVELOPS, HE WILL BECOME MORE SKILLED AT HANDLING TOYS AND BEGIN TO PLAY MORE INDEPENDENTLY

"Get ready! Your child is about to embark on an exciting journey into toddlerhood."

LOVE AND AFFECTION
KNOWING HE IS LOVED IS ESSENTIAL TO YOUR CHILD'S DEVELOPING SELF-ESTEEM AND SENSE OF SECURITY

Your toddler's development

Your baby's first birthday will be a significant and emotional milestone for you and may trigger mixed feelings. The past 12 months will have been life changing and it is quite normal to feel a few pangs as you put away the baby clothes and start to look forward to your child's next phase of development.

Becoming more mobile and developing language skills will dominate the next 1–2 years as your baby leaves infanthood behind and enters the brave new world of independence and communication.

He will start to experience strong feelings at this age, but will not yet have the ability to manage them so you will need to help him. The way you respond to your child over the months ahead will have an influence on longer-term social development. The emphasis should be on loving, nurturing, encouraging, and reassuring your child as he crawls, wobbles, toddles, and tumbles his way to mastering and enjoying his newfound mobility, and gradually builds a repertoire of skills that allows him to get about and communicate his needs more effectively.

Brain power

These early months are vitally important for healthy brain development (see page 71), and the way your child experiences the world during his second year of life will have a significant impact on his emotional development, as well as his learning and thinking skills. Children of this age need to know that the person who cares for them is emotionally available, can be trusted, and won't cause them harm. Incredible though it may seem, your child is already absorbing emotional messages from his environment that will contribute substantially to his later social skills and emotional intelligence.

You will soon need to start putting in place some clear behavioural guidelines and boundaries, but for the next six months behaviour management revolves more around using distraction techniques. One of the biggest challenges for you during the next two years is to make sure

"He may seem more independent, but your toddler needs you more than ever, to stay calm, set him boundaries, and encourage him."

PILE ON THE PRAISE *Your toddler's sense of self-belief develops from the feedback he receives from you. So praise all his attempts at new skills, even if he fails.*

that praise and encouragement are used frequently and that the word "No" does not dominate. Along with being given the core basics of food, warmth, and a safe place to be himself, your child needs love and comfort, and to develop confidence. These are the important ingredients for healthy development. A child who feels loved and safe will develop greater levels of self-esteem and will feel more secure – so remember to show your child how much he is loved and give him plenty of praise.

Short-term memory

Your toddler has little capacity for common sense and his memory has not yet developed sufficiently to retain information for long. You will have to repeat the most basic instructions, and may be surprised that your otherwise alert child can't seem to grasp the fact that if one plug socket is dangerous, then all plug sockets are dangerous. Be reassured that this is normal behaviour for this age.

Your toddler will be interested mainly in you – and how you respond to his needs. He will be well attuned to your expressions and responses, the way you talk, the way you smell, the way you hold him, and whether you are tense or relaxed. Months 12–18 are about beginning to learn the skills that will help him with personal understanding and sociability when he is older. As his senses and spatial awareness become more sophisticated, your toddler's memory will improve. He will be able to figure out, "If I stand here, I can reach there," and will remember, for example, what his fruit drink smells like. This is because the senses provide memory triggers that speed up recall. This recall will develop more rapidly from months 19–24, but the seeds are being sown now via your child's growing interest in, and ability to explore, his environment. By the age of two his senses will be fully developed, although the ability to interpret the simultaneous messages that they deliver will develop more gradually and through experience.

"This is a lovely period of child development, and I hope you are able to enjoy it to the full. Don't feel you need to force physical development in any way. That will all happen naturally and in good time."

New skills

The primary areas of development at this stage are learning to walk, learning to talk, and learning about feelings. While at 12 months your little one is likely to be quite shy with strangers, by 18 months there will be definite signs of toddler independence – although you will still be the central focus in your child's world.

In terms of physical development, the gross motor skills that drive large movements will strengthen to a point where a toddler will begin to learn to sit up, stand, crawl, and begin to walk. The fine motor skills, which drive the smaller movements of the body, will develop so that you will notice your child is able to pick up small objects by using his thumb and index finger (awkwardly to begin with); can point enthusiastically at anything of interest; can drop and throw things; and will start to build with blocks and learn to scribble. As he starts to develop new muscles and lose baby fat, you will begin to see physical and facial changes as he starts to look less like a baby and much more like a child.

Signs that development is on track

It is important to emphasize that all children will develop at their own pace, and rarely in a steady upward line (see page 64). The following is an approximate guide to how new skills will develop.

By the end of 12–15 months, your child:
- Can stand for a few moments without support.
- May be able to toddle a few steps without help.
- Can drop and throw toys deliberately.
- May be starting messy self-feeding with fingers or spoon.
- Can pick up small objects using pincer grip (thumb and index finger).
- May be able to say two or more words.

By the end of 16–18 months, your child:
- May be able to walk steadily and may start to do so "heel first".
- May be able to walk up steps or run.
- Can kneel without support.
- Can squat and then stand up.
- Can recognize familiar people at a distance.
- Can point at things he recognizes.
- May be able to say 3–6 words.

DIFFICULT TIMES *As your child struggles to make sense of her world, she will look to you for help. The more frustrated she becomes, the calmer and more patient she needs you to be.*

What is normal and when to worry

Many parents – especially first-time parents – worry about their toddler's behaviour, as well as the rate at which developmental milestones are reached. It can help to be aware of what is within the normal range and to know when and where to seek advice.

While many of the concerns you have about your child may be unfounded (see box, below), it's important to air them if you are worried. Talk to your GP and health visitor for advice, ask the staff at your nursery (if your child attends one), and discuss any concerns with other parents. However, try not to get caught up in competitive parenting and remember that parents may sometimes exaggerate their own children's behaviour and progress. If your child's temperament seems similar to your own, you may expect him to behave in a certain way. Keep an open mind and try not to make assumptions about how he might behave or which skills he will learn first.

Your anxiety – natural at times – needs to be dealt with in a way that does not impact negatively on your child or make him unsettled.

EARLY WARNING SIGNS

There are certain key developmental milestones that, if not met, may indicate cause for concern. I can't emphasize enough that all children develop at their own pace. If you have any concerns, please do seek professional advice rather than worrying in isolation.

▶ **Language** An absence of baby babble and not responding to surrounding

FEEDING CONCERNS *Mealtimes can all too easily become a battleground between you and your child as she develops. Try to stay relaxed about feeding and, remember, she won't starve herself.*

COMMON CONCERNS (AGES 1–3)

None of the following behaviour is a cause for concern, but you are not alone in worrying about it:

▶ Disruptive, attention-seeking behaviour when bored.

▶ Over-excitement when there are visitors in the house.

▶ Extreme messiness and inability to put things away.

▶ Throwing things on the floor, especially food.

▶ Resisting kisses, especially from those who are most likely to be offended!

The following statistics show how many other parents of toddlers wear themselves out with unnecessary worry:

▶ 50 per cent worry that their child eats too little.

▶ 64 per cent think their child eats the wrong kinds of foods.

▶ 52 per cent said their child wakes up in the night.

▶ 70 per cent reported difficulty in getting their child to bed.

▶ 68 per cent worry that their child hits other children or takes things.

▶ 79 per cent said that their child is clingy.

▶ 94 per cent worry that their child constantly seeks attention.

noise may indicate a problem with hearing. Be reassured that children with hearing problems are adept at adjusting and can learn to pick up sign language at the same stage hearing children learn words.

Remember:

▸ Using words incorrectly or being imprecise in speech is completely normal for this age group.

▸ Exposure to lots of language won't necessarily mean that your child will learn to speak by 12 months.

▸ **Movement** Floppy, poor muscle tone will show in a child's inability to sit unsupported, hold his head up, or push up on his arms. If your child is making no attempt to pull himself up to stand and shows a chronic lack of interest in moving, you may want to ask your doctor for an assessment of his gross motor skills (see page 48).

Remember:

▸ Reverting to bottom shuffling rather than crawling in order to get somewhere in a hurry is not regressive behaviour.

▸ **Social skills** Poor eye contact, lack of reciprocal smiles, not following a *Peek-a-boo* game, difficulty with sharing attention, not using skills such as pointing and looking where someone is pointing may indicate difficulties with social development.

Remember:

▸ Being clingy and shy is normal behaviour at this age.

▸ **Eating** Not maintaining or gaining weight, having reflux or allergies, and never seeming hungry, should be investigated by a doctor.

Remember:

▸ Playing with food and throwing it on the floor is normal.

ASSESSMENT

If you go to your GP or health visitor with your concerns about your child, he or she may adopt a "wait and see" approach initially. This is appropriate at this age as children develop at different rates. It does not mean that they are not interested. Do not hesitate to arrange to return to see your GP or

LEARNING TO WALK Your baby's first steps are a key milestone and cause for celebration. Remember, the age range for starting to walk is 10–18 months, and the timing bears no relation to athletic ability or intelligence.

health visitor again if your concerns about your child's health or development continue.

It's important to always trust your intuition as a parent. If something does not feel right, you are entitled to take action. There is a lot of emphasis on early intervention now, so there are lots of services and support networks to help you (see pages 310–311).

Walking and talking

Most children will take their first steps and say their first words during the next six months. It is an exciting time for both you and your toddler. Go at your toddler's pace and resist making comparisons with other children; he will reach the same point as everyone else – in his own good time!

Toddlers are very determined. As well as crawling, toddling, and running, at this age your child will probably enjoy climbing into, under, and over all kinds of obstacles, as well as up and down stairs. This natural behaviour will help to strengthen muscles and improve co-ordination and balance.

How to encourage movement and learning:

■ Allow your child freedom to move. Go for daily walks with him – both indoors and outdoors. He is much closer to the ground than you, and so every step is a sensual adventure. Talk to him about the surroundings, pointing out colours, creatures, and objects.

■ Provide safe areas to play and wander, where your child can do no damage either to himself or your belongings.

■ Give plenty of praise while your child explores and make positive and encouraging comments to reinforce his understanding of his progress.

■ If you feel nervous while you watch his vulnerable wobbling, try to keep it to yourself. Tumbling over is inevitable, but he hasn't got too far to fall and once he is comforted, without too much fuss, the experience will encourage him to keep trying and he will learn from his mistakes.

Essential balance

Learning how to balance is a vital skill that we have to learn, beginning in the womb. It is controlled via the body's balancing mechanism, known as the vestibular system. This is one of the first systems of the body to develop as we move and turn around in the womb. It helps us to understand where we are in relation to the things around us: for example, we can tell how far away a chair is from us so we don't fall over or bump into it, and we know how big we are in relation to the objects around us, so, for example, we

USEFUL PROPS *A toddler truck that is pushed along is an ideal toy for this age group. Although beginning to find her feet gives her greater independence, your toddler will still need constant adult supervision.*

LEARNING TO BALANCE

A toy such as a rocking horse is great fun for a toddler and it will help him to develop his ability to balance. Some ride-on toys can also be propelled along.

know whether we are able to fit through a doorway. Until the vestibular system is fully developed, the other sensory systems will not develop fully either. All the sensory systems need to be integrated for development of the "higher" systems to take place, such as thought and understanding (cognition) and the ability to control behaviour. An under-sensitive balance system leads to clumsiness; an over-sensitive one leads to motion problems, such as travel sickness.

As anyone who has ever watched a small child learning to walk will have witnessed, balance takes time to perfect. Childhood activities such as swinging, bouncing, and rocking, and other forms of repetitive movement, are all beneficial in helping to develop the vestibular system. It may help to remind yourself of that when your toddler next jumps up and down on a bed or sofa! It drives development of movement, head position, eye movement, co-ordination, and body awareness. Encouraging your child to do movement activities will stimulate the development of balance and help him learn to focus. Signs that the vestibular system is still developing include: squirming or rocking excessively at the table, a need to run around continuously, "hyper" activity and an inability to focus or concentrate. Most of these types of behaviour are normal and not a cause for concern, unless they persist beyond the toddler years. The balance mechanism has usually developed by the time a child is twelve months old but, in some, will continue to be developed through play, and through learning to be calm and to concentrate.

Learning to talk

Your baby started to communicate from the moment he was born, and by 12 months will be able to show you what he wants by pointing and gesturing. However, it is learning to talk that marks a true transition from babyhood to childhood. First words will be very simple and will usually involve a person (me, Daddy), an object (cup, bed) or an action (bye-bye, go), and over the next few months many children will build a vocabulary of some 20–50 words. By the time he reaches his first birthday, your toddler will be able to make himself understood verbally to some degree.

The way in which he discovers words will be largely accidental, but very exciting for you as a parent, nonetheless. He will be able to understand many more words that he can say and will start to understand and respond to simple instructions.

It is common at this stage for toddlers to use the same word to mean several different things: for example, the word "cat" may be used to mean any animal; the word "hot" could be used to mean "it is hot" or "I don't like it" or "make it cooler". This stage will continue for several more months. Don't worry if his words are unclear or imprecise to begin with – that will improve in time.

Learning to talk is very rewarding for toddlers as being understood removes a lot of frustration, so there is plenty of incentive for them to pick up new words and meanings quite fast. Giving your child plenty of smiles and positive feedback when he uses words will encourage him further and help him to see that talking is fun.

"All children develop at their own pace but, in general, most have a grasp of approximately 10 words by 15 months, 50 words by 20 months, and as many as 200 words by 24 months."

Tuning in to your toddler:

■ Tune into his style of speech and pay attention to his tone of voice. You can often tell more about what he is trying to say by noting the rise and fall of his voice.

■ Show excitement and exaggerate your responses, so that your child picks up the cadence of the words more easily.

■ Watch his body language. What is he looking at while babbling? Is he making any gestures, such as pointing or smiling? Well over 70 per cent of the messages we give out are non-verbal. What else is your child saying?

How language develops

Babies develop the ability to understand single words in the first few months of life, but won't be able to speak until thinking and reasoning skills have developed and the vocal system, including the vocal cords, have matured. An important part of language development is the experimental sounds a baby makes as these exercise the vocal cords and encourage the brain to use and recognize sounds.

▶ **1 month** Reflexive and reactive noises, such as coughing, sneezing, and crying.

▶ **2–4 months** Cooing and laughing, often in response to someone.

▶ **4–6 months** Babbling, making experimental noises, and the development of muscles and skills that move and co-ordinate the mouth and tongue.
All babies go through these first three stages, but will need external input after six months.

▶ **6–10 months** Babbling becomes more word-like and babies need plenty of chat and interaction to ensure ongoing language development; without these,

language development will slow down and then eventually stop. It is at this stage that child deafness may first be detected.

▶ **10–12 months** By 12 months, your baby will have started to use sounds and different levels of pitch to express meaning – for example, a higher pitch to express surprise or a question.

Children have an innate ability to distinguish sound patterns and word use in any language. They will learn the sounds and rules of the languages to which they are most exposed.

"Jessica learning to talk has been so exciting and rewarding. A real person has begun to emerge."

Adam, aged 34

■ Keep talking to him. The more people speak to your toddler, the more language he will learn. Get down to his level and make good eye contact while speaking. Language is learnt not only by listening to the words, but also by absorbing the tone of voice, facial expression, mood, and emotion.

■ Sing songs, tell stories and jokes, make up silly rhymes, and use nursery rhymes with actions.

■ Match your mood, facial expression, and body language to his, as this will echo back to him that you understand his feelings. This means he is less likely to become either frustrated or withdrawn. For example, if he is happy and excited, show him that you are happy and excited, too.

■ Give him time to respond. Leaving pauses will encourage your child to speak and learn to use language to tell you what he wants to do. For example, if you are tickling him, wait for a sign from him to "do it again". This also means you won't carry on with something he wants to stop.

■ Have patience with your toddler's love of repetition! It's all bedding down in the brain.

Your baby's brain

All you need to do to help your child develop healthily is to listen, observe, and keep talking and responding positively to him. His brain is pre-programmed to do the rest, so there is no need to push or force development. In fact, doing this can slow development in other areas.

Your baby's brain started to develop while still in the womb and at birth was made up of over 100 billion cells and 50 trillion pathways and connections. A newborn's brain is about a quarter of the size of an adult's and will grow to about 80 per cent of adult size by the age of three.

Brain development happens when the cells in your child's brain start to make connections to link events and experiences, and thus create meaning. This starts to happen in the womb and continues throughout early childhood. For example, as a young baby your child learned that when he contracted a particular muscle group, his leg moved. By repeating that contraction and achieving the same result several times, he formed a permanent message link in the brain. Soon, your baby will have learned how to control the movement of his whole leg. At that point, the message to the brain about the movement and the separate message about the leg will have become permanently connected. As these connections increase in number across the body, so an emerging sense of self-awareness develops, too.

How the brain develops

A baby's brain is very immature and is in many ways a blank canvas. Emotional awareness, the ability to reason and to think, social understanding, and memory development have barely begun. The experiences a baby has, and the relationships he forms, during the first three years of life will play a particularly important role in the development and "wiring" of the baby's brain – and research now shows that early experiences have a major impact on the formation of personality during the rest of a child's life.

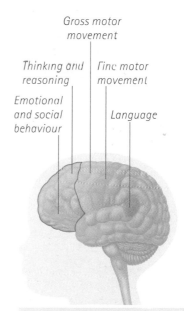

Gross motor movement

Thinking and reasoning

Fine motor movement

Emotional and social behaviour

Language

THE DEVELOPING BRAIN
The areas of the brain highlighted above are linked to development of core skills during the toddler years. Brain development continues until mid-adolescence.

"Your baby's experiences and the relationships he forms during his first three years, will determine how his brain is wired for life."

By age three, a child's brain will have twice the number of connections as an adult's, which is why your toddler is capable of learning so much so quickly. However, this does not mean he shares your ability to reason or think; his brain is still learning how to interpret information. This early phase of development is all about sculpting and refining the working of the brain. A young brain is designed to be flexible and is able to take on an array of social, emotional, and intellectual skills quite fast.

The brain continues to develop new connections until the age of 7–10 when a pruning process occurs and unused connections are wiped out. This is totally normal and is a way of strengthening the brain's connections, rather as you would prune a plant to encourage future growth. From the age of two, a substance called myelin surrounds and strengthens the brain's connections and improves and speeds up communication between the cells. Our life experiences and the habits that we form will further shape and develop these connections over time.

Influences on brain development

Baby brain development is affected by factors inherited from birth parents and by immediate environment. Parents and carers therefore play a crucial role in influencing the types of brain connections that are formed.

Important factors in the first three years of life:

■ Warm and loving behaviour involving smiles, hugs, and laughter, combined with positive mental stimulation such as chatting and play, will influence the developing chemistry of the brain and encourage a feeling of well-being (see page 88).

■ In contrast, not responding to a child, or inconsistent care, will increase levels of stress-related chemicals in the brain. This can lead to emotional, social, physical, and reasoning problems later (see page 86).

■ Once a child's basic needs have been met – physiological (such as food and warmth), safety, nurture, and self-esteem – his ability to learn new social and mental skills increases significantly (see opposite page).

■ Learning via experience is crucial to a baby's brain development. Early exposure to words through reading, talking, singing, routines, rituals, safe exploration of the environment, and play, encourages the development of language and social skills. Watching television does not have the same positive effect on brain development.

■ Children in this age group need to be allowed to develop at their own pace. Forcing the pace in one area of development can inhibit growth in another area. It is important to make time to allow a child just to "be".

Growth spurts

Brain development during early infancy is not a gradual and continuous process but occurs in growth spurts, usually at three months, 18 months, during ages 2–4, and later at ages 6–8 and 10–12. There is a growing body of research to suggest that motor, language, social, and reasoning skills develop to take place to coincide with these spurts.

A child's home environment plays a critical part in early brain development – and lays the foundations for later well-being. Warm and responsive relationships, together with the ability to listen to, watch, or relate to other people, are equally important.

Periods when the brain is going through lots of change can be challenging as well as unsettling for children, and will affect their behaviour. During these times, parents may feel their child is changing on a daily basis. Having some understanding about these growth spurts can help to allay a parent's anxieties about accelerated or delayed development.

Fulfilling your toddler's basic needs

Abraham Maslow (1908-1970), an American psychologist, wanted to understand what motivates some people to learn and develop, while others are held back. He identified four basic areas of human need, each of which is linked to the instinct for survival. He believed that until the four basic levels are met we feel insecure or unsatisfied and will be unable to achieve level 5: our future potential. There has been much debate about the prioritizing of these categories over the years, but it is probably true to say a small child needs his core requirements in place to develop his true ability.

LEVEL	NEEDS	DESCRIPTION
▶ LEVEL 5	FUTURE POTENTIAL	DREAMS, GOALS, SELF-BELIEF, FULFILMENT
▶ Level 4	Self-esteem	Progress, confidence, self-recognition, respect
▶ Level 3	Nurture	Love, affection, communication, belonging
▶ Level 2	Safety	Shelter, security, stability
▶ Level 1	Physiological	Hunger, thirst, sleep, warmth, movement, health

Raising twins

The early years of caring for twins can be particularly challenging and you will feel you need more than one pair of hands and many more hours in the day. But the good news is that double the trouble means double the joy and fun, too!

Children who are a twin, a triplet, or other multiple are individuals in their own right and also part of a distinct unit. Both aspects of their uniqueness need to be acknowledged by you, their parent. On the one hand, it can be lovely for each child to enjoy the company of their close and familiar birth-mate; on the other hand, as they start to grow up, it puts greater onus on you to ensure that each child is loved and respected for their individual talents and personality. At the toddler stage your twins need particular help in learning to understand that they are separate not only from you, but also from one another.

PRACTICAL CARE

Having two children of toddler age is always a challenge and twins are no exception. Be aware that twins are likely to take up twice as much time and energy as a solo child of the same age. If you are parenting twins you are likely to need more help from others.

It is all too easy to get into the habit of responding to both children in the same way, rather than as two individuals with unique personalities. This stems partly from practical

considerations: if you are trying to get your children to bed, it will be simpler to wash them together, read them the same story, and even dress them in similar clothes, just as you would any other children of similar ages. There is no harm in this when they are babies, but there are particular considerations to bear in mind as your children begin to talk and to grow.

DELAYED DEVELOPMENT

Research shows that parents of twins actually spend less time interacting with their children than parents of a single child. This may be because twins seem happy with each other's company and need less soothing and interaction from others. This can, however, mean they develop some skills slightly later than other children – language, for example, which they may master more slowly as a result of babbling to each other rather than to a skilled language user such as a parent. Twins may also develop skills later as a result of being born prematurely or having a low birth weight.

TOP TWINS TIPS

▶ **Individuality** Consider giving each child distinctly different names and resist the temptation to dress them the same.

▶ **Development** Remember that each twin will develop at their own pace. Try not to pigeonhole their abilities and interests at a young age.

▶ **Labelling** Don't be tempted to polarize one child as "good" and the other as "bad" – this may lead to a self-fulfilling prophecy.

▶ **Everyday care** If you find that one twin is easier to handle, be aware of the impact that this may have on the other child and make a conscious effort to spend time alone with your more challenging twin.

▶ **Siblings** Beware of inadvertently neglecting a sibling because your twins are demanding of your time. Twins can sometimes team up against a sibling, too.

▶ **Schooling** Consider whether it may be beneficial for your children to be in separate classes at nursery or school where practically possible.

ENCOURAGING INDEPENDENCE

Parents of twins can unwittingly make more work. For example, it takes a long time for any toddler to choose his clothes and begin to dress himself; imagine if each morning you have to double that time and you'll understand why many parents of twins keep on dressing the children themselves – but in the long run this help might delay the twins becoming independent.

It is important to spend some time individually with each child, but don't try to make things fair. As with all children, twins will have different needs, and it is not always a matter of dividing time equally or doing exactly the same thing with each child. You need to structure your activity and time to the needs and wants of each.

Some twins develop a pattern of behaviour whereby one of them is the follower and the other the leader, or they may switch between these roles. This tendency can extend to splitting their development progress, too. One may develop their motor skills earlier, while the other develops language ability.

They may be so used to being with each other that they behave like a single entity. This can be particularly true of identical twins – possibly because parents and other people tend to treat them more similarly than fraternal twins. Later on in life, one twin may become good at one set of skills, while the other will develop in a different direction; or they may copy one another and share many talents.

Each child will be influenced by the other's development, but this needn't necessarily be to the detriment of either child.

A CLOSE RELATIONSHIP

Twins spend an unusual amount of time in each other's company; after all, they were together in the womb prior to birth and will inevitably be compared with one another throughout their life. This can be particularly difficult as they reach toddler age where they have little control over their emotional responses. They may react intensely to one another about sharing toys, for example, but due to their closeness may seem to resent any intervention, even from parents.

There is no need to feel rejected by the close relationship between your twins, or threatened by their apparent self-sufficiency. Because they are close, twins can become so focused on each other that they are less aware or sensitive to the needs of others around them. Mixing with other children is therefore very important from an early age, so that each child develops a sense of their own social skills and individuality.

A SPECIAL BOND *Twins often form a very close attachment to each other and may compete more with each other than with other children.*

Playing and learning

At this age, your toddler's life is a constant adventure and full of the potential for fun. Every activity, journey, movement, and sound he experiences is full of intrigue and excitement. Play is a natural instinct that leads, inevitably, to him learning and developing new skills.

The activities your child enjoys naturally at 12–18 months will complement the areas of growth and development that are accelerating at this time. For your toddler, learning to walk and talk are the main priorities, along with developing finer manipulative skills. A willingness to imitate a wealth of other exciting activities, from sweeping and dusting to talking on the telephone, is a sign that reasoning ability is developing.

Toys and games that encourage movement, language, and the development of fine motor skills (see page 48) are all ideal for this age group. Activities that involve as many of the senses as possible will encourage healthy brain development and the beginnings of memory.

Every young child needs help and encouragement, but it is important to allow your child to discover things at his own rate, rather than forcing the pace. Toddlers, like adults, learn through experience. They need to be allowed to make mistakes, in order to learn and develop their abilities.

Choosing toys

Your toddler does not need elaborate toys – normal household objects may often hold more delight and are better suited to this age group than multi-functional toys. Simple household items such as pots and pans, beans rattling in sealed containers, and pieces of fabric, offer great scope for exploration, to make sounds, or to enjoy textures and colour.

"Can you find me a red fruit?"/"Shall we put a hat on teddy?"/"Can you make a big splash in the bath?" – everyday activities, such as getting dressed, cleaning teeth, bathing, shopping, and preparing food, all offer scope for fun and games. Ask simple, direct questions that encourage your toddler to start to recognize colours, shapes, and sounds, but keep it fun.

MUSCLE CONTROL *The way your toddler begins to handle objects, such as a spoon, and uses his thumb and fingers to grasp toys, is a sign of his developing muscle control.*

TODDLER POWER *As your child learns that his actions can influence his world – "cause and effect" – knocking down objects will become a favourite activity. Needless to say, it's better if he does this with his own toys!*

CREATIVE PLAY *Painting is a fun activity that will help your child learn about colours and improve his fine motor skills. Strip him off so that he can be free to get in a mess.*

Games and rhymes

Young children love to giggle and have a finely tuned sense of silliness. Finger games and action rhymes are old favourites and the perfect way to nurture language skills and co-ordination – especially if combined with a surprise ending. Rhymes and singing encourage word skills and build confidence, and are a great way to bond with your child, too.

Try these finger games and action rhymes:

- *Incy Wincy Spider* (climbed up the spout…).
- *This Little Piggy* (went to market…).
- *Round and Round the Garden* (like a teddy bear…).
- *The Wheels on the Bus* (go round and round…).
- *Head, Shoulders, Knees, and Toes* (knees and toes…).
- *Row, Row, Row Your Boat* (gently down the stream…).
- *Humpty Dumpty* (sat on the wall…).

Nursery rhymes and songs that have been repeated for generations all have their value. A favourite for helping children to learn animal noises is *Old MacDonald Had a Farm*.

Dance and music

- Swing your toddler gently round as you sing along; balance him on your feet and dance with him.
- Make your own music using rattles, a hooter, or a bell. Encourage your child to make his own sounds and, within reason, don't worry about censoring the din.
- There are economically-priced CDs and cassettes on the market that can transform a rainy day or a tricky car journey into instant playtime.

Toys and activities

Your toddler may repeat a simple action again and again, observing how something falls, moves, or lights up. Toys that are too complex will either over-stimulate and lead to him "switching off" or, conversely, create a need for him to be constantly entertained to tune in and learn.

He is developing the ability to lead his own play, and although it will become more pronounced during months 19–24 and beyond, if the signs are there, encourage him as much as possible. Playtime is a wonderful time to be with your child and, once the pattern is established, can become a great habit and wonderful pastime for years to come.

Hand–eye co-ordination, reasoning, and fine motor skills:

■ Things to puzzle over: simple jigsaws with knobs on the pieces, nesting toys that stack (rings and blocks).

■ Toys to build with: large building blocks, and to dig with: spade and sand.

■ Toys that flash, beep, and ring: simple cars, trucks, lights, and phones.

■ Toys to splash with: water, buckets, and bathtime toys.

Movement skills:

■ Toys to push and pull: toys on wheels, self-propelled cars and animals.

■ Games that involve movement and copying, such as *Simon Says*.

Helping your child learn:

■ Don't overload him with complex instructions and elaborate toys.

■ Help him to figure things out (by hiding objects), to interact (by playing *Peek-a-boo*), and to fetch things.

■ Show encouragement and demonstrate the activity, but let him lead.

■ Allow play with simple household objects – for example, a cardboard box, a saucepan, or a washing basket – to help develop your toddler's imagination through play.

"Hide and Seek": learning about "object permanence"

If your young toddler can learn to understand that objects that are hidden still exist, he will be closer to understanding that you still exist when you are not with him. The knowledge will help to soothe his separation anxiety. Try the following:

▶ Choose a familiar toy or ball or other item and show it to your toddler.

▶ Then hide it beneath a cushion or beaker (or empty container) that is close by.

▶ Next, lift the cushion or beaker and show him where the object is hidden.

▶ Use your voice, open your eyes wide, and smile to show surprise and pleasure at finding it, before covering the item again.

▶ Then encourage your child to seek the object out. (You may have to show him what to do a few times first.) "Where has the blue ball gone?"/"Where is the red sock?"

▶ When he finds it make sure you pile on the praise so he knows that he has been very clever.

▶ Then do the same thing again.

Once he has got the hang of the game, try moving the object and hiding it somewhere else nearby. With encouragement he will gradually learn that hidden items still exist and that if you look you may find them. It is the younger toddler's version of *Hide and Seek*!

A word to the wise Young children love this game, and catch on quickly. Don't be tempted to hide things like car keys or the remote control. You may find they will go missing mysteriously, for months to come!

What toddlers want and need

You'll soon learn that what your toddler wants and what he needs are not always the same thing. Toddlers are very egocentric; they have no appreciation of the rights of others, and if they want something they want it *now*! This is because they have no sense of time and live in the here-and-now.

It is important to remember that a toddler brain is not an adult brain – nor even a 10-year-old brain. What your toddler needs, apart from environmental stimulation and plenty of love, is a calm and consistent approach towards managing the hotspots of eating, sleeping, and calming down. Young children thrive on routine rather than discipline.

Repetition in every aspect of life and learning will help reinforce the messages to your toddler's brain and enable him to learn. Be aware that this can be a force for bad as well as good if a child is being repeatedly exposed to a negative behaviour or routine.

"Thank goodness for friends. We were at our wits' end with Sam's behaviour, but other parents' stories put things in perspective. Now we know this is normal, it is a phase, and it will pass." Carole, aged 40

Your toddler's newfound language and movement skills will give him an innate sense of achievement and power. Like most young children, he will discover he has immense influence over the important people in his life (usually parents and siblings) and will enjoy being contrary! The power of "No" is a great source of fun for him and frustration for you! This does not mean your toddler is naughty or "bad" – it simply means he is normal. The need for attachment to a safe and familiar adult figure remains very strong during months 12–18 (see page 90). A small child who is hungry needs to be fed, if he is frightened he needs to be reassured and comforted, if he is crying he could probably use a cuddle, and most of all he needs to be loved – consistently and unconditionally.

Guidance and boundaries

Praise and associated rewards need to be immediate and frequent at this age. Behaviour guidance or intervention also needs to be immediate, or not at all, as a toddler will not be able to link behaviour and consequence if you wait. Rather than wear out the word "No", show your child what to do and steer him out of trouble through your actions and facial expression, instead. It is your actions, not your words, that will have the most meaning and impact at this age. All too often, parents reinforce unwanted behaviour by trying to chat to their toddler about it, but he can't process the information. Instead your attention tells him that his behaviour has brought a positive reward. It becomes an incentive to do it again.

Your child's behaviour and capacity for self-control may fluctuate markedly. At this age, so much effort is being put into learning to walk and talk, that progress seems to halt or even regress in other areas of development. When a child is having to concentrate a lot of energy into one area of accelerated development, he will have fewer physical and mental resources available for other areas. That is why trying to manage

Your toddler's view of the world

Here's an insight into what your toddler might be thinking...

▶ "The world is a very large place. I am very small, so it can be overwhelming at times."

▶ "I used to think that Mummy and I were the same person. I seemed to be physically attached to her in some way. Of course, now I know that she is just here to look after me! That's why I hate it when she leaves the room. She just disappears. I can never remember that she will come back, and so it's pretty distressing."

▶ "Falling over when trying to walk is still a bit of a shock – but it seems to bother Mummy and Daddy more than it bothers me."

▶ "The changes in my mood are so sudden that it is overwhelming. I don't know what to do to calm down. I get even more stressed out if someone picks me up roughly."

▶ "I don't know what to do with all my energy sometimes – I hate having to sit still and keep quiet when there is so much to do."

emotions so often leads to frustration for this age group. Parents are often full of concern that their toddler, often a little boy aged somewhere between 1–2 years, seems intent on destroying his home and everything in it. His tantrums may be so bad that his parents are left feeling socially isolated and ready to take their child for psychological assessment! There is usually nothing wrong with these children. They are simply behaving like normal, healthy toddlers.

Parents faced with extremes of toddler behaviour should take courage. This phase will pass – and you need to remember that your child is learning valuable skills that will allow him to become a lively individual in later life. However, effective behaviour boundaries (see page 151) will be important in helping him to learn to manage his behaviour as he gets a little older.

Plenty of sleep

Children in this age group need approximately 11½ –12 hours' sleep each night, plus 1–3 hours of naps. If your child hasn't had enough sleep it will reflect in his behaviour. It is a good idea to start to get into the routine of putting your child to bed at the same time each night to establish good sleep habits from an early age (see page 136). Food, bath, story, bed is a useful and calming pattern. Make sure that your child falls asleep in the calm and quiet of their bed, not in front of the TV or in your bed.

How you respond

The toddler years are a combination of letting go of babyhood and starting to put into place the behaviour guidelines that will help shape your child's behaviour in the future. Later chapters will outline practical guidelines for routines for eating, sleeping, and good behaviour. At the age of 12–18 months the guidelines are fairly simple.

Love and praise work wonders A toddler who is rewarded for good behaviour by having your warmth and attention will not need to "play up" to get noticed. Use positive eye contact and body posture by getting down to your child's level to talk. Remain calm and consistent in your response – a child of this age will be confused by inconsistency or extremes of mood. Look for the positives in all that he does. Your child is not deliberately defiant, but is learning self-control and testing his limits and boundaries.

"I was determined not to become a part of the potty-training posse and decided I would not worry much before my son was three."

Saira, aged 30

Encourage self-feeding By 15 months, children have developed the fine motor skills needed to feed themselves. The process will be messy to begin with and should never be forced, but now is a good time to let your toddler start to hold a spoon and to experiment with self-feeding. You will probably value a very large bib, as not much will reach his mouth to begin with! He will learn very fast, though, and by 18 months is likely to be able to guide a complete spoonful into his mouth and consume most of it. Resist the temptation to keep wiping his mouth clean, though.

Feeding is a highly sensitive area of development and there are detailed guidelines on pages 206–211. At this age your toddler is too young to be fussy, and if he's hungry he is likely to eat… eventually. The most important thing is to ensure that your child is getting regular meals that are nutritionally balanced. In the majority of cases the rest will follow quite naturally.

The question of potty training By 18 months your child has enough muscle control to begin to be able to hold urine for short periods, but is unlikely to become fully dry much before 2–3 years old. Parents have a tendency to become strangely competitive about the speed with which they potty trained their child, but each child is different, not all children use a potty, and the issue should never be forced (see page 128).

Safety Your home environment is all that your toddler knows. It includes all the people, sights, sounds, and sensations that make up his world. Toddlers are children on the move, usually at floor level – and their curiosity knows no bounds. Children at this age cannot remember information for very long and have no concept of danger, so it is important to start to "toddler-proof" your home for their safety and your sanity (see page 274). Look at your home through your child's eyes and plan ahead to make potential trouble spots safe.

Make way for messy play For the sake of everyone's sanity abandon all hope of an immaculate house for the next few years. Embracing mess and chaos is all part of the child development process. Cleanliness is always important, but not when taken to extremes. An excessive focus on tidiness and hygiene may lead to undue anxiety in small children and restrict their development through play. Those who become excessively fussy eaters or unusually neat and tidy in their play are often reflecting their parents' anxious preoccupation with cleanliness and orderliness.

I WANT IT NOW!
A small child who is hungry will let you know – and will need to eat straight away.

Managing behaviour

At this age, your toddler is not being deliberately naughty and does not know how to manipulate. He is simply attention-seeking and exploring, with no capacity for common sense and little memory or reasoning ability. He simply can't understand the world from someone else's perspective.

All children have the right to be respected for who they are and for their views, but not at the expense of those around them, or society as a whole. Chapter one explains the true nature of child-centred parenting (see page 38) and the need for a careful balance between parental warmth and control (see page 27). This section is called "managing behaviour" rather than "disciplining your child" for a reason. For your child to learn to manage his feelings appropriately and develop good social skills, he needs you to set behaviour boundaries. Behaving well is the result of good behaviour habits, a routine, and plenty of praise, rather than enforced obedience.

"The phrase that I repeat to parents constantly is 'Praise the good and ignore the bad'. The earlier you can begin, the easier it will be for you and your child."

The dilemma is that we want our children to understand that when we say "No" we mean it, but we also want them to have the knowledge and strength of character to be able to refuse if an adult or child tries to coerce them into doing something they don't want to. By learning boundaries from you when he is young, your child can begin to develop self-control, which is the key to both self-esteem and personal safety.

Your toddler's response

At 12–18 months your toddler is still too young to have much control over his personal response as the frontal lobes of the brain (see page 164) are still developing. So the onus at this age is very much on you, the parent, to help your child to control his behaviour. He will experience very strong feelings at this age, which may overwhelm and scare him, but there is a host of strategies available that will keep the mutual stress to a minimum and encourage your toddler to get used to these new feelings.

Small children cry because they are distressed, not because they are being manipulative. It may be because they want something, need something, are frightened, or are ill. It is important to make sure that there are no signs of fear or sickness. Sometimes the problem can be as simple as tiredness or the need for a nappy change.

Toddlers can be surprisingly determined, so if your child wants something specific, you may be in for a long haul unless you can figure out quickly what is needed. In these instances, using distraction techniques (see below) is probably the best option.

REASSURANCE *If she is distressed, your child will usually be pacified by your presence and the pleasure of your attention. The reward of a smile and a cuddle often restores order.*

Distraction techniques

Reasoning with your child at this age just will not work – he does not have the language or reasoning abilities to follow your logic. The same is true of asking him to wait. If he needs distracting, you may have to physically move him somewhere else, and offer something to occupy him, rather than get locked into a battle of wills and mounting frustration.

If you are away from home and foresee a problem, it is helpful to be prepared in advance. Make sure you take a couple of favourite toys or books with you and, if necessary, ask another adult to come along and help you. The toys can be used as a distraction in case of upset or, even better, used as a reward for good behaviour or as entertainment to avoid any difficulties. A screaming toddler will have less impact on the rest of the adult world if he is outside, so don't be afraid to remove your child from an indoor environment and let him exercise his lungs in healthy fresh air. If you have older children, you may find that they are more adept than you are at diverting your toddler.

Sending messages to the brain

There is a growing body of research that shows that our ability to regulate the impact of stress develops in the first three years. The messages sent to the brain in early toddlerhood can affect the way the brain becomes wired and so influence how we respond to situations as we become older.

It is never a good idea to allow a child to become out of control and consumed by distress, particularly at such a young age. When we experience intense feelings, either of joy or sadness, the body sends chemical messages to the brain. These messages either take the form of feel-good hormones (opioids and oxytocin) or stress-fighting hormones (cortisol, adrenaline, and noradrenaline), and the level and frequency of these at a very young age will have an impact on how the brain develops, and how your child will grow up to deal with challenges in later life.

Minimizing stress

A child who experiences a great deal of shouting, anger, or other kinds of stress during baby and toddlerhood, will produce permanently high levels of stress-fighting hormones, especially the chemical cortisol, which is released by the adrenal glands. A constantly high level of cortisol can be overwhelming because the body is left in a high state of tension, and set for "fight or flight" from whatever is causing stress. Adults who have had a highly stressful childhood will continue to produce high levels of cortisol quite easily, and will find it hard to react appropriately to high-pressure situations. It is as if the body is in a constant state of alert, always looking for threats. This can lead to anxiety (see page 168). Ultimately the body and mind cannot cope with this state of high alert and become exhausted.

Physical intervention, shouting, and other violent techniques do not work between adults and will certainly not work on a defenceless child. We know much more now than we did a generation ago about how corporal punishment and other forms of aggression impact on the brain and it is now clear that smacking, shouting, or neglect are very likely to cause damage to a young child's development. The child's physical response will also lead to an increase in cortisol production. A child who is brought up in an environment of chronic tension or anger is likely to develop an easily aroused sense of dread about life in general, and will find it harder as an adult to find comfort in physical warmth, kindness, or affection.

"I still find it hard to cope when Liam screams and cries. I feel so helpless. We talk to him softly, which seems to calm him down."

Lucy, aged 22

PLAYTIME BATTLES *Conflict between toddlers sharing a toy is normal. Distracting one or both children with another activity is a more effective tactic than "telling them off", not least because they're not being purposefully naughty.*

Positive ways to manage behaviour

Using positive tactics to deal with your child's behaviour will encourage a feel-good response in his brain and build resistance to stress in the future. The core message behind these tactics is to love your child unconditionally and to make sure you focus on modifying his behaviour rather than criticizing. For example, saying, "Harry, that behaviour is not allowed" or "Harry, we are going to do something exciting now" will be more effective and nurturing than saying, "Harry, how many times do I have to tell you? You're a very naughty boy."

Your child's self-esteem is very vulnerable to damage. Being constantly criticized and shouted at can have a negative effect on his sense of self, and self-criticism may become a part of his identity.

It is very hard to change who you are, but we each have the power to change a pattern of behaviour. As your child gets older he will learn that he has control over his behaviour and people's reaction to it.

Positive tactics for this age group:
▶ Staying calm.
▶ Using love and comfort.
▶ Finding child-friendly areas for safe play.
▶ Using distraction techniques.
▶ Ignoring bad behaviour.
▶ Praising good behaviour.
▶ Keep instructions simple.
▶ Using short-term time out techniques (see page 270).
▶ Routine, routine, routine.

▶ A consistent approach.
▶ Rest, food, and sleep.
▶ The outdoors effect.
▶ Sibling influence.
▶ Treats and incentives.
▶ Forgiveness.
▶ Patience, tolerance, and humour.

Tactics to avoid at all costs:
▶ Smacking and any form of physical punishment.
▶ Shouting, neglecting, or extreme disapproval.
▶ In-depth explanations.
▶ Too much choice.
▶ Extreme threats.
▶ Delayed punishment.
▶ Shaking or rough handling.
▶ Deprivation or withholding of comfort.
▶ Isolation and rejection.

This, in turn, can impact on the attachment between parent and child (see page 90). There are negative effects on learning, too, because when the brain is in a state of high alert or stress, a child will be unable to learn and develop other skills.

A natural sense of well-being

Feel-good hormones are the chemicals that help us to deal well with times of distress, pain, and stress. A child who is confident that he is safe, who has plenty of fun and affection, and who is comforted when distressed, will produce more opioids than cortisol. These hormones are natural pain relievers and give us a sense of well-being. They are produced by the hypothalamus from deep within the instinctive "lower" brain. Oxytocin is released and triggers a series of chemical responses that reduce the negative effects of stress on the body and help us to enjoy life, to go with the flow, and to question and explore the world we live in.

Your feelings

When handling difficult behaviour, your mood is important because when you are stressed your toddler may become anxious. This will lead him to want more attention and be more clingy. You can only teach your child to manage his feelings if you can regulate your own feelings, such as sadness, anger, frustration, or hurt. Regulating feelings doesn't mean ignoring them, burying them, or not reacting. It means recognizing the feeling you are having and managing it in such a way that it does not overwhelm you.

Parents start to model self-regulation when they respond in different ways to a child's emotional needs. For example, if a child is screaming in frustration your reaction will be completely different to your response when he is screaming from hurt. Parents naturally pick up on the smallest of cues and respond accordingly. This kind of sensitivity and flexibility is difficult, however, if you are frequently overwhelmed by your own feelings – because your toddler will pick up on your distress and you may model ways of not managing instead. If you are unable to regulate your feelings, you may be driven to act impulsively, and perhaps inappropriately, or unable to respond at all. If you find it hard to cope, do seek help.

Getting it right

There will be challenging times during early toddlerhood, but if you get the parenting right now, your child will be much less of a handful when he is a teenager. The easiest way to navigate these years is to ensure your home is fully toddler-proofed and to swap the dread of frequent humiliation in public for a good sense of humour and some advance plans and tactics. Your armoury will need to be stronger with an older toddler, and variations on strategies will be explained in subsequent chapters.

"Remember to say 'No' to the behaviour, rather than criticizing your child."

NATURAL INSTINCTS *Your baby has an automatic reflex that makes him cry when in need of food or comfort, and you are programmed to protect him and respond to his needs.*

The bond between you and your child

You and your baby will have a deep instinct for closeness and bonding which is driven by your need to nurture and his to survive. "Attachment" is a child's overwhelming need to be near to a particular person who represents safety and comfort – this is usually, but not always, a parent.

Once your growing toddler learns who "Mummy", "Daddy", and his other main carers are, the attachment to those individuals increases and his cries will become targeted more towards them. Your toddler may develop attachment relationships with more than one person and each relationship is unique. It is at this age that anxiety about separation peaks.

Fathers are much more involved in childcare today than in previous generations and may be the primary carer in the family, and the person the child becomes the most attached to in the early months. Boys, in particular, benefit from having a positive male role model as they grow up; it is important for their sense of identity and developing self-esteem.

Attachment behaviour was written about by psychoanalyst John Bowlby (1907–1990). It is a deeply instinctive response and ensures that your toddler gets the attention he needs. It is an important factor in the development of his identity, and a strong motivator for keeping him safe.

Attachment between carer and child represents:

■ Safety – a safe base from which to explore the world.

■ Survival – ensures the proximity of the carer and therefore better care.

■ Learning – about personal needs and personal control, as well as the understanding that the way he behaves can have an effect on someone else. It's important to try not to allow your own need for closeness to overwhelm or inhibit your toddler's ability to learn his own way and become more self-sufficient.

■ Closeness – provides a model for later relationships and can teach us how to empathize and see situations from another's perspective.

By allowing your toddler the freedom to experiment and learn from new experiences, without judgement and criticism, you will be helping him to build self-confidence and self-esteem. Attachment starts as a survival mechanism, but also helps us learn about emotions and intimacy in preparation for relationships in later life. Many children need help in learning to be separate from their trusted person or family as they get older. This is all part of growing up.

A child's attachment behaviour is most likely to show when he is stressed: perhaps when separated from a trusted adult, or because of an overwhelming need for something he wants immediately. A toddler's brain does not yet know how to cope with time and so does not know how to wait; nor will he understand that when you disappear you may still be nearby and will return. This leads to separation anxiety. The intensity of the separation anxiety and how long it lasts depends on both the child's need for the parent, and the parent's need for the child. Every parent–child relationship is different, even within the context of a single family.

Early baby bonding

During the first year of life a baby moves quite rapidly through different stages of bonding and acceptance of the people around him. In comparison to toddlers, many babies are quite relaxed with new people. Separation anxiety begins later and coincides with the development of language and memory, peaking during months 12-18.

AGE	STAGE	BEHAVIOUR
▸ 0-2 months	Asocial attachments	Babies respond similarly to both people and things until they are around two months old when they start to recognize faces and voices and will settle more easily with someone who is familiar.
▸ 2-7 months	Indiscriminate attachments	Small babies will have some preference for familiar faces, but are generally at ease with new people, too.
▸ 7-9 months	Specific attachments	Will have formed a main attachment to their primary carer and can be very anxious and distressed around strangers.
▸ 9 months +	Multiple attachments	By nine months will become attached to several familiar and important figures, such as relatives, siblings, and frequent visitors.

Flanagan, C. (1996)

It depends on the unique mix of the child's temperament and how the parent responds to it. Every parent was once a child and seeing your own child grow and responding to his vulnerabilities can trigger deeply held memories of your own experience of childhood, and will affect your style of response (see page 22). For some parents this can be a challenge.

The parent–child connection

Young toddlers may find it hard to cope when their parent or carer is not there. This is because they cannot yet understand that someone or something that is out of view still exists and can reappear. This is not a matter of philosophy! It is simply that the memory systems of the brain are not fully developed. For the same reason, your toddler has no real concept of time and can't tell the difference between 10 minutes and one hour, or yesterday, today, or tomorrow. He knows only what he can see and what he wants, in the here and now.

Understanding this is important because your child might find separation from you difficult until he has reached a certain level of cognitive development. A baby as young as six months old will catch on to the fact that an object still exists even when it is hidden, but may struggle for much

Real life

I had always said I would go back to work after Pippa was born. I was looking forward to having my baby, but it was a personal wish, as well as a financial necessity. However, nothing could have prepared me for the strong feelings of love I have for my baby girl. When she was 12 months old I returned to my full-time job, but I still feel dreadful about it every day. Pippa now spends two days a week with her grandparents and three days with a childminder. She often cries when I leave her, which wrenches my heart, even though I know it's normal and she's perfectly happy and safe.

All the time I feel guilty at leaving her, worried about whether I have done the right thing, and sometimes quite resentful towards our lovely childminder – simply because she spends so much time with her. I tell myself that Pippa is well looked after, she is not coming to any harm, she is getting used to other people and that she is very well loved. In truth, I think it is harder for me than it is for her. She is getting loads of attention and having a lovely time. I just didn't realize how hard the adjustment would be. Her father and I try to make up for it by spending as much time playing with her at the weekends as possible. So Pippa gets the best of both worlds, really!

longer to cope with or understand that Mummy and Daddy still exist when they are in another room. A parent's absence is more stressful than the whereabouts of a hidden toy, and so a baby brain will find it harder to hold onto the concept that Mummy or Daddy will return.

Interestingly, separation anxiety is at its peak at about 15 months and then slowly reduces; this coincides with the development of language, which is linked to the development of memory and reasoning skills. By now your child will have had more experiences of separation, too, and will have begun to learn that Mummy and Daddy always return.

"Learning to 'let go' is a challenge that is faced by parents at every developmental milestone as their children begin to separate from them and grow up."

Coping with your own anxieties

Parents feel separation anxiety, too, and it may be you rather than your child who feels the pain of separation most acutely when you have to leave him with a carer.

To make the process of leaving him easier, remember:

■ Make sure your toddler feels comfortable and is familiar with his new surroundings before you leave him for the first time.

■ Don't be tempted to fuss too much before you go, or he may pick up on your anxiety and become upset.

■ Your child will be more comfortable if you leave him with familiar toys and encourage the carer to keep to a routine (but if this is not possible, a change in routine will not be damaging to you or your child).

■ Have enough faith in your parenting to know that your child has the skills to cope and is not going to fall apart without you.

■ If you are a working parent, make a conscious effort to build up your support network of family and other parents, so that you have people you can call on in an emergency, or if you are held up at work. Knowing you have other people to rely on can help to minimize your stress.

■ Even though you may have a busy evening ahead, take some time to reassure and reconnect with your child in a relaxed and unhurried way when you first return to him at the end of the day.

Choosing childcare

"Should I work and pay for childcare, or look after my child myself?" This is the very difficult dilemma faced by thousands of parents with pre-school aged children. The fact is that the right to choose to work has fast turned into an economic necessity.

The long-term ramifications for today's children, or society as a whole, of being in childcare while their parents go to work are not known. The work/childcare debate is an emotive issue that will run and run.

While there is no doubt that children benefit from the constant care of a loving parent, there is no reason why a child should be disadvantaged by being looked after by someone else as well. In fact, there are advantages to getting small children used to the company of adults outside the immediate family, provided they are helped to manage their natural anxiety (see page 91).

CHOOSING A CARER

A young toddler needs ideally to be with someone who listens to him, notices his needs, responds accordingly, and makes a positive contribution towards shaping his behaviour, without trying to take the place of his parents. This is the key to successful childcare. You need to feel comfortable with the childcare you have chosen, otherwise your child may pick up on your anxiety and become anxious himself.

Decide in advance what your main concerns are for your child and what qualities you want in your carer. Make a note of your toddler's likes and dislikes and the family routine, if you would like it followed. If you are able to call on a relative or friend to look after your child, you should go through the same briefing process as you would if leaving your child with a total stranger, so there can be no room for later misunderstanding. A work crèche is an ideal scenario for both child and parent, but unfortunately these are still the exception to the rule.

INTRODUCING A CARER

It can be valuable to make time for your toddler to get used to the new carer before you return to work. A child can become overwhelmed easily by a stranger, or even a relative or

YOUR FEELINGS

In reality, it is you as the parent, rather than your child, who may feel an acute sense of separation. It can be hard to return from work to find, for example, that your child has spoken his first word or taken his first steps with the childminder rather than you. But once you have made the decision to use childcare, a sense of pragmatism is essential, coupled with the desire to make time for your children when you are at home, instead.

THE RIGHT ENVIRONMENT

Whichever type of childcare you have chosen, word-of-mouth recommendations and feedback from other parents can be very helpful. There is also a wealth of professional organizations that can offer advice (see page 310–311). Spending some time in new surroundings with your child before leaving him for the first time will make it easier for both of you; and seeing how the other children respond to the carer will help you to make a judgement about whether the environment is right for your needs. If you know your child is happy, rather than distressed about your return to work, you will be free to focus instead on your career and developing another side of your life.

"It is completely natural to want to compensate your child for your absence, but giving her extra treats to make up for the time you are away can be counter-productive in the long-term."

friend, who wants to hold him or make close facial or eye contact far too soon. You can make sure this doesn't happen by explaining that you would like to allow time for your child to relax and get used to the new situation at his own pace.

▶ Don't leave the carer alone with your child initially. Allow him or her to chatter or interact while your child is close to you. It is too soon for any physical contact at this stage.

▶ Let your child lead the first contact with the carer. Watch for eye contact or a smile and make sure that your child is comfortable before the carer begins to focus on him.

▶ Once your child seems interested and comfortable, encourage him to play alongside you while you and the carer talk.

▶ After a while, encourage the carer to play with your child at his level. Watch the body language and eye contact between them – and especially notice how your child is reacting.

▶ Once your child is warming towards the carer, try retreating a bit, or perhaps leave the room.

▶ See what happens. Don't allow your child to become severely distressed, but don't fuss unnecessarily. An able carer will have lots of effective distraction techniques.

AWAY FROM HOME Children are very adaptable and if you have found the right carer and environment, your child will soon settle.

COPING WITH SEPARATION

How a child copes with being separated from you depends on his innate character, and how you cope with leaving him. Some children's first experience of separation from a parent may coincide with their first experience of being with other children. There is bound to be a period of adjustment, but provided the carer is responsive and the environment positive, he will probably adjust more quickly than you.

Just for parents

Perhaps the most important, but also most challenging, part of being a parent is finding personal time. You have taken on a role, a label, and a host of expectations about your behaviour, your priorities, your choices, and the use of your time, that will transform your life and your vision of yourself.

While your toddler is enjoying his first experience of independence, you may be wondering where your own has gone! Babies are much more portable than toddlers; even so, parents may be under the illusion that life can continue much as before. But not for long! The onset of toddlerhood, or having more than one child in the family, changes everything, and personal needs and interests can often take second place to parenting. Work, on the other hand, can often become a place of refuge.

Getting the balance right

Some parents feel guilty when they find they miss their previous life, or feel pangs of envy when talking to childless friends; others are happy to stay cocooned in their family world with their children, and feel they don't need anything else. As we all know, achieving balance in all things is the healthiest way to live, but can be hard to achieve and maintain. A parent who is unhappy or frustrated will convey that mood to their child; if both parents are in the same state, then ructions and frustration are likely. Parents who live solely for their children inadvertently make it harder for the children to separate from them and develop self-confidence. Early interaction with others is great for your child's social development.

"As a parent, I'm finding the financial pressures are a lot greater now, so I am working longer hours and am tired when I get home. I'm not sure I could face an evening out, even if we had the money." Louise, aged 37

The great secret of successful parenting is planning ahead – and sticking to those plans. Many parents are great at cramming the diary with priorities to fulfil their children's needs, but are less consistent when it comes to their own. It is usually possible to find someone suitable to babysit and to allow enough time in advance for your child to get used to the person who is to look after them. It is essential to have a "back-up" person, as you never know when it might be necessary for you to be away from home in an emergency. Take a moment to ask yourself the following questions.

How long is it since I…

- Saw friends without my children?
- Went out for an evening with my partner?
- Had quality time on my own?
- Saw a film?
- Got dressed up?
- Took up a hobby?
- Took physical exercise (other than pushing a buggy)?
- Bought new clothes that weren't easycare or practical?
- Went on holiday?
- Sat and read a book?
- Felt on top of things?

"I love my children, but I really long for some real conversation so that I feel like an adult again."

Maya, aged 25

BEYOND PARENTING *Your children have to be a priority, but it isn't beneficial in the long run to you or to them if they take over your life completely. It's positive for you all to have time out from each other occasionally.*

- Had a full night's sleep?
- Got home from work on time?
- Accepted a social invitation?
- Felt really good about myself?

Now try another set of questions:

- How would you like to spend more time for you?
- How would you like to spend time with your partner?
- What is getting in the way of you doing it?
- Is there someone who would be willing to spend a few hours babysitting one evening every week/month and how soon could you arrange this?

So often it is pressure or tiredness that gets in the way of having private time. Money is rarely the core issue as there is usually someone who would be willing to give some time in exchange for a return favour. If you feel your child would be a bit of a handful for someone outside the family, try taking the risk and you might get a positive surprise. Becoming a parent doesn't stop you being an individual.

"I look at myself in the mirror sometimes and don't know who I am any more. In spite of the enjoyment I get from being a parent, I seem to have lost all my self-confidence and our relationship is under strain." Joanne, aged 29

Your health and relationship

As a parent you have to be physically and emotionally well. Poor nutrition and a lack of exercise can contribute to feelings of tiredness and ill health. There is a wealth of information available on the essentials of healthy eating so get some advice if you have gone off track. Keeping on the move, looking after your health, and eating well are the essentials for feeling energetic and positive and great traits to pass on to your children.

Just as important is making time for your partner. Communication and affection are important aspects of a relationship that need nurturing. If necessary, make a date to be together at home, but try not to talk about the children! The same is true for lone parents. For those facing the challenge of parenting without a partner, friends are particularly important. You owe it to yourself to have a social life and your child will benefit, too.

Dear Tanya...

▸ **It is a year since my daughter was born and I still feel fat and unattractive and not myself. I can't find the time or the motivation to get fit. How can I get some of my old self back?**
The feelings you are describing are shared by the vast majority of mothers at some point. Finding time for yourself is a challenge when you have a toddler, but your weight gain is as much an emotional issue as it is a physical one.

Becoming a mother does not have to mean saying goodbye to your old self and you owe it to your child, as well as to yourself, to rediscover interests that do not involve the home and motherhood. Your toddler can cope with periods of separation from you and it will help her own development to understand that Mummy has friends and hobbies of her own.

If you have a partner and he likes you the way you are, he will also like you when you return to liking yourself – and chances are your weight will then be much easier to lose once you have regained some of that lost self-esteem.

▸ **My 18-month-old son likes to say goodnight to his Daddy before he goes to bed, so I let him fall asleep in front of the TV until my partner gets home from work. Is this a mistake?**
The danger is that you are creating a habit that will be hard to break. He is beginning to associate TV and Daddy waking him as part of his night-time ritual. A child who has a disrupted sleep pattern is more likely to play up during the day and at this age your son needs at least 11 hours' sleep a night. It would be wise to start to introduce a regular routine with bathtime, followed by a short bedtime story, and then into bed. He is old enough to have a phone call from Daddy as a comforting alternative.

▸ **I feel very feel guilty about being at work all day and away from my son and then find it hard to say "No" to him when I come home. I don't want him to resent me or to stop a close bond developing between us.**
Provided your son is happy when he is with his daytime carers, you have no reason to feel guilty. Spending time away from you will help him to get used to other people and to develop social skills. Nor do you need to worry about jeopardizing the bond between you. Your son loves to be with you and during the toddler years will crave your approval and affection. However, showing him that you love him includes having the commitment to create and stick to behaviour boundaries. He needs you to help him to learn how to contain the extremes of his behaviour, and he needs to know that you need time for yourself, too.

Being a lenient parent may seem kinder or easier than putting some rules in place, but you are setting up a pattern that will lead to long-term problems. If your child has no boundaries, your evenings will become tense and fraught. Instead of having quality time together you will feel out of control and so will he. The older he gets, the harder it will become to change his behaviour. Don't let your feelings of guilt hamper your parenting skills and prevent you helping your son to learn positive and healthy behaviour management skills.

A LITTLE INDIVIDUAL *Think of your child as her own person and remember she will grow up to be uniquely herself. She will develop into a strong, positive individual with your love and support.*

5 points to remember

1 Don't feel you need to force development in any way as it will all happen in good time. Try not to get hung up on milestones and comparing your child with others.

2 One of the biggest challenges is to make sure that praise and encouragement are used frequently and that the word "No" does not dominate. Behaving well is the result of good behaviour habits, a routine, and plenty of praise, rather than enforced behaviour.

3 Your toddler does not need elaborate toys – normal household objects may often hold more delight and are better suited to this age group than multi-functional toys. Everyday activities, such as dressing and shopping, can all offer scope for fun and games.

4 Your child's behaviour and capacity for self-control may fluctuate markedly. This is normal and is the result of him having to adjust to so many changes.

5 For the sake of everyone's sanity, abandon all hope of an immaculate house for the next few years. Embracing mess and chaos is all part of the child development process, and while cleanliness is important, it shouldn't be taken to extremes.

HOW SHE PLAYS *At this age, it is normal for your toddler to play by herself. She won't be ready to play with other children for some time yet, but she will love you to be her playmate.*

18–24
MONTHS

YOUR GROWING TODDLER

NEW ACTIVITIES AS YOUR TODDLER BECOMES MORE ADEPT AT HANDLING SMALL OBJECTS, THERE WILL BE GREATER OPPORTUNITIES FOR CREATIVE PLAY

LITTLE DAREDEVIL
NEW ADVENTURES WILL BRING TUMBLES AND MINOR INJURIES, BUT TRY TO GET THE BALANCE RIGHT BETWEEN KEEPING HIM SAFE AND BEING OVER-PROTECTIVE

"She's becoming more aware she's an individual – and won't you know it!"

LEARNING FROM YOU ALWAYS GET DOWN TO HER LEVEL TO PLAY AND REMEMBER TO PRAISE, PRAISE, PRAISE AS SHE LEARNS

Your toddler's development

In the next six months your toddler will be walking, and even running, more steadily, freeing her brain to focus on another vital skill: improving her ability to talk. A great deal of learning continues to take place through play and almost everything you do will offer potential for fun and ways to develop new skills.

Since her first birthday, you will have seen dramatic changes in your toddler's ability to move about and during months 18–24 she will become even more steady on her feet. You will start to see more and more signs of independent toddler behaviour and her need to be heard and understood will increase steadily. These changes coincide with ongoing brain and memory development, which means there will be lots of excitable toddler chatter and she will be learning new words almost every day. Although she will learn a great deal through play, there is no need for formal lessons or anything too structured at this stage; over-controlled playtime will inhibit rather than encourage development.

Children in this age group are ready to start self-feeding with a spoon (with some extra help from their fingers); some may enjoy periods of time without nappies; most are starting to be more inventive and creative in their play, and you will probably be feeling you have much less time to yourself than you did when your child was a baby.

Early behaviour and routines

Some clear behaviour boundaries will become necessary as your child becomes more experimental and challenging, not only to help her to stay safe but also because she is now ready to begin to learn to control her own behaviour and will be able to understand the difference between "Yes" and "No". Setting your limits will help her to start to set her own, and to begin to understand some of the rights and wrongs of social behaviour.

By 21–24 months you will notice a significant difference in your toddler's reasoning skills and she will be very keen to "help" you as much as possible, perhaps by starting to put her toys away. Toddlers are often

"Amy is wilful and determined, but we love her spirit. We choose our battles wisely, but she knows that 'No' means no!"

Lisa, aged 36

very keen on order and the "rightness" of things. You don't have to be too rigid, but this period is the ideal time to introduce more routine and structure to your child's day, especially at mealtimes, bedtime, and getting up time – if you haven't already done so. She still needs your help and intervention to manage her behaviour, but if she gets used to the routines now, your life in a few months' time will be a great deal easier.

"I always remind people that the toddler of today is the teenager of tomorrow. You owe it to your child – and to yourself – to put the ground rules in place early."

Emotional development

Separation anxiety (see page 90) will still be a big issue for your toddler during this six-month period as it coincides with an increase in her ability to reason, and the development of her imagination. Whereas you were previously able to leave the house to go to work with no problem, you may suddenly find that your toddler is distraught, and may weep and cling to you as you try to leave.

If you are happy with your childcare arrangements and know that your child is neither ill, nor at risk, then you can comfort yourself that this is all part of the current development stage. Young children find partings quite a wrench, and in the moment of distress will not be able to believe you will be coming home later. Give your toddler a reassuring hug and explain you will be home "soon" (or, as she gets older, "when the little hand of the

What's mine is mine

Your toddler is very egocentric (see page 55) and is becoming much more aware of "me" as a separate person from "you". She will be developing a strong sense of ownership and find it hard to let go of possessions. This is not selfishness so much as a growing awareness of herself as an individual. Once she is secure in the knowledge of what is "mine" and "yours" she will become able to share, but might not want to! The development of self-control will begin over the course of this year, but at this age she stills lack the ability to regulate her emotions and will quickly become overwhelmed by her own feelings and the extreme feelings of others.

clock points to the six"). Be understanding, but firm, and don't delay your departure (or return). She will soon settle.

Toddlers are like miniature teenagers in some ways. They are fraught with rapidly changing emotions that are very hard to handle. They will be smiley and giggly one moment and a picture of rage and despair in another. Their tears are often related to frustration and anxiety but, with reassurance, will pass very quickly.

At this age your toddler might find the transition from one activity to another quite a challenge: getting dressed or undressed may be an issue; saying goodbye or meeting someone new may be stressful; stopping play in order to eat may cause tears. This is partly because she is feeling overwhelmed by change and has an intense desire to be in control of her environment. Her attention levels are also increasing, so she may become more distressed than previously when you interrupt something she is enjoying. She can now focus on a new activity for up to five or seven minutes without a break, although she is still easily distracted by factors such as noises, people, bright colours, and movement.

Her relationships

By now, your child will be able to recognize family members, as well as regular visitors or friends, and will be able to cope with playing a short distance away from you. There will be a very strong sense of connection to you and she will know that she enjoys your attention.

You may also find that she becomes demanding as soon as you are speaking to someone else – especially if you are on the phone. You can either distract her by providing an activity while you complete your task or ignore her demands, thus giving a clear message that you are not available to her all the time.

LEARNING ABOUT HIMSELF *Asking your toddler to point to body parts gives him a sense of self-awareness. He'll realize he's "like Mummy and Daddy" but that he's also his own person.*

Signs that development is on track

It is important to emphasize that all children will develop at their own pace, and rarely in constant progression (see page 64). The following is an approximate guide to how new skills will develop in the coming months.

By the end of months 18–19, your child:

■ Can probably link together two or three words in a basic fashion ("me dog play"/"Mummy go stairs").

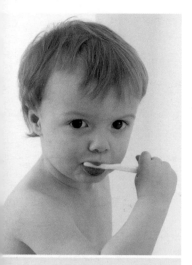

SELF-CARE *With growing independence, your toddler will want to brush his own teeth and begin to help to dress himself. Being allowed to try will increase his self-confidence.*

■ Will have stopped putting objects in her mouth to explore and learn about them.

■ Could self-feed if encouraged and may be able to use a spoon or fork as well as her fingers when eating.

■ Knows and can point to one or two parts of the body, such as her toe or ear, when asked.

■ May walk into a ball in order to kick it forward.

■ Can understand, but may not follow, simple instructions.

■ Will be enjoying imitative play, such as "feeding" a doll.

By the end of months 20–21, your child:

■ Will be able to throw a ball overarm.

■ Will be able to scribble with a pencil or crayon.

■ May be able to speak well enough to be understood half the time.

■ Can help to undress herself.

■ Will be able to start helping to brush her teeth.

By the end of months 22–23, your child:

■ Will be able to use at least six words and understand about 50.

■ Will be able to walk up stairs, putting both feet on each step, and may be able to kick a small ball forwards.

■ Will be starting to understand prepositions, such as "on" , "in", and "under".

■ Can recognize people she knows at some distance away from them.

By the end of month 24, your child:

■ Will be starting to undress herself and may be starting to dress herself too (with help).

■ Can build a tower four blocks high.

■ Can point at one or two pictures in recognition.

■ May be able to jump.

■ Can respond to simple questions, such as "Where is Daddy?"

"Remember that it is easier for a toddler to start something new than it is for her to stop what she is doing. Try saying 'Walk slowly,' rather than 'Don't run,' next time you want her to stop."

JUST LIKE YOU *She will learn so much from copying the things you do and say, and she will love it if she is allowed to be "the grown-up" sometimes.*

And then there were two...

Just as your toddler is getting used to the idea that she is the centre of your world, as you are in hers, something happens to transform the family dynamic... there is a new kid on the block! She will need all your help and understanding to adapt to this change.

It is fairly common for a new sibling to arrive while other children are still at the toddler stage. The arrival of a new baby requires adjustment on all fronts and the smoothness of the change depends on factors such as how many children you have, the age differences, any special needs, your health, and your commitments. But with a happy temperament and effective nurturing, your children will eventually learn to be co-operative and loving. Older siblings can play an important part as role models, playmates, and partners in crime! But this is a long way off yet, and when a new baby first arrives your toddler may show a range of responses varying from slight interest to excitement, protectiveness to distress, or ambivalence to jealousy. None of these is unusual – and all are normal.

REAL LIFE

We hadn't planned to have another child so soon after the arrival of Justin, who had been quite a challenging baby. Justin was only 21 months old and still very clingy when Ed was born. Soon after Ed's arrival Justin started to bite me and have tantrums. Ed was a totally different character. Relaxed and smiley, he was a very easy baby. I tried to spend lots of time with Justin while Ed was sleeping, but kept him away when he was awake in case he hurt him. As a result, Justin seemed to crave even more time alone with me. He started to use baby language when I was with Ed, and was showing signs of increasing jealousy. My husband and I then realized it was time to take a different approach, to help the two children to get used to each other. So we started to bath them together and to have family storytime in the evening. We would pay lots of positive attention to Justin, while encouraging him to help hold and soothe Ed while we got him ready for bed. I cuddled the children, while my husband read a story of Justin's choice. It wasn't an overnight success, but they adore each other now. There's lots of giggles and Justin is very protective of his baby brother.

WHAT ABOUT ME?

To help your toddler get used to the idea that a new baby will soon be arriving, involve her in your preparations. Simple tasks, such as choosing a teddy for the newborn or helping to choose the name, will reinforce feelings of family belonging, rather than feeling pushed to one side.

Although your toddler may have been making steady developmental progress, don't be surprised if she shows signs of regression, such as using baby talk or wanting to be breastfed, when the new baby arrives. This is common behaviour, and it is fine for you to baby her at times as well. She will find it reassuring to know that she has not been replaced. Now can be a good opportunity to show her that it can be special to be older. You might consider moving her out of her cot and into a bed of her own (with side-guards); or if she is still feeding from a bottle you could arrange to say "bye bye" to the bottle and give her a special beaker.

Your toddler will want and need quality time with you, but beware the trap of feeling you need to overcompensate for the attention you are paying your new baby, as this is likely to backfire. Find ways to involve both or all of your children with one another, rather than trying to slice yourself too thinly. The more quickly your older child is able to form an early bond with her new brother or sister, the less likely she is to feel overwhelmingly jealous or excluded from your world.

Dads play a vital role at this time because mums are inevitably less available. It is a nice time for dads to spend more solo time with their children, who may start to associate Dad with more fun and games. Asking friends and relations to spend time with your toddler can also offer her more playtime.

TOP TIPS FOR FAMILY ADJUSTMENT

▸ Praise your toddler to her face and to the new baby while she is with you.

▸ Read bedtime stories to your toddler and make special time to say goodnight to her.

▸ Allow her to sit on your lap and help to "hold" her new sibling. Let her express her feelings and acknowledge that the noise and mess that go with having a baby around can be annoying.

▸ Respect your toddler's space and belongings. Remember, it is normal for her to be very territorial and wary of potential rivals.

▸ Try not to compare your children or to show signs of favouritism.

▸ Be patient with your toddler's behaviour. It can be easy to label her as your "bad" child in comparison to your "good" baby, but remember that she is just adjusting to her new status and will get used to it in time.

▸ Your toddler is not yet ready or able to take on the role of caring, older sibling, and deserves to enjoy her toddler phase as long as possible.

INCLUDING HIM *Asking your toddler to "read" a story to Mummy and his baby brother while you breastfeed is a great way to involve him and have some family time together.*

▸ Set clear limits on behaviour at an early stage. Biting, hitting, punching, pushing, and grabbing should never be tolerated.

Learning to talk

Over the next six months your toddler will start to replace her baby "babble" with real words to describe things. Her ability to understand what you say will improve much more quickly and you may be surprised to find how easily she follows basic instructions, too.

Although your toddler's language skills will be improving, there won't be an overnight transformation and there will be times when it seems impossible to interpret what she is trying to tell you. There may be a gap of 3–4 months after she says her first words before her growing vocabulary takes off. By the time she is 18 months she will know about 20 words and be able to link two words together at a time; this will increase rapidly to between 50–300 words by 21–24 months. Unfortunately, the choice of words may not always make sense to you, which is why this is often known as telegraphic speech. Like an old-fashioned message by telegraph (or modern-day text message), the style is so condensed that you will have to fill in the gaps. However, your toddler will have a clear idea of what she is trying to say, so watch her body language and listen to her tone of voice.

Trying to communicate

At this age toddlers do not yet have enough words to make their meaning immediately clear.

Issie, aged 18 months, suddenly exclaims, "Big dog!" Issie's Daddy responds, "Can you see a big dog?" Issie excitedly says, "Big dog!" Daddy, determined, says "Are you thinking about Granny's big dog?" Issie, even more excited, says, "Big dog, big dog!" Daddy is none the wiser and will need some non-verbal cues if he is to get to the root of the matter. He has no idea whether Issie is saying, "I want my big toy dog," "Remember that big dog we saw," "I want the book about the dog," or just "I like the sound of the words 'big dog'!"

While it is important to give your child lots of encouragement with speech, there is not always obvious logic to the words.

Try echoing the mood and the phrase back to your child, ask her to show you what she means, or if she is becoming frustrated, try changing the subject.

Helping your child

The more you talk to your child, the sooner she will learn the fundamentals of language. It is important to sometimes repeat back to your child what she is saying to reinforce the process of talking. It may feel patronizing, but it is not. Reflecting your child's style speech back to her by using her phrases and simple adult words, will help her to develop an understanding of the to and fro of conversation, and recognize that her words will be responded to by other people. For example, if she points at the cat and says "Loo-, dat!", reply "Yes, look, it is the cat!"

At other times, by repeating and echoing back the corrected version of her words, you can help your child to become familiar with pronunciation. However, over-correction may put her under undue pressure to get things right. Trying to force early language development is generally ineffective since a child's vocal cords and control over the tongue have not yet developed fully. As the voice box (larynx) gradually strengthens along with other motor skills (see page 48), so she will learn to speak more fluently.

Describe to your toddler what you are doing while you are playing, washing, and dressing: "Shall we wash your hands now?" "This is your nose," (touch your child's nose), "This is my nose," (touch your nose), "Let's make it go 'beep'," (press your nose and make a "beep" noise; then do the same to your child). The combination of touch and sound will help to remind her of where her nose is and will reinforce the similarity between you. Introduce the idea of textures, sounds, colours, and smells: "The cat's fur is lovely and soft," "This is a lovely crunchy apple," "Have your juice in the red cup." Although children start to speak at different ages, the general process of development differs very little. Children learn mainly by listening to language and by imitation, rather than via direct instruction.

Communication without words

Until your toddler can express herself through speech, she will use a whole range of other gestures to make her needs known.

Pointing Learning to point is an important stage in learning to communicate. For your toddler to decide "That's what I want" and to reason that "If I point at it you will understand and get it for me" takes immense concentration and skill. Children of this age still want their needs fulfilled immediately, so it is wise to respond to your toddler's pointing and then use words to

"Your toddler may get frustrated at times. Imagine if you did not have full control over your mouth but were expected to speak clearly."

USING BODY LANGUAGE
She is learning to talk, but using her hands and pointing may still be the most comfortable and accurate way your toddler can show you want she wants.

reinforce her message. If you try to encourage your child to use the correct words before responding, the resulting stress may stop her memory absorbing your language lesson.

Showing you Your toddler will enjoy using her newfound speed and skill to find things and to show you what she wants. Let her explore and physically move around in order to make her own choices, rather than helping her. Imagine how frustrating it would be if you were browsing the shelves in a bookshop, only to find you kept being removed to an armchair before you had reached the section you wanted!

Facial expressions Children are extremely expressive and you will already know many of your toddler's mood cues. A simple glance at her face will tell you immediately how she is experiencing something and, more importantly, whether she is happy, worried, or anxious.

Keeping in tune with your toddler's evolving expressions can be a very useful way of helping her to understand and cope with her feelings. Even if you cannot see or sense an obvious explanation for the feeling you see written on your child's face – respond to her anyway. Your toddler will be sensing the world in a way that is vastly different to you and without language, so may need some help in learning to interpret her experiences and deal with them.

Co-operating Children love to mimic; it is a natural instinct that enables them to learn new skills through play and watching others. This evolves gradually into co-operation, and is a useful way for a child to show her understanding without the need for words. Watch out for your child reaching for her spoon to feed herself; offering her foot when you reach for her socks; lifting up her arms when it is time to take off her T-shirt. These are powerful signs that your child is learning to understand, and is gradually developing the skills required to help herself. Give her plenty of encouragement and follow her leads promptly – for example, by putting on her socks rather than ignoring her gesture.

If your child is showing you that she understands what is needed, she is also telling you that she is ready to "have a go". Whenever you have time, let your child try to do things for herself: such as putting on a shirt, feeding herself, and cleaning her teeth. With patience, encouragement, and quite a bit of support, she will soon show you that she has the skills to succeed, and is ready to learn more.

Language activities

Language development at this stage should be about fun, not flash cards. Small children are generally very ready to smile and laugh and love new and silly sounds. The more light-hearted and fun you can make the process of learning for your toddler, the more easily she will be able to grasp new words and ideas.

Rhymes, songs, and word games Singing songs and making up silly rhymes will teach your toddler about sounds and rhythm; using fingers and toes to tell a story will combine words and actions – and can be a fun way to help your child learn the parts of her body.

Traditional nursery rhymes are still used the world over for the simple reason that they work so effectively in helping children to enjoy language and learn the sounds of words. *Incy Wincy Spider, This Little Piggy, and Round and Round the Garden* are reliable old favourites.

The same is true of songs that combine words and gestures, although your toddler will be following your movements rather than listening to the instructions on the CD or tape at this stage. This is important as it helps

"Toddlers love to do things again and again. They get great joy from repetition because it reinforces their learning and gives a great sense of satisfaction – especially if it is drawing a response from you, too."

children to learn the social side of interaction, including making eye-contact, sharing smiles, and giving attention; all of which are important for building later friendships and reinforcing natural methods of communication. Your toddler will absolutely love it if you make up word games of your own, especially games that include a sense of anticipation and surprise. These are especially good for encouraging interaction and trust between playmate and child.

Picture books These can be a lovely way to get your toddler used to recognizing different shapes and textures, as well as learning animal sounds and everyday noises, such as car horns. Picture books play an especially important part in encouraging your toddler to observe and learn

Common toddler-speak

Your toddler may omit or change the sounds in words she finds difficult. If this happens, echo the word back correctly, with slight emphasis on the corrected sound. There is no need to ask her to copy or imitate you. She will gradually take it on board through experience and exposure to more words. Your toddler may:

▶ Drop the first sound from the beginnings or ends of words, especially ones starting or ending in consonants, such as b, d, or t.

▶ Swap sounds, such as d and g.

▶ Make generalizations and turn nouns into verbs, for example, "I songed," rather than "I sang a song."

▶ Extend the meaning of words, so that all machines are called "car," or all animals are called "cat."

▶ Reduce the meaning of words, so that only Daddy is a "man."

▶ Simplify the rules of grammar, so that all plurals have an "s", even "sheeps"; and all words in the past tense end in "-ed", so instead of "I ran" she will say "I runned."

▶ Stammer or stutter when trying to get her words out. This too is common at this stage, so don't worry. However, a persistent stutterer may need help from a speech therapist (see pages 310–311).

new words, sounds, and the context of things. She is too young to be able to imagine ideas and storylines for herself, but will listen enraptured if you tell her a tale – especially if it includes lots of actions and noises.

Bathtime fun Playing at bathtime is an easy way to get your child washed without her even noticing and encourages her to feel at ease in water, too. If you have more than one child, bathing them with each other is a nice way to enjoy some togetherness – and saves you precious time.

Who is in charge?

By 18 months your toddler will understand simple instructions such as, "Stop," "No," and "Come here." As well as basic concepts such as "Time for tea," and "Bathtime," and questions such as "Where is teddy?" She will also develop the ability to mimic and pick up words that have been overheard. Parents often wonder why children have an uncanny ability to pick up inappropriate swear words at a very early age. This is because they tend to be single syllable words that are used with emotion or emphasis – so they stand out in conversation. It could also be due to the reaction toddlers get when they use them: laughter, shock, and lots of attention (whether good or bad). Toddlers love to mimic – so now would be a good time to curb your language if you are likely to be embarrassed by your toddler copying you!

Your baby's brain

A big priority for your toddler during months 18–24 will be multi-sensory development. Sights, sounds, smells, and textures all contribute to the hands-on experience that will develop memory and help children to remember things far more effectively than simply by telling them.

Your toddler's brain will continue to develop during months 18–24 in much the same way as it did during months 12–18, but the impact will be more dramatic, as the information bedded in her brain accumulates, and her memory gradually increases. Chemical and neurological changes (see page 71) that take place during brain development will continue as she gets older. All areas of the brain will continue to develop during the next six months (and into puberty). During this time you will notice an increase in your toddler's ability to reason, remember, pay attention, and respond. Each time she listens and speaks, she is developing her language ability. Although we take it for granted, talking is a highly complex skill that requires many areas of the brain to function together.

Learning to speak

To use language effectively, we need to be able to produce it – by speaking, and also to understand it – by listening and comprehending. These skills develop in tandem, but are processed via different areas of the brain. Speaking and understanding rely heavily on memory and are closely linked to the ongoing development of the thinking and reasoning areas and the memory centres of the brain.

The memory centres are believed to hold information about the meaning of words and objects based on physical description, personal experience, and connections to other words and meanings. The memory centres influence which words we know, select, and use. They link to the speech areas to influence the way we produce and understand language. The thinking and reasoning areas of the brain influence our attention and when and where we speak. The emotional and social behaviour area is involved

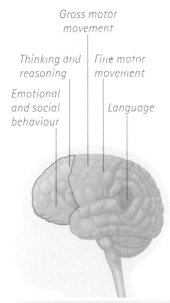

Gross motor movement

Thinking and reasoning

Fine motor movement

Emotional and social behaviour

Language

LANGUAGE AND MOVEMENT *Gross motor and language areas develop connections rapidly to improve co-ordination and develop speech. Fine motor skills mature later.*

GAINING KNOWLEDGE
Through experiencing many different sights, sounds, and objects, he builds a rich tapestry of information, which gives meaning to words and develops memory.

in decoding the language and gestures of others and influences our feelings and what we say.

When your toddler wants to say something, her brain will speed rapidly through a series of processes to see whether her memory has what it needs to communicate the information. She cannot yet think consciously, in the way that an adult can; but she can pay attention to what it is she wants to describe (what does it look like?). She will then visually process the image in her brain and the information it gives her (does it look familiar?). Next she will instruct her brain to assess the meaning of it (does she recognize it? What does it represent?) before assessing whether she has the words to describe it.

For example, if your toddler is looking at a large animal with four legs, her brain will try to figure out whether it matches any of the mental images stored in her brain. She then has to find the part of her brain which has stored the necessary word and can remind her how to say it out loud. To form the words, she will then shape her tongue and vocal cords, and pronounce it accurately, sound by sound. She may then look at you, point, smile, and say, triumphantly, "Big dog."

Learning to understand

The brain uses a different sequence to the one above to listen to and understand spoken language. As well as using the ears to hear the sounds and interpret the *literal* meaning of the spoken words, the eyes and other senses are also used to decipher the *social meaning* of what has been said, by decoding information about the speaker (gender, age, tone of voice) and the context (familiar, dangerous, new, interesting, hostile) and so on. The words are decoded as they are spoken, and matched against a memory of stored words and meanings. Hearing skills are used to gain contextual clues about the meaning of the words and lip-reading also plays a part (and is of great importance for children who have hearing difficulties).

Using the example on the opposite page, when you receive the information "big" and "dog" that your toddler has given you, you will be able to look at the picture and from the context and your larger memory bank may see that the picture is, in fact, of a horse. Your toddler describes it as a big dog, because it comes close to the "dog" she has in her mind and she hasn't learnt the word "horse" yet. Smile at your toddler and say, "Well, it does have four legs, and it is very big, but it is too big to be a dog. It is an animal called a horse." When you correct your toddler, she will be able to store new information for the future. Point out the horse's mane and its long legs and face; describe the sounds that the horse makes ("neigh"/ "clip clop"), and compare it with the dog's "woof". She will watch your mouth as you shape the words, look at the picture as you describe it, and hear the new sounds. All of this data is absorbed by your toddler's brain and stored for future use.

Your toddler's language and understanding will become both more specific and also more general as usage and personal experience increases. For example, she will begin to make associations, such as, "Patch is Granny's dog. He is white with brown spots," and "Dogs are pets. They are usually friendly. But I should not stroke dogs I don't know."

Left brain/right brain

The brain is divided into two hemispheres. Although they work in partnership, they are newly formed and immature in young children.

In the majority of people, the left brain (which controls the right side of the body) is great at logical thought: it governs understanding and language. The right brain (which controls the left side of the body) is more instinctive and creative: it picks up non-verbal cues and is more closely linked with the responses of the physical body. The two sides are linked by a network of nerve fibres that is the bridge via which words are delivered. Words to describe a feeling travel in one direction (from left to right); and the information about what that feeling represents and how to respond to it travels in the other direction (from right to left). As this bridge strengthens, emotional understanding and sensitivity develops. These connections are immature in young children and co-ordinated thinking is difficult, hence they shift rapidly between appearing calm one moment and emotional the next. As the connections gradually strengthen, (together with the frontal lobes – see page 164) the logical, rational left brain will start to communicate better with the emotional, instinctive right brain and a child develops more balanced responses.

Playing and learning

Play, fun, and learning are all the same thing to your toddler. She loves learning new skills and making new discoveries and you will notice fast and significant changes in her levels of understanding, reasoning, and speed of response during the months ahead.

You will need immense patience and humour at this stage of development. Your toddler will often approach tasks in an unconventional way that may challenge your view of how things should be done. She will want to repeat what she does more times than you would have believed possible. Do spend lots of time with her and show her how things work and what to do; your involvement and encouragement are vital to developing her future potential. You will also need the tolerance to allow her to make her own discoveries, without too much direction and correction.

Child-centred play

Playtime, at this age, is all about the development of your toddler's senses, and exploration, which is why she will love playing with sand and water, finger paints, play dough, and other messy substances. The texture, shape, sound, feel, and movement of the objects she is playing with are completely absorbing. Your toddler's agenda is different from yours. She may not be interested in making things look perfect, or learning how to do things "properly" as you would see it, but is more fascinated by repetition, cause and effect, and discovering what she can make happen. You needn't fear that her progress is slow. She will figure things out and learn more complex reasoning skills as the brain develops.

Remember, it is not all about control:

■ Let your toddler choose the activity or toy.

■ Let your toddler start the talking or activity.

■ Let your toddler lead the play most of the time.

■ Resist the temptation to correct what she is doing.

■ Don't worry about mess and resist the temptation to keep tidying up.

FAVOURITE ACTIVITIES *Your toddler will begin to lead his own play and show clear preferences – for example, he may run straight to the slide at the playground. This ability to decide for himself is positive and should be encouraged.*

See life through your toddler's eyes:

■ Play on the floor at your toddler's level, where you can make eye contact.

■ Let your toddler finish her go before you start.

■ Allow time for taking turns in play and talking.

■ Make the object of your toddler's focus, your focus, too – so that you are talking about or sharing the same experience, not just playing side by side.

■ Accept her way of doing things.

■ Being "right" is not the main priority at this age.

Give your toddler your full attention:

■ Show you are listening and attending to what she is doing by watching, and echoing speech and action.

■ Create a commentary of what your toddler is doing, and accept the way she is doing it. Avoid asking lots of questions or correcting her behaviour.

■ Praise what your toddler is doing as often as possible.

Adapt your style of language:

■ Use short, simple words, to encourage development and understanding.

■ Don't contradict what she is telling you, but echo back to her what she is saying, to show you are listening.

■ Be very positive, affirmative, and enthusiastic in your responses.

Learning to take turns

At this age, your toddler is still very self-centred and is too young to understand that another child is a potential playmate. She may, however, be happy to play next to another child and they may watch each other intently, or copy each other. This stage is known as parallel play and will soon lead to co-operative play and sharing. In the meantime, any interaction at this stage is likely to involve some minor scrapping. Toddlers of this age have a strong sense of ownership – everything is "mine"!

You can help your toddler to begin to learn about "taking turns" by joining her in play and making it into a game. This is a far more effective technique than intervening when there is an upset. Remember that your toddler is still developing her social skills. She finds it hard to manage her feelings, and can feel frustrated at being unable to express herself. It is an explosive combination that can often get physical. Hitting and biting is not unusual between toddlers. You will need to be watchful and intervene fast when things turn angry, before anyone gets too hurt or upset. Do not try to reason with a disruptive child. A simple "No!" before removing her from the situation is most effective at this age.

Taking turns can be introduced as a part of almost every game and activity, from putting plastic bricks into separate pots, to sharing food, to catching a ball, to turning the pages of a book. Your toddler is too young at the moment to be able to cope with taking turns with another child of her own age, but may well enjoy playing with an older child or brother or sister who can show patience and negotiate turns in a calm way.

The value of repetition

Your toddler may repeat a simple action again and again, watching how something falls, moves, or lights up. This repetition may be challenging for you, but is about your child consolidating learning skills and is also a sign of her increasing attention span. She is also developing the ability to lead her own play, and if the signs are there, encourage it as much as possible.

Toddlers become more aware of change and transitions at this age. Action songs that describe a sequence of events such as, *"This is the way we brush our teeth/comb our hair… early in the morning"* help them rehearse and practise a series of actions in a safe and fun way, and help them to adjust more readily to the range of skills and instructions that their developing brain is having to take on board.

Restoring the peace

All parents of toddlers need to become referees as well as skilful mediators at playtime.

Sally, aged 23 months, and Malik, 14 months, are making music with wooden spoons and empty pans. Sally abandons her spoon in favour of a saucepan lid, at which point Malik picks up the spoon. Sally screams in frustration and drops the lid with a loud clang. She tries to wrench the spoon from Malik. Both children start to cry. Dad says "Sally! Stop that immediately. Malik is smaller than you. How do you think he feels when you do that?"

Sally is too young to understand another person's feelings. She wails and tugs at the spoon… "Mine! Give me now!" "Sally…" (he speaks slowly and calmly). "Let go of the spoon. It's Malik's turn. You can have it back in a minute. Come and play with this special shaker instead." The calm instruction plus distraction, or a clear "No" followed by ignoring, help prevent the ensuing tantrums.

YOUR BUSY TODDLER *Play is essential for your toddler's physical, mental, and emotional development. Giving her a wide range of activities will stimulate her and help her develop a broad skills base.*

Playtime ideas and games

MOVEMENT ACTIVITIES

Most childhood games, involving walking, running, jumping, and climbing, are useful for the development of the large movements of the body. All your toddler needs is a safe place to play and explore without too much restricted movement, and the knowledge that her carer is not too far away. Children are "all-weather" creatures and will really benefit from fresh air and a change of scene.

Different textures and challenges are intriguing at this age:

▶ Walking on grass or sand, jumping on and off a step, walking, running (and later rolling) up and down hills, and crawling through tunnels, help children to strengthen their muscles and their reflexes.

▶ Swings, slides, and balancing are all fantastic for encouraging brain development. Your toddler may be ready to try some climbing, too. Make sure you balance your anxieties about your toddler's safety against a need for her to explore and learn from her environment.

The smaller and more controlled movements continue to improve as your toddler gradually learns to grip things and to control small-scale movement. Her drawing skills will begin now (although she has a very immature pencil grip), she will try to fit shapes together, and can hold a spoon and fork. Try:

▶ Toys to encourage holding, scooping, squeezing, and pouring.

▶ Games and activities that encourage repetition of movement.

▶ Sand and water play, finger paints, jigsaws, and wooden blocks.

▶ Running, jumping, and climbing.

▶ Kicking and throwing a ball.

▶ Blowing bubbles.

▶ Chasing and tickling games.

▶ Dancing to encourage a sense of rhythm and co-ordination.

LANGUAGE AND SENSES

▶ Things to read and look at: board books with large pictures and pages, illustrated food packages, and glossy magazines that include pictures of babies and toddlers will all appeal.

▶ Things to write with: fat crayons and pencils, and plenty of paper (if you don't want scribble on the walls).

▶ Things that make noise: beans in sealed containers, wooden spoons, saucepans, flower pots, bells - the list is endless. Also, try making noises in unusual ways - for example, by shouting into a tube to create an echo. Make animal noises that your child can copy.

▶ Toys that are bright colours and made of contrasting textures.

▶ Nursery rhymes and action songs help develop language.

MAKE-BELIEVE AND COMFORT

▶ Toys to cuddle: so many to choose from, but there is often a favourite.

▶ Make-believe toys: puppets and action rhymes, or funny, made-up rhymes and stories.

▶ Toys that imitate you and your actions, such as sweepers, tools, and telephones.

CAUSE AND EFFECT TOYS

▶ Toys that light up or make a noise, for example, when a button is pushed - these help your toddler understand how her actions impact on things.

INTERACTIVE GAMES

▶ *Peek-a-boo* will still be a favourite.

▶ Hiding an object under a cup and finding it together.

▶ Copying your actions and exaggerated facial expressions.

Thinking about potty training

There are many aspects of your child's babyhood that you will feel sad to say goodbye to, but the chances are that changing nappies will not be one of them. It is important to make potty training a positive experience, not a pressure, for your child.

Parents can become surprisingly pushy when it comes to potty training. This is mainly for reasons of practicality. A child who is out of nappies is far more portable and less labour intensive. Some schools and nurseries will not accept children until they are dry. For working parents, in particular, that is a real pressure. However, the most important guidelines for beginning potty training nevertheless remain:

▶ DO NOT start too early.

▶ DO NOT hurry the process and be willing to resist any pressure to do so.

▶ NEVER force your child to use the toilet.

▶ REMEMBER all children are different.

▶ NEVER criticize a child for having an accident, no matter how exasperated you are by it.

There is a huge variation in the age at which children become dry at night, from anywhere between 18 months and eight years. One in ten five-year-olds is still wet during the day and more than one in ten is still wet during the night. Studies show that children who are pushed to become dry before 18 months are likely to take until the age of four to become fully potty trained, whereas those who begin around the age of two will often become dry almost immediately. In reality, children only become toilet trained when they are ready, and when the nerve pathways necessary to control urine flow have fully developed. This can happen anywhere between 18 months and three years old.

BECOMING DRY

▶ Let your toddler sit on his potty fully clothed to begin with, until he feels familiar with it. If using the toilet, get an adjuster seat insert that makes the loo seat smaller. It also makes it less scary for a child who worries about falling down the hole. You might also want to get a step for your toddler to rest his feet on so that he feels more stable and safe.

▶ Once he understands what the potty is for and wants to try to use it, take his nappy off and let him settle. If you change his nappy at the same time and empty the contents into the potty, he will get the idea more quickly.

▶ Encourage him to sit on his potty or the toilet after eating and drinking.

▶ Make sure he knows where his potty is when he is playing and encourage him to use it or bring it to you.

▶ In the summer months your toddler can run around freely without clothes and use the potty when he needs to.

POTTY TRAINING FACTS

▶ Not all children use a potty.

▶ Urination often happens at the same time as a bowel movement, so it can be hard for toddlers to tell the difference between the two functions.

▶ Boys usually sit to begin with, then move to the standing position later.

▶ Boys, in particular, may find the transition to the toilet daunting and often do not like the sensation of pooing. If there is any anxiety, be patient.

▶ Do not be surprised if your toddler becomes fascinated by the results and wants to show them off! This is normal behaviour.

▶ If you can let your toddler run about outside in the summer, the process may happen quite fast after the age of three.

It is the ideal way for him to learn about his body and weeing.

▶ Take him with you when you go to the toilet so he can learn by observing what you do.

▶ Do not force him to go, but give him lots of encouragement.

▶ If he has learnt the difference between feeling wet and dry, trade his nappies for trainer pants during the day and ask him to tell you when he needs the toilet.

▶ Night-time dryness will take longer to achieve, but making the bed with alternate layers of plastic and ordinary sheets will make changing in the night a whole lot easier.

NO MORE SOILING

▶ Do not expect your toddler to control the urge to poo until at least 18 months, and 2–3 years old is ideal. It can take some children until the age of five to be completely clean.

▶ Help him to stay calm and relaxed when using the potty or toilet. Tension can inhibit his ability to poo.

▶ Get him used to sitting on the potty three times a day after meals, for a maximum of three minutes, bearing in mind his short concentration levels.

▶ Try to make the experience fun, and get him used to sitting and aiming. Alternatively, if your toddler has a very clear pattern of when he soils his nappy, get into the habit of sitting him on his potty at this time.

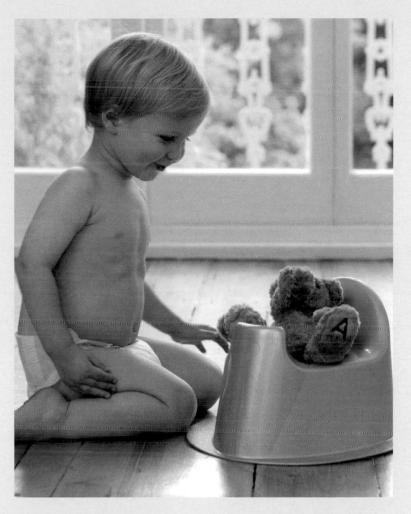

▶ If he is successful give him lots of praise and rewards; if not, ignore the outcome and let him try again later.

▶ If he says "No" do not force the issue or show disapproval or impatience. This is a potentially tense and anxious situation and his wish to say no should be respected.

▶ Give him lots of praise when he shows interest in trying again.

You can reassure yourself that all will be well in the end. After all, you

A GRADUAL INTRODUCTION *Using teddy in role play can be a good and fun way of familiarizing your toddler with his potty.*

don't find 15-year-olds still walking around in nappies! Let things happen at a natural, stress-free pace. If you have any concerns, keep a careful eye on his progress and ask your doctor for advice. See pages 310–311 for more help and information.

What toddlers want and need

During this six-month period, your toddler will go through a very complex series of changes, but will want a very simple range of responses. She will thrive on love and comfort, but also need an increasing number of very clear behaviour guidelines and boundaries.

Without any boundaries, your toddler will try to create her own and may push you quite hard to get some resistance. She is beginning to understand who she is and what she thinks of the world. She needs you to be strong and consistent concerning her behaviour. This period is also a time of transition: her newfound language skills mean she understands more than she has before and her awareness of being separate from you means that she understands that you may go away (and worries that you may not come back). There may be big changes in the family, such as the main carer returning to work, or perhaps a new baby arriving in the family.

There are also changes in the way she is being nurtured. You may have decided to wean your toddler off the bottle altogether; she is adjusting to a new range of flavours and textures on her plate each day; and she may have moved from a cot to a bed. Combine this with the new range of feelings that she is experiencing and it is unsurprising that your toddler will be very sensitive to your feedback and needy of your approval.

"We found it hard to set consistent routines at first – but we persevered and Ali is definitely much more contented as a result."

Sayed, aged 32

How you respond

How we shape our children's early behaviour will have an impact on the way they view themselves in later life. A child who is out of control and has no boundaries can feel both powerful and afraid, which leads to poor behaviour as well as emotional outbursts. Your toddler will be excited by her newfound communication skills and be starting to enjoy toddler-style "conversations". However, she remains egocentric (see page 55) and will still be preoccupied with her own needs and wants. She will want to act independently and be in control, but often becomes anxious and frustrated; and so need you to be consistent in her care and attention. Managing behaviour at this age is about helping your child to learn to manage her big emotions as well making sure she feels secure. It is about ensuring that you can keep enough control to protect her physical safety when necessary, and put in place the routines and boundaries that will help her to start managing her own behaviour as she develops, without crushing her spirit. Until she is three years old, you will need to show her, not tell her, what to do.

Mealtime anxieties

One area of confrontation that may begin to develop at this time is battles over food. As the chart below shows, this often develops from parents misunderstanding what triggers their toddler's behaviour.

Toddlers and tastebuds

Children's food and family mealtimes can become fraught with anxiety if parents have not devised a workable routine or have unrealistic expectations about their child's needs and wants. It is all too easy to misunderstand a toddler's reaction to food by interpreting it from an adult perspective.

TODDLER'S ACTION	PARENT'S INTERPRETATION	OTHER POSSIBLE MEANINGS
▶ Pushes plate away	Is misbehaving	Is bored or full
▶ Spits food out	Is misbehaving, ill, or doesn't like it	Food is too hot/too cold/is not used to the flavour or texture
▶ Plays with food/won't eat	Is misbehaving/will starve	Has been snacking/is full/has been given too large a portion
▶ Throws food on floor	Is misbehaving	Is experimenting/playing/having fun/likes to see parent's reaction
▶ Leaves food on plate	Is a fussy eater	Has been given too large a portion
▶ Won't eat a new food	Is a fussy eater	Isn't used to it yet; may eat it next time
▶ Won't make up her mind what she wants to eat	Is being awkward/is a fussy eater	Is too young to make her own decision about what to eat
▶ Licks food and then leaves it on plate	Is playing with food/misbehaving	Is experimenting/getting used to new texture and taste; may eat it next time

GROWING UP *Make change positive – tell him he's a big boy now so he can have a beaker instead of a bottle. Give him encouragement as he begins to use it by himself.*

Useful tips for happy mealtimes:

■ Be a role model and show your toddler how to use a knife, fork, and spoon. She will soon copy you, but don't worry if she still prefers to use her fingers most of the time.

■ Avoid constant fussing. She is less likely to eat if you are anxious.

■ Be ready to trade your toddler's baby bottle and highchair for a beaker and booster seat.

■ Introduce food play and allow eating with her fingers, to get her used to the feel and smell of new foods.

■ Introduce new foods and textures one at a time.

■ Keep the portion sizes small; remember. your toddler has a very small stomach (approximately the size of her fist).

■ Be patient when introducing new foods. Add small amounts and don't force her to eat the whole portion.

■ Expect as many as 15–20 mealtime attempts before your toddler accepts a new flavour or texture.

■ Keep a close eye on snacking between meals. It could explain why your toddler cannot eat her meal.

■ Remember, if your toddler is still using a bottle or breastfeeding, that she will be partially full when she sits down to eat.

■ Encourage other older children to model "good" eating behaviour. Your toddler will pay great attention to siblings.

Your toddler's view of the world

Here's an insight into what your toddler might be thinking...

▶ "We go for walks in the park and there is so much to see, smell, and hear. I like to take things slowly so I can explore and remember, but grown-ups are always in such a rush."

▶ "It's hard to know how to please them: one moment they want me to learn to climb on to a chair, the next they put up gates on the stairs so I can't practise climbing on my own!"

▶ "There are so many different words for the same thing. Why can't all animals just be called 'dog'? I seem to be an 'Eric' – at least, that's what they call me."

▶ "I am chatting away much more now, but Mummy and Daddy don't always understand. I get so fed up with trying to tell them that I get angry and sometimes scream."

▶ "We like playing together. My favourite is the "No" game. I throw something on the floor and then Mummy screws her face up and says 'No!' I don't think she likes this game."

Managing behaviour

Your toddler is too young to understand "right and wrong" or why certain behaviour is unacceptable, but she understands and likes routine, and thrives on your approval. As she gets closer to two years, she will understand that most behaviour has "good" or "bad" consequences.

Behaviour boundaries work best if they are part of a daily routine. This sets up clear expectations and eventually your child will develop control over her behaviour and emotional reactions.

The most effective routes to taming behaviour at this age are:

■ Routine – if she knows what to expect, she is less likely to "play up".

■ Rewarding – help her to learn to associate "good" behaviour with positive attention.

■ Distraction – she has a low attention span and will be easily diverted.

■ Ask once nicely, tell once firmly (see page 135) to get a message across.

■ Ignoring – this stops attention being given to tantrums/whining.

The comfort of a routine

A good routine has regular structure and familiarity, which will make your toddler feel safe, as well as reinforcing behaviour boundaries. If she knows that bedtime happens after supper and a bath, and that it comes with cuddles and a picture book, she will come to expect the pattern to be repeated and will enjoy and encourage it. Importantly, a good bedtime routine will encourage and help healthy sleep habits, too (see page 136).

Ignoring bad behaviour

A common mistake parents make when trying to stop children of this age from doing something "naughty" is to discuss it with them. The approach won't work because what your child really wants is more of your attention. By talking about the behaviour, you are rewarding her with exactly what she wants – lots of attention! It is hard not to give children more attention when they play up, but this can cause problems in the long term.

"All children crave praise, warmth, and positive attention, but if it's not forthcoming they will settle for negative attention."

Rewarding good behaviour

The more you praise and reward good behaviour, the more good behaviour you will get. Your toddler will crave your approval and affection. If you reward good behaviour with warmth and positive attention, she will gradually learn to associate the good behaviour with good feelings and learn that it is more fun to be good than not.

"Praise the action, not the child, so that your toddler learns what it is about her behaviour that is good. She will learn much more that way, and your encouragement will have more value."

Distraction in action

Techniques to distract your toddler work because they put a few seconds between her thought and her behaviour, and in that moment of curiosity her mood can change, for the better. With the immediate crisis over, you can both enjoy the more positive outcome. The following interaction between 20-month-old Callum and his mum show how a distraction technique is much more effective than a "telling off":

Scenario 1 Callum is repeatedly throwing his plate of food on the floor while eating. His mother is desperate for him to eat his food. She snaps at him: "Callum, STOP IT! You can stay in your chair until you have eaten what's left." Callum bursts into tears, and she tries to spoon-feed him – with difficulty, as he wriggles his head from side to side and pushes the plate to the floor yet again.

Result Callum is unhappy, but has Mummy's attention. Mummy is annoyed, has a mess to clean up, and feels like a failure.

Future prospect Is likely to repeat the action.

Scenario 2 Callum is throwing his food around and wriggling. His mum really wants him to eat his lunch, but she recognizes that he is bored. She says, "Callum, there is an aeroplane here that wants to deliver your next mouthful! Are you ready? Open wide…" Callum sits stock still and opens his mouth in anticipation. His mum takes the spoon again, makes another aeroplane noise, and swoops towards his mouth! Callum takes a mouthful of food, and swallows. "Here comes another aeroplane…" Callum is giggling and enjoys this long enough for the plate to almost empty before announcing, "Callum do it!"

Result Callum is happy and fed and Mummy is pleased. She has managed to transform the difficult behaviour into something much more positive. This is not a case of making mealtimes a game; the key is that the technique distracts from the disruptive behaviour and not from the food and eating.

Future prospect Less chance of repeat pattern and self-feeding is progressing nicely.

Asking once, telling once

If you want your child to do something, you shouldn't need to ask her more than twice. It is important for safety reasons for you to know that she will obey not only you, but any adult who is looking after her, especially in an emergency. Ask her once nicely, and then tell her once firmly. You will need to use your facial expressions and body language to emphasize what you are saying.

Your child knows you well by now, and she will be very sensitive to your tone of voice, or a particular look on your face. If you are consistent in your response, you will gradually be able to teach her that you are serious about the consequences if she misbehaves. You don't need to resort to shouting to get her to do what you want.

Ask once, nicely "I'd like you to get in the buggy now, please."

Tell once, firmly Get down to her level, look her in the eye, and say slowly and firmly, "Get in your buggy now, please!" Be patient and don't say anything more until she has done as you have asked. If that doesn't work, you will need to take an action-based approach; that is, put her in the buggy to show her that you mean what you say.

Use distraction "Did you see that squirrel run up the tree." While she looks, pick her up and put her in the buggy.

Stand firm Do not give in. If a massive tantrum or aggression results, ignore it, and remember she will grow out of this phase before long.

BEING ATTENTIVE *Smile at your toddler and give him lots of positive encouragement. If he has your attention and feels contented, he will be less likely to misbehave.*

A good night's sleep

There is nothing more restorative than the power of a good night of uninterrupted sleep – and toddlers need more sleep than most. For many parents, however, bedtime battles and night-time waking deprive the whole family of sleep.

A toddler who has less than 10 hours sleep per night is in a state of chronic sleep deprivation and her exhaustion will have an effect on her behaviour during the day, too. Her brain will be tired, her physical and mental responses will be slow, and she will experience even more frustration than usual. The result: more tantrums and less chance of being able to control her behaviour – at any time of day. Inadequate sleep in toddlers is often at the root of their behaviour problems during the day. If you create a good sleep pattern, you may solve the daytime problems, too.

RELYING ON YOU

Your toddler needs to be able to settle herself to sleep without your help, so that if she stirs in the night she can settle again without waking herself up, and without becoming distressed.

Most problems occur because there is no routine at bedtime, and the toddler hasn't learnt the right cues for when she is meant to go to sleep. For example, if a child is used to falling asleep in her parent's arms in front of the TV, her sleep cues will be her parent's body warmth, and the TV.

Cuddling your toddler is very loving and comforting, but you are sending her the message that she cannot sleep without you being there, and cannot get back to sleep without having you as comfort. The longer this goes on for, the harder it will be for her to settle or sleep on her own when she gets older.

"We used to be so exhausted by Robbie's night-waking that we gave up and let him sleep in our bed." Liz, aged 25

A HEALTHY SLEEP ROUTINE

The key to ensuring sweet sleep at 18-24 months is to develop a healthy sleep routine:
▶ Plan your routine.
▶ Use appropriate sleep cues.
▶ Use the gradual withdrawal technique (see page 202).
▶ Be patient.
▶ Be consistent.
Life and work patterns often mean that children see more of their parents and get more one-to-one attention in the evenings than at any other time of day. Understandably, toddlers will try to extend this attention as long as possible – preferably with lots of fun and games. If you have been parted from your toddler during the day she will be excited when she first sees you, but try not to over-stimulate her if it is less than an hour before her bedtime. It will be harder for her to calm down before going to sleep.

Playtime and mealtime often go together very well as your toddler can play while you prepare food, or play with you while it cooks. Digesting food will give her energy levels a boost, so try to feed her early in the evening, so that she has time to burn off some energy, before her bath. Bathtime is the ideal time for winding down, ready for a cosy night's sleep.

The easiest way to give your toddler what she wants, while managing to get her to bed, is to create a routine that gives her warmth, fun, and attention, but also gives her very clear and positive sleep cues that let her know she is in the process of going to bed and to sleep.

An ideal bedtime routine might go:

▶ Mealtime.

▶ Playtime.

▶ Bathtime.

▶ Into pyjamas.

▶ Final drink.

▶ Teeth cleaning.

▶ Into bed.

▶ Bedtime story.

▶ End of story warning.

▶ Finish story.

▶ Kiss and a cuddle.

▶ Lights out (or leave a nightlight on if necessary).

BEING FIRM

Do not give in to pleas for longer bathtime or more stories, or you will reinforce them as habits that mean settling your toddler takes longer Simply put her to bed and leave the room quietly. Of course, this is often easier said than done.

A child who has got into the habit of getting out of bed, or waking in the night, will take time to adjust, but be patient. If your child is very anxious, you may need to take a more gentle approach, by using the gradual withdrawal technique (see page 202).

Even in exceptional circumstances, it is a good idea to keep to the sleep routine if possible. Perhaps your child has been ill, or you have been staying away from home, you may be potty training (page 128) or a night-time disruption has meant your child has needed reassurance. Whatever the reason for your child requiring extra attention at night, bear in mind that learning to sleep through the night on her own is essential for her healthy development and well-being. Even if your child is suffering from night terrors (see page 205) or nightmares (see page 264) she is probably better

BABYSITTERS *If your child has a consistent routine, it will make it easier for others to put her to bed, giving you more freedom to go out!*

off learning to settle in her own bed. However, this is much more about personal choice and you must do what works for you and your family.

HOW MUCH SLEEP IS ENOUGH?

The chart below shows the average amount of sleep that is recommended for children from one to four years of age. All children are different, so this is not a strict regime, but dropping significantly below these levels at night, could cause problems – as could too much napping during the day.

AGE	NIGHT	DAY NAPS	TOTAL SLEEP	IDEAL BEDTIME
▶ 12–18 months	11½ hours	2 naps (2¼ hours total)	13¾ hours	6–7pm
▶ 18–24 months	11½ hours	2 naps (2 hours total)	13½ hours	6–7pm
▶ 24–36 months	11 hours	1 nap (2 hours)	13 hours	6–7pm
▶ 36–48 months	11 hours	1 nap (1 hour)	12 hours	6–7.30pm

Your toddler's wider world

Your toddler may oscillate between being clingy – wanting lots of affection; and wanting to be highly independent – pushing you away, resisting kisses, and not wanting to be hugged. This can make it difficult for her to get on with others at an age where she is particularly reliant on you, her main carer.

It is important to help your child to broaden her awareness of the world as new experiences will develop her ability to learn, as well as enhance her memory development and reasoning skills. She is now ready to start making friends, but will need your help in learning how to behave.

"It can be hard to 'let go' of your toddler, but it's essential to let her socialize as widely as possible in order to expand her horizons and develop social and communication skills."

Starting to make friends

Up until now the adults in your family will have been your toddler's main focus, but now she will start to have more interest in other children, especially toddlers of her own age. Try to create opportunities where this interaction can happen.

Be aware of the differences between your nature and your child's developing personality. The shy child of more outgoing parents may need careful handling. Don't force or criticize your child if she does not adapt readily to playing with others or to a new environment; instead use gentle introductions to new experiences, praise her, and do not expect co-operative play immediately. Encourage her to mix widely with children so she gets used to a variety of temperaments. Although managing to cope with all sorts of people is a necessity in life, it might be wise not to mix an acutely shy or anxious child with a boisterous or confident one until they are ready to choose each other, unless they can be supervised in a positive way.

Understanding others

Your toddler may start to become more aware of the needs of others during these six months and you may notice her comfort a crying child or become distressed if you are upset. This is a useful trigger to start to talk about what feelings are and to describe to your toddler how she might be feeling. She can only begin to understand the concept of emotions and feelings once she has the language to describe them. Your comments can help her to start differentiating between different sensations such as anger, sadness, sickness, and joy.

Feelings such as anger and excitement will prompt the same physical sensations in the body and young children can't tell them apart. They need help with labelling these feelings and understanding them. For example, your son may notice that his friend is agitated. You will be able to interpret the situation and might explain to him that "Jack is *angry* because he can't get out of his seat" or "Chloe is *excited* because her friend is here to play."
A similar process applies when interpreting your child's symptoms if she is poorly. When a child reports a sore tummy, many doctors will look first at her throat. The toddler knows she has pain, but is unable to tell where it is coming from. All pain therefore becomes tummy pain.

Playing alone

Children need to learn to occupy themselves and not to rely on you for everything. Playtime can help develop this skill. Give your toddler activities that will ensure her safety while she plays, but give her some space to play and try things on her own. Playing alone and talking to herself are valuable learning experiences and will help to develop her imagination. She will learn to be happy in her own company, too.

PLAYMATES *Your toddler will gradually enjoy spending time with other children, but let her take things at her own pace and don't force friendships upon her.*

Just for parents

One of the largest areas of contention in any home is the tricky matter of chores. When children are added into the mix, a simple discussion about who could do what can easily descend into a row about what is fair, who does the most, and whose fault it is that you have a messy toddler.

You know the scenario. It has been a long, hard week. You've barely had time to speak to each other each evening before collapsing into bed with exhaustion, and now it is the weekend. There is the weekly shop to do, a mound of ironing, endless washing up, and tidying – and the carpet hasn't seen a vacuum cleaner for a while. Household chores don't complete themselves; they steal time when you would much rather be doing something else. With small children in the mix, running a household can seem a never-ending challenge, and the jibes start to fly: "You never do anything."/"You never ask me."/"I have to do everything."/"But you're never here."/"Look at this mess. *Your* children are out of control."/"What do you mean, *my* children?!' and so it goes… What both voices are saying is: "I don't feel appreciated enough and I'd much rather be doing something else – and to top it all, you never listen to me."

How you can help each other

Your time together is precious so try not to "sweat the small stuff".
Most of the tasks can be tackled with the minimum of fuss:
■ Make a pact that you will tell each other clearly when you would like help. Both sexes can develop a martyred air when they feel life is unfair – especially when one partner has done more of their fair share of the nappy-changing lately. You need to explain how you feel and what you need help with.
■ Agree to disagree and find a compromise. If one of you likes the house pristine and the other can live with the mess, find mutual ground. For example, cleanliness takes priority over tidying.
■ Agree on a division of labour.

■ Agree to sharing the children, so you each have child-free time to complete a few things without interruption.

■ Restrict the number of toys or rooms that your child can play in so that the chaos is contained to some extent (although not to the extent that he or she is constrained or restricted too much).

■ Swap roles occasionally so you can empathize with each other's needs.

■ Spend time with parents of children of a similar age, who can help to normalize your concerns, and remind you that you are not alone!

■ Appreciate and thank each other – as often as possible. Children are a joy, but they are exhausting, too. It is a treat to have a home that feels like yours for a few hours before it descends back into a toddler zone.

Dear Tanya...

▶ **We have been feeling guilty that our second-born is not getting the same amount of attention that his sister did at the same age. He is not speaking as early but seems happy enough. Should we be worried?**

It is inevitable that your son won't have as much one-to-one time with you as your daughter did, because you will be busier, but he will have other advantages.

His sister will be playing an important role in his development, being both a role model and playmate. He will understand more words than he is speaking and she may also be speaking for him some of the time. Boys' language skills often develop at a slightly slower pace than girls anyway, but they catch up later. He will certainly benefit from having personal time with you to play and bond, but will have different needs to his sister, and a character all of his own.

What second children lose in one-to-one time they gain in having less anxious parents and an exuberant playmate. So try to lose the guilt and enjoy your son.

▶ **My partner says our toddler is turning into a "Mummy's boy" and he should be disciplined and "toughened up". Is he right?**

The idea that young children of either sex will benefit from "toughening up" is an outdated concept. Children are far more likely to be adventurous if they know that they will receive comfort rather than criticism if things go wrong.

Your partner is right to believe that behavioural guidelines need to be put in place, but it sounds as if he may also be feeling jealous of the closeness that you share with your son. If he is feeling "second best" in your affections, or an outsider in his own family, this will impact on his attitude.

You need to allow your partner to be a father to your son in his own right and to form his own bond with him. Their relationship will be of increasing importance as your son grows up and will benefit from them having got to know each other in these early months.

QUESTIONS AND ANSWERS

EMOTIONAL INTELLIGENCE *Your toddler will have to learn to handle some big and all-consuming feelings. He needs you to help him feel secure at these times and manage his emotions as he grows and learns.*

5 points to remember

1 The more you praise and reward positive and fun behaviour, the more of that behaviour you will get. Your toddler will learn that it is more fun to be "good" than not.

2 Toddlers are often very keen on order and the "rightness" of things. You don't have to be too rigid, but this is the ideal time to introduce more routine and structure to your child's day. It will give her a sense of security, as well as making everyday care easier for you.

3 The more you talk to your child, the sooner she will learn the fundamentals of language. Reflect your child's speech back to her and use simple adult words to help her learn.

4 When your toddler plays, she does not need to know how to make things look perfect. She needs the freedom and encouragement to experience and make sense of the world in her own way.

5 Inadequate sleep is often at the root of a toddler's behaviour problems during the day. If you can create a good sleep pattern, you may be able to solve the daytime problems, too.

LET HIM SCRIBBLE *There is no need for formal lessons or anything too structured at this age. Over-controlled playtime will inhibit rather than encourage your child's development.*

2—3
YEARS

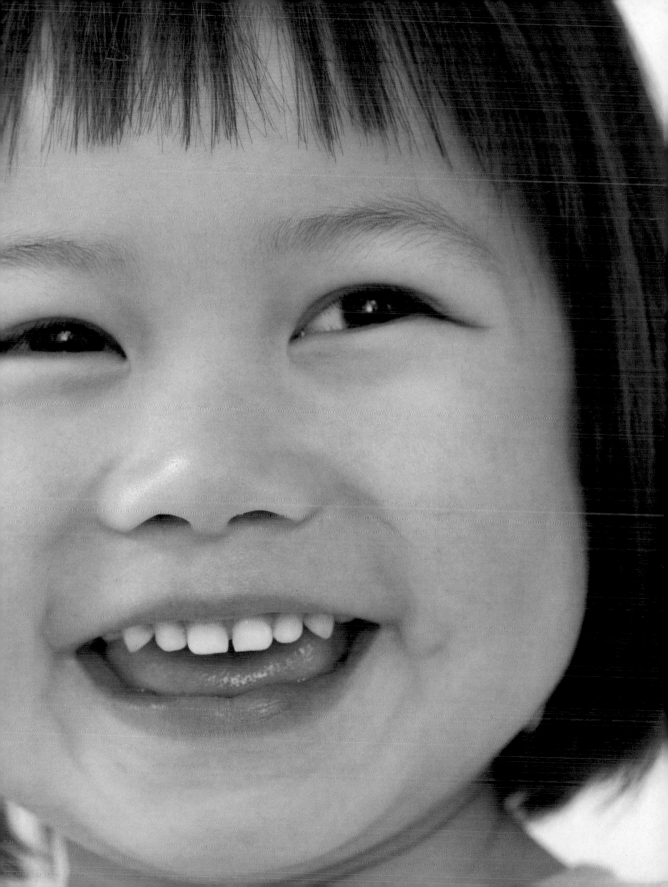

YOUR OLDER TODDLER

DISCOVERING HER WORLD AS HER AWARENESS OF HER SURROUNDINGS INCREASES, SHE WILL BE INQUISITIVE ABOUT EVERYTHING AND WANT TO EXPLORE

BECOMING MORE CAPABLE YOUR TODDLER IS BEGINNING TO UNDERSTAND MORE ABOUT HOW HER TOYS WORK AND WILL REMEMBER HOW TO PLAY WITH THEM

TIME TOGETHER HE WILL BE HAPPIEST WHEN HE HAS YOUR ATTENTION – YOU ARE STILL HIS FAVOURITE PLAYMATE FOR NOW AND HE WILL BE DELIGHTED IF YOU JOIN IN WITH HIS ACTIVITIES

"She may be laughing and having fun one minute and crying and screaming the next – life certainly won't be dull for any of you!"

Your toddler's development

Toddlers tend to get a bad press – the "terrible twos" is a label they carry with them wherever they go. But for your child, months 24–36 are not so much a battlefield as a period of enormous adventure and personal transformation and for you, as a parent, they will be more rewarding than difficult.

What is it about your two-year-old that makes him so different from when he was one? You may be so busy that you hardly have time to pause and reflect on how much your child has matured, but you will be well aware that he is now highly mobile, adventurous, vocal, and increasingly sociable. He is also very loveable, and knows how much he loves you, although he does not yet have the words to express the depth of his feelings. You and your home are the centre of his world, but he is increasingly questioning and testing to find limits and develop independence.

Significant changes

Although he is still very egocentric (see page 55), your toddler has also become far more aware of himself as a human being, and is developing thoughts, desires, and opinions of his own that will continue at an ever-increasing rate over the year ahead. He is keen to become more independent, and wants to learn for himself. "Me do it" is a common phrase for this age group (along with "No!"). During the next twelve months he will be using all his mobility and language skills to learn even more about his world; his brain and his memory will develop at a significant rate. The speed and range of the emotional changes that are taking place can be overwhelming – for your toddler, as well as for you.

Your toddler needs you more than ever during this challenging and exciting period. You are his anchor, his safe haven, and his external control. He needs you to help him to manage, understand, and direct his feelings in a way that makes him feel comfortable, and in control. By understanding what triggers his behaviour, you can use practical strategies to tackle it (see page 193) and make life more fun and loving for all of you.

"I am not sure which word I hear from Jemma more often at the moment – 'No!' or 'Again!'"

Tina, aged 38

Your toddler's personality

By the time your toddler reaches his second birthday he will already be developing his own distinct personality, which will be even more apparent six months later. All children are unique, with their own mix of genetic inheritance and personal response to their environment, but it is all too easy to start to label or compare children of this age (see page 43). Perhaps your son is more chatty, shy, quick, or difficult than his older brother, cousin, or sister. Or you may find Grandma saying he is just like his father

"It can be all too easy to demonize a small child who gets easily frustrated and finds it hard to control his tantrums. Remember that this is a developmental phase."

was at the same age. In reality, your toddler's brain has not yet developed to a point where his true talents and social skills can emerge so his unique personality is not yet fully formed – he is simply being himself. Try to resist pigeonholing your child; instead focus on developing the special relationship you have with him (and each of your children). The better you get to know him at an early age, the better you will be able to understand him as he gets older, when keeping the lines of communication open may become more of a challenge. Playtime is the ideal time to encourage your child to develop his personal skills and to recognize his individuality.

There can be significant differences between children's outward signs of developmental progress at this age. Some will be speaking in full sentences, others will be saying very little, and the vast majority will be somewhere in between. This is not a time for progress comparisons – the vast majority learn to speak in full sentences eventually, so there is no rush. The important thing is to make sure your toddler knows he is loved and appreciated for who he is, with no conditions attached.

At his own pace

Young children need to experience an immediate sense of progress and achievement when they are learning, which is why your toddler should be allowed to develop at his own pace. Your two-year-old is still too young to be able to cope with delayed gratification or waiting for a reward. "Instant wins" are vital to prompt the beginnings of self-confidence. Pushing your child too far, too fast, will not lead to faster development; conversely, it will cause anxiety. It may also lead to him wanting to give up too soon due to frustration or boredom because he cannot achieve the necessary results. If continually pushed, this response can develop into a pattern of learned failure that can interfere with progress in the classroom and later life.

A happy, relaxed environment has been shown to promote healthy development. The balance between pushing and encouraging a child can seem remarkably fine, but it is important to get it right. Learning to read your child's behaviour will help you to understand whether he is enjoying his learning, or whether he is feeling under pressure.

Signs that your child may be feeling under pressure to perform:
■ Avoiding tasks altogether.
■ Sticking to an activity he can do and repeating it, rather than trying something new.
■ Getting very frustrated and distressed if he is unable to do something. (To a certain extent this is normal and healthy behaviour that helps develop frustration tolerance, but if your child over-reacts to every small frustration, he may be feeling under pressure.)
■ Regression to an earlier stage of development.
■ Seeking approval and wanting to please you rather than understand and complete the task.

Signs that your child is a relaxed and happy learner:
■ Eager to try new things.
■ Keen to attempt the next step and not overly distressed by failure.
■ Readily absorbed in the task.
■ Finding fun in tasks and having a playful nature.
■ Able to adapt the task to suit his own ideas, so he might be creative rather than focusing on a perfect result.

Behaviour boundaries

Tantrums and the art of saying "No" are synonymous with this age group, but both have a very important function. A toddler's battle is both with his parents and with himself. He is learning about personal feelings and boundaries, as well as the possibility of self-control. These skills mean that he is starting to test his personal limits and to become independent.

HAPPY IN HIS PLAY
Encouragement, not pressure, is the key to learning at this stage. If your toddler is enjoying doing an activity or playing with a toy, he will be learning naturally.

Along with the joy of independent discovery will come a strong need to feel contained and secure. This is the ideal age to begin to build up simple behavioural guidelines and routines. Behaviour boundaries are not about being overly strict or controlling. They are not there to prevent your child from expressing himself or experimenting. While they will doubtless make your life easier, their main function is to help your child to know his own limits and to learn at a very basic level how to regulate his own moods and behaviour. Be careful not to pay more attention to "naughty" behaviour than to "good" behaviour, as you will be reinforcing the "naughtiness" and "good" behaviour may go unnoticed. The same applies if one child is more extrovert; make time for your quiet child as well as your noisy one.

Language development

Two-year-olds love to talk and talk. Their newfound language skills are their passport to understanding their world and they won't miss a single opportunity to flex their vocal cords. Your toddler's vocabulary is growing every day and he understands a lot more than he has the words to express. He is gradually moving from two-word sentences to six-word sentences and by the end of the year will be able to make himself understood by most adults. The priority is to help your child to enjoy and develop his language skills as much as possible, through conversation, songs, rhymes, and word play. While your toddler is busy talking, you will be busy

Helping your child to cope with strong emotions

It is an important part of social development to be able to experience all kinds of feelings, from joy to rage. Understanding that the feelings will pass, and can be controlled, will in time provide your child with tools to self-manage his emotions.

▶ Watch for signs of personal frustration, especially if he is prone to biting, hitting, or screaming.

▶ Try not to lose your cool. Give a clear instruction to stop the behaviour, but don't be drawn into explaining why he must stop. He is too young to understand.

▶ Tell your child how he is feeling so he starts to learn the language to describe his feelings.

▶ Divert your child's attention with an activity rather than focusing on the negativity.

▶ Be realistic: problems are more likely when a child is tired, hungry, bored, or over-excited.

▶ You may need to remove an angry and aggressive child from the situation for a calm-down period.

"actively listening". This means, both verbally and non-verbally, encouraging your child to talk and increasingly reflecting back to him what he has said, so that he gradually learns to express his feelings.

Learning to reason and remember

Up until now your toddler has relied mainly on his short-term memory to understand his world. He will remember *what* has happened within the past few hours and will recognize the look, smell, and sound of those

"Toddlers have a very limited concept of time and will need to be given prompts and reminders to help them understand, such as 'tomorrow is when the sun comes up' or 'later when we have eaten supper'."

people who make him feel safe, but he has had little understanding of *when* things happened. By his second birthday, however, this will have changed. His brain is developing (see page 164) and with it comes an increased understanding of time. This is an important development. An understanding of time allows us to tag and store our memories. We also need an ability to recognize things to be able to recall them. Your toddler is developing this skill, too.

He will now progress from being able to remember the last few hours, to knowing what happened "yesterday" and having an awareness of "tomorrow" as well. This may show in your toddler's style of play. He may now choose the toys he wants to play with unassisted and be quite insistent about how he wants to play with them. For example, if he played with building blocks at a friend's house recently, he might say, "build house" every time you get his blocks out of the cupboard. Your toddler now looks at the blocks and thinks, "I know what I want to do with them" rather than simply, "I had fun playing with the blocks yesterday, I would like to do that again today." His memory has been prompted by an internal cue.

As long-term memory begins to develop (see page 242) so will a gradual ability to reason and to understand. Clear behaviour guidelines and routines will add structure to your child's day and you will find that your toddler loves routine, habits, and order in his life. This is partly because his attention span is still quite limited, but also because the repetition of actions and activities will help him to learn, by "bedding down" the information in his brain. There is another benefit to instilling some routine, too. The rapid changes in development at this age can be overwhelming. Structure, routine, and consistency help create a safe and secure environment for learning and development.

"When everything around them is changing so fast, including their own abilities, young children need some things to be constant, to offer them reassurance and make them feel safe."

Your skilful toddler

By the age of two your toddler will be far more steady on his feet, and as well as walking, will gradually discover new ways of getting about, such as running, climbing, jumping, and hopping. He is now able to hold a pencil in a writing position, can manage door handles, some buttons, zippers, and lids. He will also start to draw this year, and will enjoy turning the pages of books while he looks at the pictures. Throughout the next year he will become more confident and more physically co-ordinated. It is largely through his physical skills that he will experience the world and the more time he can spend outside in the open air the better. Children of this age are starting to enjoy gentle rough-and-tumble games, piggy-backs, playing horsey (usually with a willing adult on all fours and playing the horse!), and being swung round and round (safely).

Safety note

Toddlers are very accident-prone and have little judgement. Water hazards are particularly dangerous to a young child, as he cannot hold his breath or right himself easily if he falls. Roads are another obvious danger. It is essential that a toddler is supervised by an adult at *all* times.

LETTING HER LEARN *Getting ready to go out may take three times longer these days; however, it is important to be patient and give your child opportunities to help with tasks such as dressing herself.*

How you can support memory development

Your toddler will be getting better at remembering, but there are ways you can help him:

▶ Children learn mainly through personal experience, so hands-on learning is always a good idea.

▶ Strengthen memory by encouraging the use of more than one of the senses, for example songs to help learn words; the smells of cooking to explain the name of foods.

▶ Encourage his understanding of time by looking at photos and discussing past events – "When you were a baby we..."

▶ Read his favourite story and pause before naming a favourite character or phrase to allow him to fill the gap.

▶ Give information in short chunks – say, "Get your socks" rather than, "Get your socks, and then find your ball." He may only remember one instruction.

▶ Do not expect your child to be able to tell the time. He does not yet have reasoning skills.

▶ Give him extra information to help him understand the concept of time and ground his memories. For example, when talking about doing something "tomorrow", remind him that it means: "When you wake, then it will be tomorrow, and then we will go to the park."

Your toddler's movement skills and co-ordination will really start to take off now. His brain will be sending messages a lot faster, and so his movements will look more spontaneous. By the end of the year, he will be able to walk backwards, change direction when walking and running, and he will be carrying himself differently. He will have lost the rolling gait of a toddler and will have learned to walk in a confident way.

Social development

Toddlers of 24–36 months are a bundle of mixed emotions and are still very egocentric and self-interested. However, they are becoming much more interested in children their own age and will happily play alongside another child for a while – before falling out. Differences of opinion amongst playmates can be fairly vocal, physical, and frequent. Toddlers are great imitators and will be keeping a watchful eye on those around them to learn how to do new things. Their belief that everything is "mine" and that "everyone experiences life the way I see it" will inevitably lead to tantrums and misunderstandings. However, your toddler is learning fast. It may surprise you to find out from a babysitter that he is perfectly well behaved when you are not around. A lot of his behaviour is about experimentation – and trusting that you will be there to save him if things go wrong.

Signs that development is on track

It is important to emphasize that each child will develop at his own pace, and rarely in a steady upward line (see page 64). The following is an approximate guide to how new skills will develop in the coming months.

By the end of months 24–27, your child:

■ May be able to use as many as 50 single words and will be able to understand as many as 300.

■ Will be able to combine two words or more in a phrase.

■ May be able to follow a simple two-stage instruction.

■ Can probably take off one item of clothing.

■ May be starting to try to get dressed.

■ May be able to jump.

■ May be able to wash his hands.

■ Can use a cup with few spills.

By the end of months 27–30, your child:

■ Can probably put on an item of clothing.

■ Will be able to name as many as six body parts.

■ May be able to recognize as many as four images by pointing.

■ Can probably jump.

■ May be able to name a friend.

■ May recognize himself in a photo.

By the end of months 30–33, your child:

■ May be able to build a tower, six bricks high.

■ Will probably be able to wash and dry his hands.

■ May be able to say one or two sentences in short conversation.

■ Can stand on tiptoe when shown.

■ Can often draw circles, lines, and dots.

■ May show signs of being right- or left-handed.

■ Will notice small details in picture books.

■ Will know his full name.

By the end of month 36, your child:

■ Will be able to name at least four images.

■ Will be able to wash and dry his hands.

■ Will be able to clean his teeth, with help.

■ Will be starting to use prepositions in speech such as "on", "in", "under", and "over".

USING HIS HANDS
Fine motor skills are developing but no clear hand preference is shown before the age of three. Before this, using either his left or right hand, or both, is fine.

Learning new skills

Your relationship with your toddler is gradually changing. He still needs your help for most tasks, and craves your approval and involvement, but is becoming more independent and outward-looking and more aware of influences in his life – he remembers who people are and what they look like.

"You will see more signs of self-awareness as his unique personality and self-expression begin to emerge more strongly."

During this 12-month period there will be rapid changes in brain development. Your toddler will be totally absorbed in developing a new range of skills and, in particular, trying things out for himself and wanting to be in control. This inevitably leads to the tantrums, the increase in "Nos", and the sometimes challenging behaviour typical of two-year-olds as they struggle with being frustrated and emotionally overwhelmed. Your toddler will be torn between desperately wanting to do things for himself – such as getting dressed, making things, being free to move about – and his need to remain very dependent on you. He is developing the ability to know what he wants – but knows he cannot yet get there on his own.

Dealing with his frustration

As your toddler sees the world as a bigger and more exciting place, he will want to experience everything more often, which means he needs greater supervision. He will want to do more things, but may still be developing the skills required to do certain tasks. This can lead to frustration and he may, for example, suddenly throws his toys across the room. Calmly sit with him and help him achieve what he set out to do, while giving him instructions and a lot of encouragement. This enables him to achieve what he set out to do at the same time as acquiring new skills and developing more positive ways of dealing with frustration.

Imagination and reasoning skills

Over the next two or three years your child's imagination will be developing at a rapid rate, due to the changes that are taking place in his brain (see page 165). During this year he will be learning to pretend and will be developing a growing understanding that an object (such as a toy telephone) can represent something else (an actual telephone) – provided it at least looks like the real thing. By the time he is three or four he will have developed this skill much further and will be able to imagine that anything from a shoe to a banana might be a phone! But for now, this vitally important skill means he can start to enjoy and understand pictures and stories, and later learn about letters and numbers.

Without imagination and the understanding that one thing can represent or symbolize another, your toddler would not be able to understand that a sound can represent a letter of the alphabet; or that numbers represent things, for example that the number two can represent "two apples" or "two horses" or two of anything. Nor would he be able to recognize himself or others in photographs, or appreciate that a cartoon picture of a cow represents the real thing.

By the time he is 3–4 years old his fantasy world will be well developed; even now, his ability to imagine and pretend means that the boundaries between his imaginary world and reality can become blurred and confused from time to time, as the following example shows:

"My toddler Ricky had been playing with his 10-year-old cousin, Mike. Mike kept disappearing briefly behind the sofa, using his voice to pretend

MAKING CHOICES *At this age, children begin to know which toys are their favourites and which offer comfort. This shows that memory is now playing a role as they remember having fun and how to play with something.*

there was a cookie monster there who would come and eat Ricky's cookies. To begin with, Ricky thought this was hilarious, and kept popping behind the sofa to check things out; but when Mike announced in his monster voice, 'I'm coming to find the cookies now...' Ricky's imagination suddenly took over, and it all became too much for him. He ran screaming to find me."

Watching your toddler play can give you a fascinating insight into what is going on in his mind. At this age, he may often chatter to himself and commentate on what is going on. You will be able to see whether he is acting something out that is funny, loving, or scary, and whether he is mirroring behaviour that he has seen, as the following example shows:

"Poppy had a tantrum one morning because I was giving priority to her baby sister, Rachel. Poppy had hit Rachel and I told her very firmly that

Role-play

Your toddler's ability to pretend means you can also use role-play to get him used to understanding how to behave, or to get used to situations that he could find challenging, such as starting nursery, going to the doctor or dentist, or coping with someone he finds frightening, such as an eccentric neighbour. Playing "let's pretend" helps him to put things in context.

It's important not to mock or trivialize your child's fears, but trust your judgement to decide when you might introduce a sense of fun to help normalize the situation.

For example, if he is very attached to Grandpa and becomes upset when he has to go home, you can play "let's pretend" to help him understand that Grandpa will come back the next day, and gradually help him to change his mood.

▶ **Daddy** "Luke, would you like to pretend to be Grandpa, and shall I pretend to be you?" In sad voice, (pretending to be his son Luke): "Don't go, Gramps. I hate it when you go. I feel very sad and want to cry."
▶ **Luke (pretending to be Grandpa)** "Don't cry. Don't cry. I come back."
▶ **Daddy, in worried voice** "When will you come back. Grandpa? Will you come back tonight and read me a story?"
▶ **Luke, firmly** "No. Back 'morrow."
▶ **Daddy, sadly** "But I feel sad and I don't want you to go."

▶ **Luke, gently** "Don't be sad." Strokes Daddy's head. "Back 'morrow."
▶ **Daddy, gently** "OK, Gramps. I love you." Gives Luke a hug. "I will try not to be sad but I miss you when you leave, and sometimes tomorrow seems a very long time away. Leaves a short pause... and then changes mood, with silly, happy voice: "Grandpa?" Gets Luke's attention and eye contact. "Grandpa, pleeeeease will you stay?"
▶ **Luke, giggly** "No, I go now."
▶ **Daddy in more silly voice: and giggling** "Grandpa, pleeeeeeeeeease will you stay?" Then in a calmer voice, "Will I see you tomorrow then Grandpa?"
▶ **Luke, giggly** "Yes." They hug.

hitting was bad, and to treat Rachel gently. Later that day I was moved to see her playing with her doll and saying, 'No hit little teddy. Hitting bad! Hug better.' She then helped her doll to hug her teddy better." If your toddler can use his imagination, it also means that he is developing his reasoning skills, and will link cause and effect more consistently and begin to realize that what he does has an influence on what happens next.

Learning social and emotional skills

Now that your two-year-old is beginning to understand the impact that he has on the world around him, he is also starting to become aware that other people may not see the world in quite the same way.

It is now that your toddler needs your help to begin to become in tune with his emotions, to realize that other people have feelings too, and gradually to develop his social skills. All the effort you are putting in to help him to manage and name his "big" feelings is helping him to learn and understand about his emotions. The more he is able to identify and understand the way he is feeling, the better he will be able to empathize with other people.

During this period, most children are able to openly express a wide range of emotions and are gradually learning to cope with their anxiety if separated from a parent for a while. As explained above, this is because your child now has an understanding that although you have gone, you will also come back. This level of trust and expectation explains why toddlers hate any change in their routine. They take comfort in the regularity and predictability of actions and behaviours. If something does not go as normally expected, the impact can be very distressing.

Helping your child to learn social and emotional skills:

■ When you need to discipline your toddler, make sure you use respectful language and do not insult or belittle him in any way. This will encourage him to stay in tune with his feelings.

■ Comfort him and help him understand. Children who are able to trust that they will receive comfort when they are upset, and who are encouraged to express and understand their feelings, are able to develop compassion and show empathy towards others from an early age, and grow up to be in tune with their feelings.

■ Do not dismiss his feelings. Children who experience hurt, who are

LET'S PRETEND *Toys such as plastic food help to bridge the gap between play and reality and stimulate your child's imagination, as well as enabling her to act like Mummy or Daddy.*

WAITING HIS TURN *Patience and co-operation are two skills your toddler is gradually learning and, when he does, he will begin to wait to take turns and play more harmoniously with others.*

insulted, or whose sensitive feelings are regularly disregarded, will learn to cope by gradually shutting themselves off from their emotions. This behaviour can lead to a child developing difficulties in forming deep friendships or relationships in later life.

Learning to wait

Just as you are starting to wonder whether your toddler is ever going to learn the art of waiting, a major shift in his behaviour happens. Along with the development of his reasoning skills comes an understanding that "I can't have it now, but I can have it later." Your patience is now going to pay off, because your toddler is finally starting to learn self-control. His ability to pretend means that he has the ability to imagine that things can happen later. His improved sense of time helps him to practise using more self-control because he knows he will get what he wants eventually.

You can probably remember that night-time seemed to go on forever when you were young. Long-distance time is a problem for children of this age – an hour is still an interminable length of time – and "later" may have a different meaning to him than it does to you. So bear this in mind and help him to learn.

Guidelines for helping your toddler to wait:
■ Link the time frame to an event, so that he can understand when the right time has arrived. "Not now. Later, when your sister is in her cot."
■ Use "if, then; when, then" (see page 196). "*If* you put your toys in the toy box first, *then* you can play with your trains."
■ If it is a challenging wait, add an incentive, and show your appreciation: "I want you to be quiet now, Tony. Can you be quiet until we leave the shop? Good boy. *If* you can, *then* you can play football with your brother *when* we get home. Thank you."
■ Use an incentive, such as giving him coloured balls, stickers, or building blocks to collect. Tell him that every five minutes that he can wait and behave nicely, he will be rewarded with another one.

Needless to say that in order for a child to learn to trust in the value of "later", the adults who are asking him to wait need to honour their promises and do as they say, and when they said they would. A toddler who discovers that "later" is code for "never" or "I don't feel like it" will feel let down and will be less likely to behave nicely in the future.

Your toddler's brain

This period sees a slight plateau in the speed of development of your child's movement skills, while his brain diverts its attention to another major priority: the development of the frontal lobes. This part of the brain plays an important part in developing rational thought, emotions, attention, and memory.

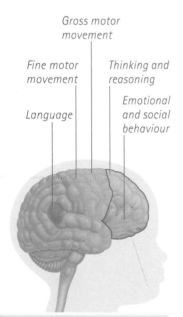

Gross motor movement

Fine motor movement

Thinking and reasoning

Emotional and social behaviour

Language

GREATER UNDERSTANDING

The frontal lobe area is marked by the darker line. The two areas within this start to mature and influence your child's under-standing of his world.

Closely linked to the improvement in your child's communication skills that occurs during this year, and the emergence of imagination and developing personality, the frontal lobes of the brain (see diagram, left) contribute a great deal to the characteristics that make us human. Both sides of the frontal lobes are inter-connected, with thinking and reasoning skills based in one area and emotional and social behaviour in the other. Together they are the driving force behind our ability to understand and reason, plan, and organize. They regulate our emotions and responses, and keep our impulses in check. The role of the frontal lobes is to direct the overall activity of the brain as a whole. Like the chief executive of a huge organization, they decide which ideas to run with, what your priority is at this very moment, and oversee the functioning of all the other areas of the brain. They give us the go-ahead to act, react, or not act at all.

The thinking and reasoning area tells us:
- Where we should be concentrating our attention.
- What we should remember.
- When and when not to act.

The social and emotional area:
- Oversees our emotions.
- Regulates our feelings and puts them into context.
- Helps govern our responses, while keeping a check on impulsive actions.

The frontal lobes continue to develop throughout your child's early years, fully maturing in adolescence and giving him the ability to deal with more complex skills, such as flexibility and multi-tasking, by the age of fifteen. They play a vital part in developing your toddler's behavioural control and his personality.

Choosing the right response

The frontal lobes play an important role in reasoning and problem-solving. They help us to decide what to pay attention to in any given moment and to respond in the way that seems best. It is easiest to think of them as the part of the brain that puts things into context. It is where thoughts about our inner world – our memories, movement, emotions, and so on – link up with thoughts about our outer world – where you are, who else is there. By taking all this information into account the lobes can decide what behaviour or action is most appropriate to take.

In the case of your toddler, for example, this could mean him understanding and choosing to respond either to hunger or excitement: "Which is more important to me right now: the awareness that I am hungry [his inner world] or the excitement I feel because Mum has just bought me a really exciting new toy [his outer world]?" In responding, he needs to decide which to attend to and how he should behave.

Thinking and reasoning

The thinking and reasoning part of the frontal lobes drives the development of our planning and reasoning skills, as well as our ability to resist the thoughts and responses that might take us off course. As the frontal lobes of your toddler's brain develop, you will notice a real increase in his planning and reasoning ability. For example, "If I drag a chair here and climb on it, I can reach the sweets on the table." He will also be able to concentrate better and to tune in to the messages that will help him to get what he wants. While he is learning self-control your toddler is developing the skills he will need to succeed in the future, both academically and socially. Once he has the experience to remember to sit and pay attention, take the feelings of others into account, and stop himself reacting impulsively, he can begin to guide his future behaviour and actions.

Attention span

Before he is able to learn to reason and plan effectively, your toddler first needs to be able to concentrate. His ability to focus completely on a task, game, or conversation will develop gradually through different stages and levels of attention, throughout the toddler years. As he develops he will become more focused on his own needs, wants, and goals (which is not always a blessing!) and will become less easily distracted. There are three different types of attention that develop over time:

Selective attention This is the basic ability to choose to pay attention to what is relevant and ignore other cues. Toddlers need to have this ability before they can begin to store information in their working memory (see below). Young babies start to develop this ability, but are easily distracted.

Divided attention When we pay attention to more than one thing at a time we are dividing our attention. This is a challenge for toddlers. Whereas an adult can listen to the radio while completing a crossword, or have a chat while planning dinner, toddlers find it difficult to do more than one thing at a time. This is why, if you want your child to focus on a task, such as eating, it is best to remove toys from the table to minimize distractions.

"Emily loves to help me make cakes, but she gets easily distracted. She loves the mixing and decorating, but we take short breaks, too, so that she doesn't become frustrated and have a tantrum." Annette, aged 27

Sustained attention Maintaining attention over a period of time is a developing skill. Your toddler is able to stay focused for only a few minutes at a time. Typically, children can concentrate for only very short periods on activities such as drawing or looking at a book. At 24 months, this time span can be as short as seven minutes, increasing to nine minutes by the age of three, 13 minutes by age four, and 15 minutes by age five. Not until the age of six or seven will a child be able to concentrate for as long as one hour. Your two-year-old may do some colouring for seven minutes, pause to stroke the cat, take a sip from his beaker, wander round the room and then go back to colouring for seven more minutes. Toddlers need to take frequent breaks from things, so you should not be concerned.

How the memory works

When the brain receives an instruction, two different types of memory work together to follow it. The short-term memory recalls and stores the information ("I need to get my coat"); while the working memory helps to put the instruction into operation, very fast and stage by stage. ("I need to reach the coat peg; I am stretching my muscles; I am going on to my tiptoes, I am reaching for my coat"). The working memory holds small chunks of information for just long enough to tell us what we need to do to achieve our goal right now. Once your toddler has his coat, he can still remember that he wanted it (using his short-term memory), but his working memory has dropped all the stages. By now his working memory is helping him to put one foot in front of the other to walk out of the door, or to pick up a toy, or to go and find his sister.

Short-term memory has a very small capacity and the ability to remember is still in development in young children. This is why toddlers find complex instructions hard to follow and may get frustrated. Your toddler may need to be given instructions in two, three, or more small chunks. (Even an adult can hold only about seven chunks of information in mind at a time.) So instead of saying: "Get undressed and washed, and then clean your teeth, and then you can say goodnight," break the information down into smaller tasks. "Let's get you undressed," (wait until task is complete)/"Now we will get you washed," (do this and wait)/"Now clean your teeth," (wait until finished)/"And now you can say goodnight."

Planning and achieving

The frontal lobes of the brain (see page 164) play an important part in enabling us to decide what we want and then plan how to get it. They also enable us to overcome obstacles and distractions to achieve our goals.

Tina has decided that she wants to play with her red ball. First she must think: "I want the red ball." She then uses her working memory to hold on to the thought while she reasons how to get the red ball: "I shall walk to the toy box and find it." Next she puts her thoughts into action, and moves towards the toy box. Looking inside, Tina spots her blue ball instead: "That's a nice blue ball..." Instead of getting distracted, the frontal lobes in her brain help her to switch off the "blue ball" message and focus back on the "red ball" message – "...but I want my red one – and it's not here!" She realizes that what she is doing now won't help her, and decides, "It might be in the garden..." Off she toddles.

If she were younger, Tina would probably forget about the red ball altogether and play happily with other toys; but because Tina is now 30 months old, she not only wants the red ball, she remembers how and where to find it. Her working memory helps her to stay on a task long enough to achieve her goal.

Your anxious toddler

Anxiety is a natural part of growing up. Your toddler's imagination and reasoning skills will develop to a point where he understands dangers and that things can go wrong. You have a positive role to play in helping your child to cope with extreme feelings.

Feelings of anxiety are a sign that we feel frightened or under threat, from something physical (such as being attacked), environmental (such as a tornado), or psychological (such as being criticized).

During the toddler years these "dangers" may include, for example, being left to cry for long periods, picking up on parental tension or unhappiness, and being shouted at.

Anxiety triggers a powerful and automatic reaction within the most primitive part of the brain that drives our instinct for survival. When we experience intense emotions, such as anger, fear, and even excitement, the brain tells the body to release stress hormones that will either make us challenge the situation (fight), or run away from it (flight). These "fight or flight" hormones, especially adrenaline

and cortisol, then block the production of "feel good" hormones, such as oxytocin (see page 86).

LEARNING TO COPE

Everyone experiences anxiety, but some people cope with these feelings better than others. We now know that our ability to cope has its roots in our childhood experiences. During the toddler years, a child relies almost totally on caring adults to help him to manage his "big" feelings.

When a child is anxious, if Mummy or Daddy is on hand to soothe him, his body will learn to produce "feel good" hormones as he calms down. On the other hand, a toddler who is not comforted will become increasingly anxious and will produce even higher levels of stress hormones. His brain is becoming wired for anxiety rather than calm.

By the age of 2–3, your toddler's anxiety about being separated from you (see page 90) is gradually diminishing, only to be replaced by a range of fears stimulated by his developing imagination and awareness of the wider world. It is natural for toddlers to be scared of new

MANAGING YOUR OWN ANXIETIES

If you find it hard to manage your own stressful feelings, you may also find it hard to tolerate extreme feelings in your toddler. If you were constantly shouted at, over-controlled, or criticized when you were a child, your brain is likely to release very high levels of cortisol when you are anxious, and you are likely to pass your feelings of stress on to your child.

▶ Make time for activities that makes you feel calm and relaxed.

▶ Make sure you have a social network that offers you warmth and support when you need it.

▶ If you have had relationship problems, a bereavement, or any other life-altering challenge to cope with, consider getting professional help to dissipate your anxiety. It will be impossible for you to protect your child from your feelings, and his emotions may intensify in response to your own.

▶ Avoid smoking, drinking to excess, and consuming high levels of caffeine from tea, coffee, or chocolate, and some fizzy drinks.

▶ Parenting a toddler *is* stressful on occasion and it is natural to feel anxious; don't be too hard on yourself and do try to keep things in proportion.

experiences at this age, but their anxiety will usually pass if it is carefully handled.

SIGNS OF ANXIETY

Children show anxiety in a variety of ways. Some cry, others may become very quiet, clingy, or whiny. Nervous tics are also quite common at this age – that is, involuntary muscle spasms that children cannot control – such as rapid blinking or twitching; but most disappear of their own accord.

Whatever the signs, your child needs to be reassured. Each time you hug him and help him to cope, you are increasing his chances of being able to manage his feelings and cope with stress as he grows up. Children who are reprimanded rather than comforted will worry and become more anxious more often. They are also more likely to develop later behavioural problems such as phobias (see page 260), bedwetting, or soiling (see page 303).

HELPING YOUR CHILD

Your toddler learns from your example, so start by learning to manage your own strong feelings and showing him that shouting or crying are not the only ways to respond.
▶ Stay calm, smile warmly, and speak to him in a gentle tone.
▶ Hug him or show him affection to soothe his fears.
▶ Never reprimand him for feeling

anxious; instead encourage him gently to try new things and praise him every time he copes with a fear.
▶ Use distraction techniques, such as singing, to help reduce your child's fear while you help him to address whatever has caused the anxiety.
▶ Never call a child by derogatory names, such as "stupid", "clumsy", or "hopeless", or label him as "a cry baby",

LEARNING TO CLIMB *It is natural to feel anxious as your toddler tries new things, but resist telling him to "be careful" when he's doing just fine,*

not even in jest. He needs to know that he can rely on you for consistent love, care, and support. If your response pushes him away or scares him, his anxiety will increase even further.

Learning through play

Play and learning are very closely linked throughout the toddler years, and your child will love nothing more than to have your involvement. The hours you spend playing with him is never wasted time; he is learning from you all the time and needs as much attention as you can manage to give.

A balance between physical and mental play is essential to help your toddler to shape up his brain and body for learning. He will learn what is important and how things are valued from the people around him. He will also make discoveries about his own likes and dislikes, how things work, and how to use and develop his personal skills. While play is a natural instinct, it needs to be encouraged so that he knows that he has your regard and approval. Without adult involvement and without playmates, your child may lose interest in playing; and his learning will reduce too. Remember it is the process not the end result that is important. It is the fact he is starting to draw that is the success – not whether the picture really looks like Daddy!

Maria Montessori

Born in Italy in 1870, Maria Montessori was the first Italian woman to qualify as a medical doctor. She became convinced that a child's true potential can only develop if given the right kind of stimulation during the early years of life and devoted her life to developing a new style of child-orientated education that has been widely adopted across the world for over 100 years. Working initially with children from deprived backgrounds, she discovered that children enjoy learning practical skills and benefit from a calm and ordered environment. At the heart of her philosophy is the belief that play and learning are inter-related because one cannot occur without the other. She identified distinct developmental stages and key "sensitive" periods of learning that Montessori schools still use today.

Montessori teachers encourage multi-sensory learning, especially through play, and help children to learn self-management, self-respect, and how to acquire skills that encourage the development of independent thought and ability.

Gender differences tend to show in levels of maturity, and in skill and language development. In both instances, girls tend to develop more quickly. These factors are connected, because language development has an impact on social skills. The differences between the sexes are thought to be largely conditioned by home environment; so by the time a toddler is aged 3–4 he will have a much clearer idea of what it is to be female or male. At the age of 2–3 years, however, toys and games are interchangeable and not all children will be certain of who is a girl and who is a boy.

Play stages

Toddler play develops through several distinct stages. Up until around 24 months, your toddler will have had very little interest in anyone other than you as he played, but his brain has now developed to a point where he is beginning to understand his feelings and to develop imagination. With this comes memory development and his ability to "tune in" to his wider world, which means he is starting to pay more attention to his peer group and wants to be with them, too.

His parallel play skills will continue to develop now. Rather than just playing alongside a child, he may start to show more interest in what the child is doing and will watch and copy some of his actions – although he is not ready to play with other children yet. In time, when he has learned to share and take turns this will develop into more co-operative play. For now, though, the change from solitary to parallel play is challenging enough and your toddler will need your help to cope with it.

Learning to share and take turns

Your toddler will like to rehearse his play actions. You may have noticed that he will try things out on himself, or on you, before he uses his imagination to apply them in a pretend play situation. For example, he might put his teddy to bed in the same way you put his baby sister to bed. This process of learning applies to sharing and taking turns, too – but he

TAKING TURNS *While she will be more aware of her playmates, your toddler still does not understand the "rules" of play and still thinks that everything belongs to her.*

will need your help to learn. For example, count out sweets – one for Mummy, one for him – or as you cut a pizza, tell him you are dividing it to share. When he is playing with another child, explain it is his playmate's turn to have the toy.

Adjusting to the challenge of socializing with his peers will take some getting used to. The problem for toddlers is that other toddlers may not seem to understand the rules of sharing and taking turns in the way that you have been showing him – so encounters tend to end in tears, tantrums, or aggression quite quickly. You can help by playing a valuable and essential support role. Your toddler needs you to help him to rehearse a co-operative style of play, in the safety of his relationship with you, where he can avoid the power struggles and fallings-out that tend to happen with his own age group. He also needs you to stay present when he is in the company of other toddlers, so that you can ease the way if there are signs of tension, and help him transfer his practice skills to a real situation.

In time, once he gets used to interacting with his own age group, you will be able to draw back slightly and allow him to negotiate his own way; but he will need to have got to grips with the basics of sharing first.

"Overseeing toddlers playing together is not about taking control and directing their behaviour; it is about keeping an eye on the situation and helping them to ease their way out of trouble when flare-ups occur."

Developing styles of play

Your toddler has been experimenting with different styles of play since he was born. As a baby, he mastered the art of dropping or banging things out of curiosity and for the sheer joy of making the sound; he will next have developed a masterful array of physical skills and has since built up his strength through experimental play and exploration. Now that he can combine his sensual awareness with his physical skills, and with his rapidly developing imaginative and language skills, a whole new world of pretend play is open to him.

TICKLE ME! *Rough-and-tumble will delight her because she has your attention. Choose your moment, however, because although these games are great at expending energy, they may make her upset or over-excited.*

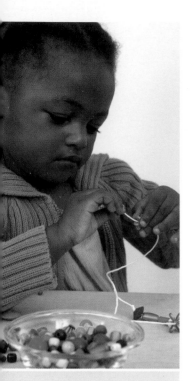

CREATIVITY *Her ability to concentrate for longer periods will give more scope for creative activities, and you can begin to encourage her to give her creations to people as gifts.*

Language play You may notice your toddler talking to himself. He will comment constantly on what he is doing, how he is feeling, and how he is playing. This important stage is helping him to develop his inner voice and helping him to understand his actions and feelings, and whether he is on track. This voice will gradually quieten and become internalized. At this stage, however, "listening in" to what your toddler is saying to himself will give you an insight into his feelings, reactions, and where his imagination is taking him.

His language play is also about the sheer joy of experimenting with sounds and words. Toddlers often chatter to themselves as they lie in bed at night, and an initial "story" can quickly transform into nonsense-speak such as, "Daddy play with Abby, go see Uncle Bob. Hello Uncle Bob, Bob, Bob. Do you go bob bob? Bobee, bobby bob, bobadob, bob dog."

We each have an internal voice that comments on our thoughts and actions. It is an important way of self-monitoring and self-control. Children who at an older age have difficulties with self-control may have had difficulties developing their internal voice and therefore self-monitoring is more difficult. You can help your toddler to learn this skill by chatting to him about what you are doing and by encouraging commentary, so he can learn to model it. For example: "Mummy is just going to tidy up her plate and mug before she plays with you," "Daddy is feeling very happy so he is going to come and get you for a big cuddle," "I am going to play ball with you and show you how I take turns."

The inner voice acts as a commentator and can therefore have an impact on developing self-esteem. If you hear your toddler making constantly self-deprecating or critical remarks, it is a sign that he does not appreciate himself or his achievements. You can play an important role in teaching him to value himself and help him to replace the negative thoughts with more positive ones.

Physical play Children love to keep on the move and at this age find it quite hard to keep still for long. Being able to play in the fresh air – whatever the weather – gives children a sense of freedom. Factors such as energy levels, tiredness, physical temperature, how long he has been playing, personal likes, and whether yours is an "outdoors" kind of family, all play their part in deciding when it is time to change focus. There is no doubt that children find it easier to concentrate on indoor activities such as drawing, puzzles, making things, and story-telling if they have had a chance to burn off some energy. On a simple biological level, physical activity gets the blood circulating and directs more oxygen to the brain and other vital organs – which will keep your child healthy, and help his body to learn more effectively.

Physical play also helps children to develop self-confidence. Your praise as he bravely tries the see-saw for the first time, or enjoys the thrill of sitting in a swing (which is very good for developing his sense of balance) will encourage him to trust his physical capabilities. In time, he will be ready to try the climbing frame, too, and to navigate space with other children. Make sure he knows how well he has done in his efforts and encourage him to try new activities. Try not to allow any anxiety you may feel about him falling or hurting himself prevent him from "having a go" in a safely supported context.

How to play with your toddler

Playtime is a creative and fun time for your toddler – and for you, too. This is a delightful time in your child's life and he will be constantly surprising both you and himself with his discoveries, abilities, and

Supermarket games

Supermarket shopping with your toddler may fill you with fear and trepidation, but with a little planning and a large dose of patience, a shopping trip can be fun and an opportunity for learning, too.
▶ On the way to the supermarket create a memory game: "We're going to the supermarket and today we're going to buy... an enormous loaf of magical white bread that can take us to the moon." Make your descriptions elaborate, colourful, and silly to help your toddler's brain create associations. Gradually add more items and see what he remembers and can imagine himself.
▶ Let him help you to push the trolley for a short distance, or to put the coin in the slot to release it.
▶ Cut distinctive labels and pictures to give your toddler his own pictorial "shopping list". Give him clues and encourage him to find the items.

▶ Play a simplified version of *I Spy* to encourage him to name things: "I spy a green vegetable... Can you see it?"
▶ Encourage him to help you unload the groceries at the checkout.
▶ Describe what you are buying and what it looks like.
▶ Reward him with lots of praise and a small treat so he associates shopping with fun.
▶ When you get home, involve him in putting the shopping away.

observations. Children can be very funny at this age (not always deliberately) and love to entertain and be entertained.

Let your child lead play whenever possible. It is important for him to be able to follow through an idea from beginning to end and to understand that he "has a say". Keep things simple: children of this age have trouble holding more than one idea in mind at a time. If he has to field your suggestions and interruptions unnecessarily, your toddler will become frustrated and temporarily confused.

Encourage your child's imagination by introducing pretend objects that represent the real thing – such as toy kitchen equipment, and gardening and DIY tools. In time, your child will be able to create the same effect by using anything at all.

"Break things down into small steps. Your toddler can't take in more than one or two pieces of information at a time, so he needs you to help him to take in what you are saying gradually."

The importance of pictures

Images play an important part in your child's learning. His brain is developing at a rapid rate, enabling long-term memory and imagination to improve. Pictures are important triggers for both memory and pretend play, which is why picture books are so important for this age group. His skills have now developed to a point where he is able to notice small details on the page and to recognize many more images than he was able to previously. Your toddler's memory is still developing (see page 242) and his attention span is still short, so he will have an insatiable appetite for repetition and will want to keep returning to the same book and the same pictures again and again.

Picture books offer great opportunities for learning and encouraging familiarity with words and sounds, as well as great fodder for the imagination. You can encourage your toddler to find things on the page and ask him what he notices and what he likes the most and least. Leave gaps when you are telling the story and see whether he can fill them. Using descriptive words to describe the pictures (focusing on shapes, colours, and sizes as well as locations) will encourage your toddler to develop the words to describe what he sees, and he can then follow your lead.

Picture books will lead your toddler gently into language learning and reading. They also offer the perfect opportunity to see your little one's personality developing and to get some insight into how he views his world.

Freedom to learn

The ideal activities for your toddler at this age are those that encourage the development of a wide range of skills and interests. He will be developing preferences, but is much too young to stop trying a variety of new experiences.

Encourage messy play Giving your toddler free reign to explore textures, shapes, colours, and the world of his imagination, will not only help him to develop his motor skills (holding pencils, taking lids off jars and tops off tubes), it will also "free him" to learn to express himself. (There is a time to learn about cleaning up, too, but not until the end of playtime.)

Withhold your judgement Toddlers are too young to "get it right". The important thing is to encourage his sense of exploration and to encourage him to try. Hold the criticism, and go heavy on the praise.

Learning new skills It is a good idea to resist turning playtime into lesson time at this age, but nevertheless a question such as "Do you know how to draw a face?" will invite curiosity and allow you to show him a new skill. Allow him to absorb ideas and take them in at his own pace.

Throw out the rule book Toddlers do not need to know the true rules of *Snap* or the fact that it is better to find the corners of the jigsaw first.

Start from scratch Remember that the latest games and elaborate gadgets tend to be there for the benefit of the manufacturer's profits rather than your toddler's well-being. Some of the greatest fun can come from making up your own games, rhymes, toys, and stories. Children have plenty of

FAVOURITE STORY *If your toddler felt good about a story last time, she will trust it again. And she will associate it with having fun and being with you.*

"Teaching him to be curious now will help to foster a healthy attitude to learning later."

ideas for how things should "be". Creating something together will have lasting value for you both.

Enjoy being silly There are plenty of years ahead for conformity and being sensible. At this age your toddler needs to develop ways to remember new information. Being silly and doing things in an original way will not only help to prompt your child's memories, but will also help him to develop the art of self-expression and original thought.

Dressing up is fun At the heart of creative play is a child's imagination. Although it will be another six months to a year before he is able to manage dressing up or enjoy fantasy play to any great extent, a hat, a cloak or a magic wand are all the props he needs to become a wizard. Create a dressing-up box of hats and bags for your child to decorate.

Never too young You can help him to understand what he sees and hears around him by commenting on it and exposing him to new experiences. Even at this age you can introduce him to different types of music and rhythms, pictures and colours, plants and seeds, and the moon and stars.

Think toddler-sized Buckets, watering cans, spoons, knives, and forks: all of these come in cheap and cheerful smaller sizes that help your little one to become more dextrous.

Show him how things work Children enjoy being shown, rather than told, how to do new things. With gentle encouragement they will develop the confidence to try for themselves.

Lev Semenovich Vygotsky

Born in 1896, Vygotsky, a Russian developmental psychologist, was fascinated by the links between the development of thought, language, and memory. He believed children's speed and level of development are greatly influenced by the help and encouragement they have with problem-solving. His theory was that children learn more easily when given assistance. He argued that the role of the parent (and later, the teacher) is important in helping children bridge the gap between their current and potential ability. For example, a child who is trying to fit shapes into a box may get frustrated. However, if handed the right shape, one at a time, he will succeed and learn. To help development further, the helper might push the right shape closer (but not hand it to him) so the child still has to choose to pick up the shape, but has been given a clue. Parents will do this naturally: helping children to take small successful steps, one at a time.

LETTING HER HELP *Move on from pretend play by involving your toddler in activities such as baking. Guide her, but let her do it her own way as much as possible, and don't worry about the outcome or expect it to be edible!*

Games for children

You may find that your child enjoys some games more than others and that he is developing a preference for playing indoors or outdoors. Free play and having time to explore are very important for children's healthy development, but it is also the ideal time to begin to gently turn play into learning, too. Messy and unstructured play is good for children. It helps them to develop skills and stimulates their imagination. Parents need to learn to relax and deal with messiness so that toddlers follow their example. Put away the wet wipes! There is a link between anxious children fearing getting dirty and problems with food and feeding.

Most of the toys your toddler had at the age of one will still be relevant now, although he will start to play with them a little differently. He will be able to cope with short trips to the zoo, to the park, to listen to music or other entertainment. Less is more at this age as he still has a short attention span and is easily overwhelmed. Imagination and simplicity are the keys to fun and games at this age.

He will be interested in:

■ How things work – zips, dials, buttons, and switches.

■ What things do – cars, dolls, and animals.

■ How things sound – bells, whistles, drums, and xylophones.

■ How we live – getting dressed, making things, and cooking.

"Nurturing creativity in all areas will help your toddler to make greater use of his mind and imagination and to develop his reasoning and imaginative skills."

Top tips for reducing playtime chaos:

■ Limit your cleaning up by allocating a messy play area, playing outside, or showing your toddler the "special play sheet" he needs to get before using paints, for example. But after that, let him be free in his chaos!

■ Try using pictures to organize where things are kept. Your toddler will then learn where things are kept as well as the object in the picture.

■ Take the time to show him how things work, so he learns how to play in a way that cuts down the chance of things breaking, but hold the criticism if he does break something. At this age damage is inevitable.

Playtime ideas and games

QUIET PLAY

▶ Jigsaws – giant floor puzzles and robust puzzles with additional grip.

▶ Matching and sorting shapes – use this to start to introduce simple rules and turn-taking. For example, picture dominoes or simple *Snap* or sorting colourful building blocks.

▶ Your toddler will enjoy hearing stories that are recognizable and predictable and is likely to have his own favourite characters.

▶ Memory tray – lay out no more than three to five items to begin with. Take something away and ask your toddler which one has gone. Add something: add a new object and see whether he can tell which it is and what it is called.

▶ Nature table – encourage him to collect leaves, shells, stones, twigs, and insects when you go for a walk. Lay them out on a table and talk to him about what they are and how they grow.

▶ Spot the difference – draw two faces that are largely similar, and then add some obvious differences (such as green hair or a red nose). Ask your toddler to tell you what is different about each picture and what is the same.

▶ Weighing and measuring – an oversized tape measure will help children develop an understanding of size. A set of scales and dry beans can be used for weighing and pouring.

OUTDOOR PLAY

▶ Sand play – with water, buckets, shells, and other accessories.

▶ Ball games – play with a football, skittles, a basic bat and ball

▶ Water play – including a paddling pool. Supervise at *all* times.

▶ Playgrounds – let him play on climbing frames, swings, and a see-saw.

CREATIVE PLAY

▶ Play dough – it is easy to make your own.

▶ Painting and drawing – give him an easel, paints, and an apron.

▶ Edible faces – make smiley pizzas or silly sandwiches.

▶ Collage – it is amazing what can be created with a glue stick and beads, pulses, glitter, string, and crayons.

▶ Cutting and sticking things.

PRETEND PLAY

▶ Glove puppets – these can be home-made really simply out of socks with sewn buttons for eyes.

▶ Dressing up – keep an eye on charity shops for flamboyant items that can be cut down to toddler size – and look in your wardrobe, too.

▶ Indoor picnic – children will love the novelty of eating with their fingers and sitting on the floor, especially if teddy can come, too.

▶ Treasure hunt – following clues (with your help) and finding surprises is fun for all ages.

▶ Playing schools – will help your toddler get used to the idea of what happens at school.

▶ Playing shop – will help him get used to the idea of coins and swapping them for goods.

ACTION PLAY AND PARTY GAMES

▶ Action songs – such as *Head, Shoulders*, *Hokey Cokey*, *If You're Happy and You Know It*, *The Wheels on the Bus*, *Ring o' Roses*.

▶ Party games – such as *Pass the Parcel*, *Simon Says*, *Musical Bumps*.

▶ *Hide and Seek* – when you hide, make sure you are easy to find.

▶ Trains and cars – pushing trains round tracks and playing with cars.

▶ Pretending to be an animal – hop like a rabbit, jump like a frog, and run like a cheetah.

What toddlers want and need

Every day is a learning experience for your toddler. Sometimes he will be confident and other days anxious and uncertain. You need to be sensitive to his changes in mood and adjust your approach accordingly, until he is at an age where he is better able to manage them himself.

What your toddler still wants more than anything is your attention. He wants to copy you and loves being with you. But be careful that your enthusiasm for him to learn doesn't inadvertently tip over into pushiness. Try to avoid encouraging him to get something right when he is too tired or hungry to concentrate; your keenness may end in tears, not progress.

Toddlers at this age are enormous fun, have a great sense of humour, and will follow your lead very easily if you choose to be "silly". Laughter is a great catalyst for learning because it means your child is having fun. When children experience enjoyment they naturally make more use of their senses to "tune in" to the experience. Using humour is one way of tagging experiences and making them distinct, which can help with memory recall. Being able to tell the difference between how something is meant to be and the "silly" alternative shows your toddler's developing ability to reason and understand that there are different ways to view the world. However, children at this age can easily become over-excited and will need help to know when they are going too far. This direction may come from your tone of voice or facial expression, or by giving your toddler a break between a period of having a laugh, then calming down.

Guidance from you

You are a very important role model for your child's behaviour; at this age he will copy not only what you want him to do, but also many things that you would rather he didn't! One of the most effective methods of getting him "on the right track" is to show him what you want him to do.

How your toddler can learn from you:

■ Is he finding it hard to put on his socks or shoes? Show him how you put yours on.

■ Is he spilling lots of food when he eats? Show him how you guide a spoon to your mouth.

■ Is he having difficulty taking turns? Show him how it is done.

This period of learning is all about showing, not telling. Let your toddler watch, observe, and try for himself. With encouragement rather than criticism he will eventually get there. This is the ideal time to involve older children as toddlers may be very attached to older siblings and be very happy to copy their "big boy" or "big girl" behaviour.

Behaviour boundaries

Getting your child to behave in the way that you, and society, would like him to will take many months and years. At its extreme, teaching appropriate behaviour is known as discipline. It can be helpful to remember that "telling off" should not be so much about controlling

"You may be so afraid of your child's tantrums that you 'give in' for an easy life. The trouble is that short-term gain leads to longer-term pain as he'll learn to use a tantrum to get his own way."

your child as reinforcing the lessons that you have been teaching him about how to behave and manage his emotions. During the toddler years this takes a very simple form. Setting behaviour limits so that your toddler is clear about what he can and cannot do is the first stage in the process of teaching him relationship and social skills.

When you set a boundary, your toddler learns that there is a point beyond which he should not go. The more clear and consistent your boundaries are, the more quickly he will learn that "No means no". By having boundaries, he also learns about self-awareness and develops an understanding that he can choose how to behave and that different choices will have different outcomes.

The principles that underline behavioural techniques for toddlers are:

- Set clear boundaries.
- Reward good behaviour.
- Ignore bad behaviour or have a clear consequence.
- Be consistent in your approach.

In many ways it really is that simple – although in the heat of the moment it is not always an easy philosophy to stick to. If you do not set boundaries for your child's behaviour he will try to set his own – by pushing and pushing you until he finds your limit. This happens because he needs to know where he stands in order to feel safe. Behaviour boundaries and routine are the ideal partnership. Once your child is familiar with a routine, he will have some idea of what to expect (bath, pyjamas, bedtime story, sleep) and he will be able to remember more easily how he is meant to behave (no screaming, no kicking) and will remember that there is a treat (bedtime story) if he behaves. A behaviour boundary only works if you are willing to stand firm and see things through.

Guidelines for setting behaviour boundaries:

- Decide what behaviour you want to achieve ("I want Samuel to stop hitting his brother").
- Decide on the consequence ("If Samuel hits his brother, he will lose his favourite toy until he plays nicely").

SHOWING HIM *Your toddler needs lots of help developing his newfound skills. Show him what to do in play and everyday tasks and he will simply copy you and gradually learn to remember.*

Your toddler's view of the world

Here's an insight into what your toddler might be thinking...

▶ "I do like chatting, but I don't always get my words right."

▶ "I like to try to dress myself, but I can't do buttons."

▶ "I see my friends but I don't like them playing with my toys. Mummy calls it sharing – but that's not much fun because they all belong to me."

▶ "The worst thing is when I get upset. They call it a tantrum. Sometimes I do these on purpose, but usually I can't help it. I get all hot and bothered and everything seems to go wrong."

▶ "I really like being silly. Words are often silly. Mummy and Daddy sing songs and say rhymes and do actions that make me laugh."

▶ "Picture books are my favourite thing. There are so many things to look at. I like cuddling up for a story before I go to sleep."

■ Tell your child in simple terms what you do not want him to do and what you do want him to do instead ("No hitting. Hitting is bad. Don't hit your brother. Play nicely together").

■ Tell your child in simple terms what the consequence will be ("If you hit your brother, then I will put your fire engine on that shelf").

■ Follow through with your intention, this time and every time. Being consistent is the key to learning and success.

Praise and rewards

Rewarding "good" behaviour works wonders. The more you praise your toddler for the kinds of behaviour you want from him, the more of the "good" behaviour you will get. Positive attention or praise will reinforce the messages that are being sent to his brain and help him to condition his brain to behave appropriately in the future. This still has nothing to do with understanding whether his behaviour is morally right or wrong; it is simply to do with the messages that you and others are giving him about which behaviour delivers the greatest rewards.

Personal success is an important cornerstone for the development of self-esteem. Praising and giving your child lots of positive attention helps him to understand when he has done something well, which encourages him to do it again, which means he will get even better at what he is doing and learn to trust himself to succeed. Your praise and recognition increase his desire to persist and to see errors as part of the learning process; they are essential for effective learning. Open any parenting book, read any problem page, or watch any TV programme and you will find that most of the expert advice focuses on solving problem behaviour: its cause, its effect, and how to stop it. Rarely will you hear someone say, "I don't know how to praise my child." However, there are two sides to behaviour shaping: replacing unwanted behaviour with wanted behaviour also means replacing criticism and negativity with rewards and praise. Even praise can backfire if it is not delivered in a way that is reinforcing.

How to encourage more good-style behaviour:

■ Praise the behaviour, not your child, to separate the achievement from his judgement of himself as a person. ("That's a lovely drawing of a flower Max", rather than just "You're so clever, darling" on its own).

■ Explain clearly and simply, and anchor your comments in time (see page 196). "*If* you are a quiet boy when Mummy is on the phone, *then* afterwards we can play in the garden and you can go on the slide." Rather than, "If you're quiet, you can have a treat."

■ Give him lots of hugs and smiles. If he is going through an unaffectionate phase, stay warm and smiley, but don't force things.

■ Praise and rewards should be immediate. "Tomorrow" is too far away for a toddler to understand. Better a small reward now than having to wait.

Family traits

As your toddler's personality begins to emerge it is easy to look for character traits that seem familiar and to make comparisons with other members of the family, especially you, the parents. This is natural; after all, his genes play an important role in the development of who he is. However, be aware that your personal history may be affecting your interpretation. Be careful not to attribute fixed traits too young, especially if you are starting to notice elements that remind you of a challenging relationship.

Perhaps you didn't get on with your mother; if your toddler looks or acts like her, then it may inadvertently make your relationship more difficult. A single parent who had a difficult relationship with her baby's father may find herself saying "You're just like your father" in the midst of her toddler's spectacular tantrum. This can have a significant impact on both the mother's feelings about her child, and in due course the child's perception of both his father and his own inner nature. At this age, it is just as likely to be developmental and environmental factors affecting personality as any long-term behavioural tendencies.

FINDING THE RIGHT REWARD *For some children, praise and smiles work; for others, being trusted with something grown up, such as holding the dog's lead, is a great motivator for good behaviour.*

Praise and rewards should ideally motivate your toddler to make good behaviour choices for the future, rather than teaching him to behave well in order to receive a treat. If the treat becomes the main incentive for the behaviour, the danger is that he will lose his motivation when there is no reward. The rewards therefore need to be everyday activities that are connected to, and reinforce, the behaviour in some way. Using everyday activities as rewards alongside lots of praise not only reinforces your child's good behaviour choices, but also develops his self-esteem by making him feel loved and appreciated.

Appropriate rewards might be:

■ You tell your toddler that if he is able to stay still in the shopping trolley and manages to behave well, you will go to the park on the way home.

■ Your toddler has behaved well in the car en route to Granny's. As a treat he can help you make her birthday cake.

■ He has gone to bed without any fuss, and has managed to put on his pyjama bottoms (back to front!). You give him a big hug of appreciation and let him choose his favourite bedtime story.

Inappropriate rewards might be:

■ Giving him sweets in exchange for being quiet in the car. Sweet treats are never a good idea for health reasons and he may begin to expect sweets every time you travel in the car.

■ Buying him a DVD because he didn't have a tantrum when you were in the supermarket. Buying gifts leaves you open to bribery in the future – "I'll be quiet if I can have…"

■ Promising him he can eat while watching the television if he tries just a bit of new food. Once the control becomes negotiable, he will want to do it more and more.

Material rewards and inappropriate treats will send your toddler mixed messages. They will not help him to learn and there is a danger that you may undermine the routines you have put in place. Treats such as staying up later are more suitable for an older child who will have the ability to understand that it is a one-off event.

Successes such as learning to walk or talk don't need to be rewarded because they are natural developments that a child learns anyway. Rewarding this behaviour raises an expectation that he might receive something, which may reduce natural motivation when a reward is not forthcoming.

"Toddlers, like adults, need to develop confidence in their ability to think, act, and achieve things on their own."

How you respond

Many parenting problems stem from a belief that a toddler is being wilfully naughty, has an ulterior motive, or is scheming to get his own way. In reality, he does not yet have any moral reasoning skills and needs your help to understand the boundaries between "right and wrong". While it is true that he is very determined and focused, and may have a specific short-term goal in mind ("I want it, and I want it now!"), he does not have an overall game plan and does not want to trigger your disapproval.

It is all too tempting, when your child is playing up, to tackle the problem by confronting him head on: "Don't do that"/"Stop it immediately" /"That's enough" and by raising your voice. There are two problems with this approach. Firstly, you have given your toddler exactly what he wanted. "Mummy is paying attention! I'll do it again!" and secondly, if you tend to shout at your child, you are increasing the levels of stress hormones in his developing brain (see page 168). Over time, this may affect his ability to cope in stressful situations in later life.

Why telling toddlers off doesn't work

Although your toddler is now old enough to understand that his behaviour has had an effect ("Daddy is pleased with me"/"Daddy is cross with me"), he is still too young to understand the reasons why it has had an effect.

Ignoring negative behaviour

Twin toddlers Piers and Rupert are playing together. Piers hits Rupert, who bursts in tears, and Piers soon follows suit. Their mother leaps across the room and focuses first on Piers. "You're not to do that, you naughty boy." She then picks up Rupert, checks that he is okay, settles him on the sofa out of harm's way and then returns to Piers. Picking Piers up, she wipes his tears and tells him sternly that he is a naughty boy to pick on his brother.

▶ **Result** Time Mummy spends with Rupert: none; time Mummy spends with Piers: five minutes.

▶ **Message to Piers** Hitting Rupert means I get more attention and get to spend more time with Mummy.

If on the other hand their mother had removed Piers to the sofa, ignored him and given more attention to Rupert, the message to Piers would have been the opposite.

▶ **Result** Time Mummy spent with Piers: none; time mummy spent with Rupert: five minutes.

▶ **Message to Piers** Hitting means I am ignored and Rupert gets lots of hugs and attention.

"Danny has already learnt that if I say 'No' there is a good chance that Daddy will say 'Yes'. It drives me crazy."

Steph, aged 34

It will be another year or two before your toddler's moral reasoning skills have developed (see page 261), enabling you to explain the rights and wrongs of his behaviour.

Your child gives you his love unconditionally and he craves your attention. He would like to have lots of love and cuddles and praise, but if he can't get those he will settle for any attention going. He is a vulnerable being at this age and will continue to love you no matter how you treat him – for now. As a result, if a parent pays more attention to a child when he is being naughty than when he is being good, he will give his parent more of what they seem to want: more naughty behaviour; or if you give him attention when he is being funny, he will continue to play the clown. If, on the other hand, you praise your child more often than you tell him off, he will understand that you like that behaviour and he will repeat his "good" behaviour.

How to be consistent

Shaping your toddler's behaviour is a team effort, involving all those who have responsibility for his care. There is little point in one parent being clear, firm, and consistent if the other is lenient, or if the person responsible for day care is inadvertently undermining all the hard work you are doing. The answer is to talk to one another and to anyone else involved in your child's upbringing.

These guidelines should apply to anyone involved in caring for children:
- Be committed to your child, and consistent in your approach.
- Present a united front. Make sure other adults involved in your child's

Real life

I was getting on the bus with my boys – Jim, aged four, and Adam, aged two-and-a-half. Jim climbed on confidently, but Adam was anxious. He hung back, fearful and hesitant and pulled away from me. With one boy on the bus, the other on the pavement, and the bus driver becoming impatient, it was getting embarrassing and I was tempted to get cross with Adam. But instead, I crouched down, spoke to him gently and encouraged him –"Take a big step, darling, you can do it." He succeeded and I lavished him with praise – "My clever boy. You are getting so good at that now!" The situation was resolved calmly, without anyone getting upset.

upbringing are following the same ground rules as you.

■ Face up to your past. Understand how your own experiences may be affecting the way you react to your child's behaviour.

■ Be a good role model and believe in yourself.

■ Stick to the behaviour guidelines outlined in these chapters.

Difficult times

You may be a loving parent, but first and foremost you are human – which means that sometimes you will feel tired, angry, or vulnerable, and unable to cope with your

It may feel like an emotional battlefield at times, but if you try to stay calm and handle the situation carefully, your toddler's outbursts will be short-lived.

toddler's whining or tantrums. It is easy at such times to question your parenting ability and to wonder if you are doing something wrong. When this happens, try to see the situation in context. Remind yourself that all toddlers behave this way and that most behaviour is normal behaviour for the next few years.

Your toddler is experiencing feelings that are new and dramatic and that he does not know how to handle. With your help he will do better next time and today's problem will be smaller tomorrow if you manage it effectively. If you are concerned that you may lash out or do something that would upset or be harmful to your child, or you simply feel you can't cope, you must take measures to calm down or seek support (see pages 310–311).

If you are not coping:

■ Put some distance between yourself and the problem – either by imagining that distance, or if it is safe to do so, by removing yourself physically from the room.

■ Relax, by breathing deeply and slowly.

■ Remember, if you shout at your toddler you will be reinforcing the behaviour by rewarding it with undue attention.

■ Look for support: from your partner, from family or friends, or from a professional person or organization.

■ Remember that feeling overwhelmed sometimes is normal. It simply means you are like everyone else – and probably exhausted.

Managing behaviour

While a toddler's tears and tantrums are distressing, this type of behaviour is a crucial part of learning to grow up. If your child does not get angry and learn to manage his rage at an early stage, he will find it harder to express his true feelings and act appropriately as he gets older.

There is no doubt that between the ages of two and three toddlers can be very challenging. Their short attention span, combined with the demands of learning a new range of skills and emotions, means they can become overwhelmed very easily. Your toddler may fluctuate from being calm and giggly to hyperactive and angry in a matter of moments – and it may feel as if you do, too. The good news is that by the time your toddler is two years old he is ready to cope with and understand behaviour boundaries and with your help can begin to control his own impulses.

A child of this age learns a great deal through imitation, so he will be learning about behaviour from everyone around him, but most of all he will be learning from you. It is a good time to start modelling the kinds of behaviour you would like to see in your toddler.

Your approach to managing your toddler's behaviour is influenced by your own experiences of discipline and punishment – or the lack of it (see page 26). Some parents may find the idea of a routine stressful because they don't like to conform; others may be tempted to establish a routine that is so rigid there is no room for flexibility. However, behaviour boundaries are about much more than instilling an element of parental control. They are an important stage in your child's understanding of "right and wrong". You are helping him to begin to learn to respond appropriately in social and other situations. Behaviour-shaping is less about restraining your

LEARNING FROM OTHERS
Your toddler discovers new things by copying, so any older siblings will invariably become role models – in both their good and their not so good behaviour.

toddler's behaviour and more about enabling him to learn skills that will help him to make friends, be accepted socially, and eventually help him to integrate in the world at large.

Managing behaviour isn't about encouraging your child to conform unquestioningly, or about being a perfectly behaved "good" boy; it is about developing self-expression and control and understanding what behaviour is appropriate in different circumstances – and the consequences of that behaviour. It is also the way that children first begin to understand the concepts of "sorry" and "forgiveness" (see page 200).

The A, B, C of behaviour

What causes us to behave the way we do? There are many theories, but it is commonly accepted that everything we think and do is learned behaviour, conditioned by the experiences, people, and events in our lives. The way we act, what we say, and even our psychological and biological processes, have all been learned over time. A lot of learned behaviour has its roots in our toddler years, which is when the brain first begins to build up its network of learned responses and develops beliefs that guide future behaviour.

Behaviour does not just happen. It always has a cause and it always triggers an effect. This is very useful for parents to remember because it is often much easier to avoid the cause of your toddler's unwanted behaviour in the first place than it is to change the outcome (such as a tantrum). Psychologists call this the A, B, C approach.

The next time your toddler has a tantrum, ask yourself:
- What triggered the tantrum? **A** cause or past history.
- How did your toddler react? **B**ehaviour.
- What happened as a result? **C**onsequence, response, or outcome.

"C" is your own response to the behaviour, as well as what happened to your child as a result of his behaviour.

Here is an example of an ABC of behaviour for a two-and-a-half-year-old:
- **A** cause: Mum (Lucy) asks Grace which dress she would like to wear.
- **B**ehaviour: Grace keeps saying "No" to every option.
- **C**onsequence: Lucy loses patience and makes Grace's choice for her. Grace refuses to get dressed and has a full-scale tantrum.

It would be easy for Lucy to focus on the outcome (Grace's refusal and her tantrum) and to think she needs to work on altering that, but by using

"Lewis is quite jealous of his baby sister. He often plays up when I pick her up, so we try to involve him, too."

Suzanne, aged 30

the ABC approach, she can look at what happened immediately before the tantrum. The real cause was giving Grace too much choice, which triggered frustration and Grace's difficulty in managing her feelings; and it was also compounded by Lucy's impatient response. Next time, Lucy will give Grace just two dresses to choose from – "Would you like to wear the pink one or the blue one?" – which is more appropriate for her daughter's level of development. She will allow more time to do things at toddler speed, too. The result is likely to be a quick and easy decision followed by plenty of hugs and smiles.

Avoiding trouble does not mean you are pandering to your toddler. Children in this age group still need adult help to manage their behaviour. The fewer opportunities your toddler has to become unnecessarily distressed, the quicker he will learn positive behaviour patterns and the less likelihood there will be for his unwanted behaviour to become an automatic response. If a pattern of behaviour is repeated often enough, then the behaviour becomes a conditioned response (see right), which can be harder to change.

Understanding his behaviour

Many of our reactions to people and events are affected by the way we have been conditioned to respond through repeated experience; either through what we have been told or because of events deeply buried in our memories. What triggers our feelings or responses (the cause) and

Recognizing patterns of behaviour

Toddlers become conditioned to respond in certain ways to particular situations, as this example shows:

Lara knows Daddy well. She has learned to recognize his mood by how he acts when he comes home from work. If he throws his keys on to the table, sighs deeply, and slumps into a chair, she knows that he is in a bad mood, which means he will have no patience with her. Over time, her response to this sequence becomes conditioned, so that thrown keys (Daddy is cross) becomes a trigger for her to stay out of the way (I feel rejected). But if he is humming a tune as he walks through the door, and hangs his keys on the hook, she knows he is in a good mood and is likely to give her a hug. In time, the conditioned response becomes Dad humming his favourite tune (Daddy is happy), which triggers an impulse to run up and hug him (I feel loved).

links them with the outcome (the effect) may not always be obvious – but your brain has nevertheless learned to make the association. There are two types of conditioned behaviour. Psychologists classify these as classical conditioning (learning by association) and operant conditioning (learning by effect).

Classical conditioning The most well-known example involves a scientist called Ivan Pavlov and some dogs. He knew that the sight and smell of food would make dogs drool, but he wanted to see whether he could introduce a new stimulus to trigger the drooling, without food being present. He began to ring a bell each time he brought food to the dogs. Eventually the dogs learned to associate food with the ringing of the bell on its own, and would drool whenever he rang it. They had learned by association.

Learning by association:

■ Original association – Jonny's mother always buys him a lollipop as a treat when he goes swimming.

■ Changed association – whenever he is given a lollipop Jonny asks to go swimming. The cause, or trigger, for going swimming has changed from being Jonny's mother, to the lollipop that she always gives to him. The lollipop has become linked strongly in Jonny's past experience to going swimming, and so now, whenever he is given a lollipop, the lollipop itself becomes the trigger (**A** cause) that makes him ask for swimming. It has become an automatic response (**B**ehaviour).

Operant conditioning A psychologist, B.F. Skinner, devised an experiment to show that if the consequences of a behaviour are positive we are more likely to repeat that behaviour. He gave pigeons a choice of red and green levers to peck to get food. Over time the pigeons learnt which colour would deliver food and which would not. They had learned by effect.

Learning by effect:

■ Original effect – Jonny bites another child and becomes upset. His mother gives him a hug. Jonny gets a positive message and does it again.

CAUSES AND TRIGGERS

There will be a reason why she has behaved in a certain way. Look back to find the trigger and you may be able to prevent the behaviour being repeated.

■ Changed effect – his mother removes him from the room. Jonny gets a negative message and doesn't do it again. The alteration in Jonny's mother's response (**C**onsequence) has altered Jonny's experience of what happens when he bites someone and therefore changed the probability of him doing it again (**B**ehaviour).

A toddler can become conditioned to react automatically when a familiar trigger stimulates an automatic response (see box, page 194). Understanding what triggers your child to laugh or cry may not be immediately obvious. Learning to decode this can take patience and increased awareness of his personal triggers and learned behaviour.

Consequences

Helping your toddler to manage his angry mood, or to stop unwanted behaviour, is challenging and time-consuming, and time is often in short supply. If behaviour-shaping is to work, your toddler will need to understand that there will be a negative consequence if he does not do as he has been asked – or a positive consequence if he does.

An important aspect of seeing problems off before they begin is to ensure that your toddler has a clear idea of your expectations. A young brain needs clear and simple instructions. Try using *if* and *then*, or *when* and *then*, so he understands the cause and effect of his behaviour.

Examples of if, then; when, then:

■ "*If* you keep screaming, *then* you can't go to the park."

■ "*When* you are nice to your sister, *then* you can play catch with her."

Your toddler will need the consequences to be very simple and immediate, as he will not be able to relate to "later". A negative consequence normally involves something being taken away, such as not being able to take teddy shopping, or not coming with Mummy. A positive consequence is usually more effective and will involve something being given, such as playing with Daddy, or having a favourite story at bedtime, if he does as you ask. The treats should be simple, everyday "favourite things", rather than sweets or gifts.

When stating a consequence, you must be consistent, and you must follow through with what you have said – otherwise it becomes meaningless. Your response needs to show your child that you are serious about the boundary you have set, and if he crosses that boundary, that his behaviour

HELP HIM LEARN
He is beginning to understand the consequences of his behaviour, but it is important to keep explanations very simple at this age.

"A behaviour pattern that has been learned and repeated over time is known as conditioning – if the pattern continues, the same result will always occur. 'If you keep doing what you're doing, you'll get the same result'."

is unacceptable. If a tantrum or aggression results, ignore it – and remember he will grow out of this phase before long. Whatever his action and response, still treat him with respect.

The art of ignoring

To be disregarded and overlooked is the ultimate negative consequence for your young child. Your toddler is used to thinking of himself as being the centre point of the family. To suddenly discover that no-one is interested in him is a powerful behaviour deterrent for the future. This style of ignoring is not about withdrawing affection and is not meant as a malicious or vindictive act. It is an immediate and effective tool to stop unwanted behaviour. It works because it isolates your toddler and gives him an opportunity to calm down.

Remember that ignoring your child is not ignoring if you remain focused on and looking at him. For it to work, you need to remove eye contact and stop talking to him, to show apparent disregard (while always ensuring he remains safe). If he is sitting on your knee just reduce your attention for a time (see page 200). This approach can sometimes work after a few seconds and at other times may take up to two or three minutes (although don't continue for any longer at this age). Once he has become calm you can re-engage with him.

If, for example, you are in a crowded supermarket and your toddler starts to grab things from the shelf, disregarding your instruction to stop and being defiant, you have two choices: either to ignore him and continue to shop, or to ignore him and leave the supermarket immediately. Leaving the shop is not a good option as it will give your child too much power – he will think that when he is bored he just has to "play up" and Mummy will take him home. Do not look at him or talk to him. Once he has calmed down, give him a hug. You could then suggest playing the "find

AGGRESSIVE BEHAVIOUR *A firm "No" and removing positive reinforcement, such as fun toys for a limited time, sends a message that aggressive behaviour is not acceptable.*

the colour" game, where you find coloured packets on the shelves, or other supermarket games (see page 175). Your toddler will learn from this that calm behaviour is rewarded with cuddles and a game, and that being defiant and ignoring your instructions won't reap rewards.

To give another example, perhaps your friend has come round who you have not seen for a long time. Your toddler has plenty to keep him occupied, but he keeps screaming because he wants your undivided attention. You both physically turn away from your toddler and ignore his behaviour completely. Once he has calmed down, turn to him and say, "Come and have a cuddle." Introduce your friend and show him that his "good" behaviour gets attention and praise.

Ignoring can also work well if combined with distraction techniques (see page 85). Distraction works well as a way of changing your toddler's mood in an instant. This is less likely to work, however, if a full-scale tantrum is in place. "Time out" (see page 270) and variations of this, such as "the naughty step", are other forms of ignoring that can be used briefly to calm your child if he is aggressive or out of control.

"Even though we are separating we have promised each other to try to be consistent in the way we parent Bella. A united front is crucial if we are to help her learn how to behave appropriately and not confuse her." Ben, aged 35

Selective behaviour

You might discover that your toddler only behaves in a certain way when he is with you, and that he does not play up for other people. There could be several reasons for this, but often it is because you are the only one that responds to his behaviour. It has worked. He has got the attention he wanted (for example, you have given him treats). You can take strength from the fact that children grow out of this phase. Your toddler will gradually learn how to manage his feelings appropriately and find better ways to get what he wants. In the meantime, however, remember not to reinforce his behaviour by reasoning with him. Withdrawing attention is still more effective than talking and negotiating at this age.

Letting go and moving on

It is always a relief to be able to make up after a disagreement, and nevermore so than when your child is calm and ready to apologize. The time to ask him for an apology is after the consequence of his behaviour has run its course. The tears are over, he is calm, he has had time to reflect, and everyone wants to be friends again. It is a hard lesson for a toddler to learn, but it is important that he understands that he has to learn to say "sorry" as part of the process of taking responsibility for his behaviour.

At 2–3 years, it is unlikely that a toddler will truly "feel" sorry – he has not yet developed sufficient empathy and understanding of others to feel the effects of his behaviour on someone else. However, it is an important response to begin to teach. When your child has done something to physically or emotionally hurt someone else and you prompt him to say sorry, you are teaching him an important social skill. Over the next 18 months he will start to feel increasing levels of empathy and will begin to really mean it when he says it. An apology is a vital part of behaviour-shaping because it will help him to understand that we must take

Managing extreme behaviour

Some toddlers take their behaviour to extremes. Occasionally this is about attention-seeking and finding their parent's weak spot, but more usually it is triggered by overwhelming feelings that they cannot control.

Actions such as banging his head as a tantrum reaches its peak; holding his breath; shrieking in a hysterical high-pitched way are all alarming, upsetting, and very hard to manage. No parent can ignore a child who is distressed or hurting himself, so what is the best course of action and coping?

Firm holding is a useful technique:
▶ Minimize the amount of attention you are paying to your child and his actions. It is possible to hold your child firmly, to keep him safe, without giving him positive attention.
▶ Hold him firmly, facing outwards, against your body. His head should be against your chest so that he doesn't smack it into your face. (Say no more than "No, calm down," occasionally and very softly).

▶ If your child is holding his breath, he will eventually gasp for air and cannot harm himself, but you can also try splashing a little water on or blowing gently into his face
▶ Do not rise to the bait and panic, and do not give in to the temptation to talk to him or pay attention to what he is doing or saying. If you give in once, then next time it will be twice as difficult to handle.
▶ Wait until he is calm to give him positive attention. See page 302 for more information on head-banging.

responsibility for the impact of our behaviour on others. Your toddler does something wrong, you put him right, he apologizes – everyone moves on. He needs to feel safe in the understanding that no matter what he does, you will still love him. Making up and moving on is vital in showing him that his behaviour was unwanted, but he is still loved and wanted as a person. Your challenge is then to "let go" of the event and to try not to use it to label his behaviour, or to bring it up again when he misbehaves at a later date. Do be aware, though, that your toddler saying "sorry" shouldn't stop you following through with a consequence for bad behaviour.

Putting space between thought and deed

As a parent, it is normal to frequently overestimate your child's ability to understand the reasons why you are unhappy with his behaviour. Even now his brain has developed further, he will learn more by what you show him than what you tell him. Putting space between his thoughts and his deeds is the most effective way to stop the unwanted behaviour.

Distraction, ignoring, holding, and "time out" are all ways to help him learn to calm himself and choose to act differently. In the next chapter there is a description of how to use "time out" (see page 270), a more extreme form of ignoring. It is more suitable for slightly older children and is used as a technique to help children to cool down and reflect on their actions. It should ideally be used only after all other methods have failed. If your child is completely out of control, has been aggressive – especially towards another child – or is being extremely anti-social in some way and needs to learn to modify his behaviour, then "time out" can be used in the 24–36 month age group as well, but for no longer than two minutes. A more appropriate technique is firm holding (see box, left).

Seeking help

Poor toddler behaviour can instil intense feelings of guilt or hopelessness in many parents. If you are having ongoing problems with managing your child, do not suffer in isolation. Ask your health visitor for help, join a parenting class or workshop, ask other mothers for advice, or go to your GP. Some of what you are experiencing will be normal toddler behaviour, which will pass in time; it can be helpful to speak to other parents to keep things in perspective and normalize your child's behaviour.

TIME TO REFLECT
Sending your toddler to a safe place to calm down following unwanted behaviour is a good technique, which can be used more as he gets older.

Overcoming sleep problems

Your toddler is on the go from morning till night, and requires your help to understand when he is tired and needs to get some rest. Life is far too interesting for him to want to go to bed of his own accord, but he needs his sleep and will benefit from having a routine.

With your guidance, your toddler needs to learn how to go to sleep, stay asleep, and how to settle himself if he does wake up. Common sleep problems at this age are: taking a long time to settle, waking frequently throughout the night, and needing comfort to go back to sleep.
This year is an ideal time to introduce a more regular sleep routine if you haven't already done so (see page 136). Many parents find bedtimes are a challenge. Rather than going to bed and staying in bed their child or children are up and down like yo-yos, refusing to settle and waking frequently through the night. If this kind of pattern is combined with biting, hitting, or tantrums the whole family can end up feeling unhappy and exhausted. The following series of time-honoured and successful techniques can, if you are persistent and consistent in approach, transform your toddler's sleep habits.

Gradual withdrawal technique

A young child who is used to you being close by at bedtime, or finds it difficult to fall asleep on his own, may be anxious initially when you try to leave and will need your help to become more independent. This technique, if followed consistently, will help your toddler to feel safe and secure while he adjusts to the new routine.

How to use the gradual withdrawal technique:
■ Every night after saying goodnight, turn out the light, but stay close by.
■ There is no need to say anything, but simply be there.
■ Do not be tempted to turn on the light or to respond to his chatter.

HELPING HER SETTLE
Calm things down and minimize your toddler's excitement before bedtime by enjoying quiet reading together.

■ Do not give in to pleas for cuddles. Turn away and be boring and quiet.

■ As the days pass, gradually move further away – to the foot of the bed, to a chair, closer to the door, to the door, to just outside the door, and finally away altogether.

■ If your toddler is settling but still anxious, you could pop back to check him every few minutes, but do not say anything. The purpose of this is only to reassure your child that you are still there and that he is safe.

■ Gradually increase the length of time in between your checks, and eventually stop checking altogether.

Children who are unused to being on their own will take some time to unlearn their old behaviour and relearn the new one. Your toddler may seem quite frightened or unsettled during the first few days. Be patient. He will adjust, and so will you, given time. Learning to fall asleep without your help is an important skill for an increasingly independent child. The aim is to eventually be able to leave the room while he is still awake.

Rapid return technique

The gradual withdrawal approach does not work in all instances and if you find your toddler is resisting your new routine, you may need to try a different approach. Rapid return is a simple sleep management technique with an immediate "no-nonsense" message. It is particularly useful for managing children who wake in the night and come and join you in your bed rather than resettle in their own. It works because it does not reward your toddler's sleep-resistant behaviour, and in time he will become bored, and sleepy, and will stop trying to resist your new boundary. But be warned, this technique can be tough to put into practice. You will need to be determined and consistent for it to work – and you may well need some help to put it into action. If the rapid return technique is to work, it is vital not to chat, make eye contact, or pay attention to your child, so that you are neither acknowledging or rewarding his behaviour.

How to use the rapid return technique:

■ Settle your child, turn out the light, say goodnight, and leave the room.

■ If he gets out of bed, take him back straight away without getting cross and without speaking.

■ Even if your child is kicking and screaming, remain calm but firm and put him into his bed. Then leave the room.

"I am so tired of the battles that I find it hard to be consistent with my daughter's night-time routine."

Ashley, aged 28

■ If he gets up again, pick him up and put him back into bed, with no fuss. Keep repeating this process as necessary until your child falls asleep. You must not make eye contact or give your child attention.

■ If your child stays in bed, but is crying and finding it hard to settle, do not go back to him straight away, but leave him for a short period of up to 1–5 minutes. He needs time to gradually learn to settle himself to sleep, as well as back to sleep when he wakes up.

■ Then, go in briefly, say "Shh, shh," and leave. Keep repeating this process until your child falls asleep. In some situations, where the sleeping problem has been going on for a long time, you may need to keep this pattern up for a couple of weeks. It can be exhausting to begin with, so try beginning the new routine at a weekend, when you need not worry about being fresh for work, and can arrange some other adult support.

"Rapid return works especially well where sleep problems are long-standing, or if your toddler tends to show very angry behaviour at bedtime."

Praise and incentives

In the early stages of using the rapid return method it may be helpful to use basic rewards or incentives to encourage your toddler to settle more quickly. These should be simple and appropriate. The idea is not to make bargaining a habit, but to distract your toddler away from his old sleep behaviour pattern and help him to start to learn a new one. Remember that the point is not just to get him to go to bed, but also to encourage him to stay in bed until morning. Praise works wonders with small children. They love to know that they have pleased you and that they have done something well. If your child manages to sleep through the night, or has stayed in his own bed, don't hold back on the hugs and the praise. Keep setting new goals. It will help him to get a sense of his own success and progress and will help him to understand that he has control over his own behaviour. As your child gets older he will also be able to understand that there will be consequences, and the withdrawal of treats, if he does not do as he is asked. Don't expect instant success, and you may have to be satisfied with small results to begin with – but be patient, and believe in your ability to make the change happen. Stick to your routine when you are away from home, too, if possible.

How to use praise and incentives:

■ Tell your toddler he can choose which story to read if he behaves. The longer he takes to get to bed, the less time there will be for a story.

■ If your child has a favourite book character or teddy, involve it in your bedtime routine – "Put teddy to bed now. Shh. If you're noisy you will wake him, and he's had a very long day. You go to sleep now, too."

■ Most children love stickers, and they enjoy seeing how well they are doing. A simple promise of a favourite sticker from the night-time fairy if he can stay in bed until morning, can work wonders.

■ The promise of one balloon to be fixed to the foot of the bed for each night he manages not to get out of bed also works well.

PEACEFUL SLEEP *Tackling sleep problems requires your patience and perseverance, but remember it is in your child's best interests to settle and feel secure in her bed at night.*

Night terrors

Night terrors are common at this age. They differ from nightmares (see page 264) in that your child does not wake up and will have no memory of his dream. They usually occur within the first 1–4 hours of a child falling to sleep. They can be very alarming for a parent to watch, but are nothing to worry about. Your child is unlikely to wake up and will have no memory of his experience in the morning. Typical symptoms include: rapid heartbeat, sweating, signs of fear, may not recognize you if woken, may scream, cry, or moan. His eyes may be open, but he will be sound asleep.

A night terror can last as long as 30 minutes. Although frightening for you to watch, there is no need to wake your child during one. There is nothing you can do, apart from keeping him safe if he is thrashing about. However, if you see a fixed time pattern to the terrors, you can wake your child just before that time each night. Night terrors are more distressing for a parent to witness than they are for the child experiencing one. Children usually grow out of night terrors as they become older.

Encouraging healthy eating

What toddlers should eat, how much they should eat, and how to get them to try new foods are perennial dilemmas for all parents. The good news is that most fussy toddlers are normal toddlers – and they grow up to become healthy adults who eat a wide range of foods.

Guidelines for healthy eating can seem full of contradictions, and concerns about allergies, food additives, and organics put additional pressure on parents who are anxious about whether their children are eating well or enough. Combine this with the average toddler's tendency to be restless, fussy and, occasionally, explosive at mealtimes and the mix can become a potent cocktail of tension and trouble.

Eating is about more than health; it is a social skill, too. Sharing food and eating together have an important role to play in the way we communicate with one another; family mealtimes are a great opportunity to get everyone to sit together and share their day. By the time your toddler is 24–30 months, he will be able to manage three meals a day,

A balanced diet

You don't have to spend a fortune on food to raise a healthy child, but avoiding junk foods is advisable. Steer clear of foods containing unsaturated fats and refined sugar (which has no nutritional value and may contribute to disruptive behaviour), and limit salt intake.

Include foods from these food groups daily for a nutritious diet:
▶ Milk and dairy foods.
▶ Meat, fish, eggs, beans, peas, and lentils.
▶ Bread, rice, pasta, cereals, and starchy vegetables.
▶ Plenty of fruit and vegetables.

Toddlers have very small stomachs and small appetites, too. It is therefore very important that what they eat is as nutritious as possible.

Don't consider giving your toddler semi-skimmed milk until he is two years old. Fully skimmed milk is not suitable.

and will have the ability to self-feed using his fingers or a spoon. He can sit unsupported at the table with everyone else, although he may need a booster seat to help him reach. This may disrupt grown-up plans for a peaceful meal, but the involvement will speed your child's development much faster than one-to one spoon-feeding or watching over him. He is more likely to act "grown-up" if he doesn't feel different from everyone else. There are general tips in the previous chapter (see page 132) to help you to enjoy mealtimes with your toddler, but if there appear to be problems developing there are other strategies listed below.

Your toddler is a fussy eater A great many children develop fussy eating habits at some point, and it may feel as if your toddler is letting you know that "Any food is acceptable except the food that is on the menu today!" Try the guidelines for introducing variety, below. If that doesn't work, your toddler may have fears linked to food, mess, or texture (see page 210).

Your toddler misbehaves at mealtimes It can be hard for a toddler to sit still for extended periods of time, and if there is any family tension at the table you can be certain it will affect his behaviour. Minimize distractions, ignore the unwanted behaviour, and follow behaviour guidelines. Encourage him to model his behaviour on yours, or an older sibling if he has one. Check that he is sitting comfortably. If he still uses a highchair, consider whether now would be a good time to introduce a normal chair. Likewise, if he is still using a bottle, its purpose will now be comfort rather than practical necessity.

You are worried that he eats too much or not enough Most toddlers will eat when they are hungry, so it is unlikely that he will go without what he needs. However, he will need your help to regulate his eating and to eat in a healthy and balanced way. Regular mealtimes and clear behaviour boundaries will help him to get into the routine of eating. Small healthy snacks a couple of times a day, rather than "grazing on demand", will prevent him from filling up between meals. Make sure that he is always given plenty of fruit and vegetables and hold back on sugary snacks that may encourage unhealthy cravings.

You are worried that he is too chubby or too thin All toddlers are plump. However, a toddler who does not exercise, or who is lethargic and sits around a lot, may be putting on weight and storing up health problems for the future. Consult your GP for advice and healthy weight guidelines.

LEARNING ABOUT FOOD
Involve your toddler in the kitchen. An early interest in cooking may give her a more positive relationship with food and make her more willing to try new things.

FUN WITH FOOD *Being creative with a new food, such as making it into an interesting shape, will get your child's attention and increase the chances of her trying it.*

If your toddler is thin, but you are slim too, there is probably little to worry about as long as he is eating a balanced diet (see page 206). However, any sign of dramatic weight loss or gain, or change in appetite, should be investigated by your GP. Important note: do not be tempted to put your toddler on a low-fat diet. He needs his full-fat foods for healthy bone growth and development.

Your toddler eats too slowly There is no shortcut to overcoming this. All you can do is be patient and remember that it is better to eat slowly than too fast. Keep mealtimes fun. Don't force him to eat more than he can manage. Remember that his stomach is very small. If he has stopped eating, take the rest away; it means he has had enough.

Your toddler won't try new foods Children need time to get used to new foods before tasting them. Encourage your toddler to help you to prepare ingredients; describe them and let him play with them. Don't worry about mess as undue worry about being clean and tidy may inhibit him from trying certain textures, such as chunky or wet foods. Don't be surprised if he licks unfamiliar foods and then puts them back on his plate. He is not being naughty; this is his way of experimenting with the flavour and texture. Be patient and he may well choose to take a bite next time.

Keep the focus on food and fun

If food looks fun a child will decide that it must taste good, too. Use your imagination when serving your toddler's food.

Try the following:

- Cut sandwiches into interesting shapes.
- Make a mashed potato face using other vegetables.
- Use toddler-friendly china that reveals a character once the food is eaten.
- Make a plate of sliced fruit or vegetables into a face or other picture.

Having meals in front of the TV may seem like a fun idea, but even if that is the choice you make for yourself, try to make your toddler's mealtime a more interactive and personal experience. The idea is to get him used to self-feeding and consciously enjoying food, without distraction. His brain is not able to concentrate on more than one thing at a time (see page 166), and so watching TV whilst eating is not a good idea for him at this age. He will take much longer to learn if there are non-food-related events going on at the same time. Mealtime and playtime tend not to go together for the same reason. At this age, your toddler may need to be artfully distracted to encourage him to eat or to try new things (see page 134), but toys at the table are not good practice as they will always be more tempting to your toddler than the meal on his plate, leaving you no further forward.

Eating out

Having a meal away from home may not be the treat for a small child that it is for an adult. If you are going on a car journey, consider taking familiar and child-friendly foods with you. If a stop-off is easier, do not plan a long meal. It will be very tiring for your toddler.

Introducing new foods

Try alternating a small quantity of a new food that he is resisting with a "treat" of something that he loves, such as sliced banana or soft cheese – or even chocolate buttons! The idea is that you are creating a positive association (see page 195) between the new and unfamiliar foods: "I like that food, therefore I may like this new one." If his food range is extremely limited (for example, to bread, baked beans, and chocolate buttons), do not worry about introducing bizarre food combinations. Giving your toddler a chocolate button immediately after he has tried a piece of carrot or chicken may seem weird to you, but it will be a treat for him – and will send a message of familiarity and comfort to your fearful child. Once he is happy with the new foods, gradually phase out the treats.

How to keep a food diary

If you are concerned about your toddler's diet, then keeping track of what he eats, and when, will help you to spot if he is getting a balanced diet (see page 206) and whether he has been snacking between meals or filling up on liquids. The list does not have to be scientifically precise to give you a clear picture of your child's eating habits. If necessary, cut down on and substitute heavy or sugary foods for healthy portions of fruit and raw vegetables. Don't forget that liquids are filling, too.

Simply create a new page for each day of the week and keep a list of:
▶ The time of day.
▶ The type of food or liquid.
▶ The amount of food or liquid.
▶ Where he ate it.
▶ Whether he finished it.

Food games

If your child has fears associated with trying foods, show him that food can be fun. Children who have no issues with food will find these activities fun, too, so there is no need to draw attention to one particular child.

Have a messy food picnic Jelly, cream, ketchup, rice pudding – you name it; provided it is not hot, it can be smeared on your toddler's nose or face, or he can smear it with the hands, like finger paints. The more odd the food combinations, the better. If your toddler seems nervous or distressed, calm him, smile and show him that you are comfortable with the mess. With your encouragement, he may then follow your lead.

Have a new food race Set up two sets of very small quantities of new foods in a row on a table. Keep each food covered. On the shout of "Go" your toddler and another child or an adult tastes each food in turn. Reward your toddler with a very small quantity of something that he likes each time he tries the new food. (These tactics are an effective short-term tool in this extreme situation, in order to build up positive food associations.) When he reaches the end of the course, provided he has licked, touched, or tried each of the foods he can have a suitable "prize".

Being positive

The more positive and encouraging you can be about food, the more relaxed your toddler is likely to be about eating. Involve him in food preparation from an early age so that he accepts it as a normal part of

Does your child have a food phobia?

Toddlers are commonly neophobic, which means that they are instinctively nervous or scared of anything that is unfamiliar. In the case of eating, each new food, flavour, and texture is a new and sometimes daunting experience for a phobic toddler.

▶ Is your child uncomfortable with any kind of mess?
▶ Does he hate to touch anything wet or slimy?
▶ Will he eat only foods that are dry and crispy?
▶ Do you take pride in having a very clean and tidy house?

▶ Have you any history of personal issues around food?

If the answer to several of these questions is yes, then your toddler may have developed a food phobia. He will need help to overcome his fears and to understand that food and eating can be fun.

everyday life. If you know you have had problems related to food – such as a history of extreme dieting or an eating disorder, get help from your GP or a nutritionist so that you can be sure that both you and your child are eating well. This will also help to reduce the level of anxiety that exists around food in your home.

Top tips for easy mealtimes:

- Encourage self-feeding.
- Create a balanced diet (see page 206).
- Introduce healthy eating habits.
- Introduce variety slowly.
- Be patient and relaxed about food.
- Praise your toddler when he does well.
- Keep eating and mealtimes sociable and fun.

Overcoming problems

If you have real anxieties about your child and his eating habits, make a note of your concerns over a period of a few weeks and keep a food diary (see page 209) – noting all you can about the amount and times that your toddler eats, and the types of food and drink he likes and dislikes. It will help your GP or health visitor ascertain whether the problem relates to the food, an allergy, the eating routine, or a more deep-seated family problem. If your child has an extreme food phobia (see box, left), see your GP and ask for specialist help. You may need support to overcome it.

Finally – don't forget to praise the "good" and ignore the "bad" at mealtimes. The more you can encourage your toddler to have good feelings about food, or simply to accept it as a straightforward part of the day, the healthier he will be.

PICNIC TIME *A lot of mealtime problems stem from things being rushed and stressful. A picnic is a great way to enjoy food with your toddler in a relaxed environment.*

"Don't forget to take care of your toddler's teeth. By the time he is 36 months old, he will have all his baby teeth and they will need looking after. Help him to brush thoroughly at least twice a day."

Communicating with your toddler

Your toddler needs to learn to communicate so that he can relate to other people and develop the social and inter-personal skills that are so important for building friendships and being understood. He relies on non-verbal, verbal, and listening skills and in many ways operates at an intuitive level.

"Karl is a real chatter-box. His conversations are a lovely mix of fantasy and reality."

Angela, aged 25

Much of what is now referred to as emotional intelligence has its roots in our childhood experience of learning language and communication skills. What we say to our children is important, but so is our choice of language, tone of voice, how we ask questions, how we listen to their replies, what we hear, how we respond, whether we empathize, and how our body language echoes or contradicts what we are saying.

The art of toddler conversation

Now that your toddler's memory is so much more developed and he is able to use his imagination to cope with the idea that one thing (such as a doll) can represent another (such as a baby), his language skills will quickly develop and he will be ready to start having conversations.

When we talk, we use words to represent the things we want to talk about, so the word "apple" represents the fruit, even if there is no apple in sight. Your toddler is beginning to understand this and is developing the ability to link the right word to the right object simultaneously. He can remember and talk about things that he can't see, and his newfound ability to take turns in conversation means that he is getting more used to being able to listen to what you say and then respond to you.

At the age of two, however, your toddler is still unable to hold lots of information in his mind at one time, so his conversations may not follow a logical sequence, and he will probably answer no more than one in three questions, as the following sequence between Aaron, aged two-and-a-half, and his Daddy, shows:

Daddy "What would you like to do today, Aaron? Would you like to go to the park? Or would you like to play a game?"

Aaron "I play with Daddy."

Daddy "That's a nice idea. What game would you like to play, Aaron?"

Aaron "Mummy goed in car." Aaron has split his focus of attention.

Daddy "Yes, she has gone shopping in the car."

Your toddler will also begin to realize when he has not understood something, and will start to ask for clarification.

Daddy "Aaron, would you like to come to watch me play football?"

Aaron nods and says "Aaron come play."

Daddy "No, Daddy will play football. Aaron will watch Daddy play."

Aaron looks puzzled and says "Huh?"

You can help your child to understand how to make things clearer by asking him to repeat what he has said.

Daddy "So, Aaron, would you like to come with me?"

Aaron "Yes."

Daddy "And what are we going to do?"

Aaron, smiling, says "Me watch Daddy play foo'ball."

Daddy "That's right, Aaron. You can come and watch."

Aaron pauses, and then grins and repeats "Me watch Daddy play foo'ball … and me have ice cream."

Daddy, laughing, says "We'll see about the ice cream later!"

Aaron "Huh?" He is seeking clarification.

By the time Aaron is three years old, the same conversation will become strikingly different. Instead of saying "me watch" and "Mummy goed" he will probably be able to use "I" correctly and will have a better understanding of how to use words in the past tense. He is very likely to be able to say: "Mummy went shopping, Daddy. In the car," and "I come and watch you play football." Toddlers can never have too much conversation time with Mummy, Daddy, or anyone interested enough to

BEING INQUISITIVE

He will begin to converse with you by making comments and asking questions. Take time to talk to him and give him the opportunity to respond.

chat to them. It is valuable to make special time to talk to your toddler and have a proper conversation, rather than chatting absentmindedly while doing other things. First thing in the morning, after coming home from work, while eating a meal, or at bedtime: all these are ideal private times for uninterrupted talk.

Learning about feelings

Communication is about body language, too. Every hug, kiss, glance, smile, frown, or laugh sends a clear message to your toddler and tells him how you feel about him, what sort of mood you are in, and what kind of response you are expecting. He probably knows your body language better than you do, but make sure that your non-verbal signals match your words. Having your hands on your hips while saying "well done", or saying "good boy" with a frown on your face, is likely to confuse your child and send him a mixed message.

"Be aware of the power of your body language. When you praise your toddler verbally you need to look and act like you are interested, too!"

Are you in tune with what he is saying to you? Watch his facial expressions and physical stance when he is talking to you. Does his voice match his body language? If his eyes and stance say one thing and his words say another, gently encourage and help him to try to tell you how he feels. Toddlers know the power of eye contact and are able to win over a total stranger at 10 metres in a shop queue, simply by staring and smiling. However, his language skills are not as mature and he will need your help in learning how to translate his mood and feelings into words.

How language develops

How we learn language is not fully understood, although the work of linguistic experts such as Noam Chomsky and Jerome Bruner (see pages 216–217) plays an important role in our current beliefs and understanding. It can be helpful to know that when your toddler speaks he is actually grappling with four different areas of language development, simultaneously.

These four areas are:

■ How to use sounds and how to pronounce words (phonemics).

■ How to understand individual meanings of words and learn to use them in a way that makes sense, such as using plurals or the past tense (semantics).

■ How to combine several words into sentences in a logical order and a meaningful way (syntax).

■ How language is used in different situations and contexts (pragmatics).

That is a lot for a developing brain to take on board, so it is no wonder that your toddler gets frustrated sometimes. When he is older he will learn his letters, spelling, and grammar, how to use tone of voice appropriately, and how to use language sensitively. But for now he is concentrating on building his memory bank of words so that he has enough words to choose from to be able to communicate at a basic level.

During year 2–3, his language skills will race ahead. First of all, his phrases will lengthen from two words to three or four. Instead of "Daddy work" he might announce at 24 months, "Daddy go work now," and by 36 months may have progressed to, "Daddy going to work now." By 30 months he will be able to use the personal pronouns "I", "me", and "you" in the correct way. He will probably develop his own shortened version of some words and phrases, often based on the beginnings and endings of words, such as "chocake" for chocolate cake, or "su-ket" for supermarket.

Learning to listen

Listening to your toddler is about more than hearing the words that he says. He needs to know that you are on his wavelength, and that you are really engaging with how he feels and what he needs to tell you.

Make eye contact, touch his head or cheek while he speaks, smile or look quizzical. Use your face and your body to show him that you understand and are interested. By watching your reactions he, too, will learn how to empathize when people talk. You are helping him to learn how to read people's faces and develop understanding.

Top tips for effective listening:

▶ Use all the patience you can muster to let your toddler tell it his way.

▶ Echo back what he has said to show that you have heard and understood him.

▶ Don't interrupt him to correct his speech.

▶ Ask questions to encourage him to repeat and clarify what he's saying.

▶ Look enthusiastic. Your interest will help to boost his self-esteem.

▶ Praise him for being so clever at talking.

(Obviously some words just have too many syllables to be useful!) He will also start to learn how to ask questions, often by simply adding "Why?" to his sentence. Before he might have observed that, "The baby cry." Now, at 24 months, he is asking you, "Why baby cry?" and by 36 months he might say, "Why baby crying?"

Probably the words with the most impact, however, are your toddler's understanding of the importance of "Yes" and the overwhelming power of "No". Over the weeks ahead you will probably hear the words "No" and "Why" more often than you would have thought possible.

Language development – taught or caught?

Until the late 1950s there was a common belief that children learned language on an individual basis, either by hearing and imitating sounds or by interpreting other people's responses to sounds. The linguistic expert Noam Chomsky believed that this was too simplistic to explain the complex process of learning the meaning, structure, and grammatical rules of language. He pointed out that children as young as three will show awareness of grammatical rules, such as making plurals.

He also pointed out that children show a clear pattern of language development across different cultures and this could not be the case if all language was individually taught.

Make language learning fun

Keep up the songs, rhymes, and word games that you have been enjoying with your toddler. Don't worry that you are out of tune or haven't sung a note since you left school. Your toddler won't mind. He just loves the sounds of the words and the actions. Each repetition helps bed down his word memories even more. Do also let him lead when it comes to learning letters and numbers. He may enjoy learning about the sounds of the letters, but don't force the situation. There is plenty of time for spelling, grammar, and counting when he is a little older.

Making up stories and reading storybooks with your child is an excellent way of accelerating his language learning as well as ensuring that he is involved and enjoying the experience. If he has a favourite story (and toddlers are often word perfect with favourite books), pause while you are reading and see whether he can remember the missing word, or tell you what comes next. Be tolerant and full of praise, not critical, as he learns – this way he will progress quickly and enjoy the experience.

Chomsky believed that we have an inborn ability to learn the rules and meanings of any language from birth, depending on what we are exposed to. He pointed out that all children, whatever their cultural roots, show similar errors at different stages of language development, which are the result of getting used to grammatical structure.

Chomsky's ideas were developed further by Jerome Bruner in the 1980s. He believed that language results from a combination of innate ability plus exposure to language in our personal environment. Social interaction starts when, as a small baby, your child learns to direct his gaze to where you are looking. By 12–18 months he learns to look at objects not only from his own perspective, but also to move position, to see what you are looking at. Bruner and others argue that this stage connects to language development. This is the point where a child first starts to share meaning with another, as this example shows:

Daddy "Look at the beautiful green bird, Tariq." Tariq looks, but he can't see a bird.

Daddy, pointing, says "There, look, on the tree." Tariq follows the direction of his Daddy's pointing finger.

Tariq "I see bird! I see green bird, Daddy." Tariq is saying, if I look where you look, I can share your perspective and understand what you mean.

Sharing the meaning of words and a point of focus is known as "joint attention". Once a child can manage this he becomes ready and willing to communicate and converse, and will start to develop ways to do so.

I CAN SEE IT, TOO!
Once your toddler learns to look where you look, he can begin to learn the meaning of words by both verbal and non-verbal means, such as pointing.

Bilingual families

Children under the age of three who are raised in a bilingual environment are believed to learn both languages simultaneously, with no detriment to developing language skills. The easiest way to support language-learning is to be consistent in approach, perhaps by adopting a "one parent/one language" approach at home or by agreeing that one language will be spoken at home, and another outside the home. When conversations consist of mixed languages, a child may have difficulty working out which vocabulary applies to which language. Bilingual children appear to develop greater dexterity in their language-learning than those with a single language, once at school. This may be because they pay greater attention to language, which helps when developing literacy skills later.

How to talk with your toddler

Communicating with your toddler at this age is all about encouraging him to talk. He probably knows between 200–500 words, but won't be able to use them all comfortably. The more he talks to you and others, the more fluent and confident he will become.

There is a fine line at this age between encouraging your toddler to take the lead and controlling the outcome of the conversation, but he will benefit if you can help him to expand his language skills.

▶ **Keep up the commentary** – he still needs you to describe and reflect on what he is doing, so that he learns to understand and think about his actions, and so that he increases his sense of himself in action. So, for example, you might say, "You are pedalling your cycle very fast, so that you can get to the park quickly."

▶ **Keep things simple** – be as clear as possible when you describe something to your toddler or give him a direction, so that he understands what is expected and what he is experiencing. "You slid down the slide really fast, Nathan. Well done."

▶ **Encourage description** - increase his vocabulary by building on the information he gives you. Describe everything in more detail. "Your tummy felt whizzy did it, darling? It sounds as if you went very fast and it was very exciting. I expect you landed on your bottom with a bump!"

▶ **Ask questions** – about things he knows, to stimulate his language skills; but don't overwhelm him. "Closed" questions invite a specific answer: "Did you make new friends?" "Open" questions encourage him to chat: "What did you like playing best?" A mix of questions allows him to express himself and gives you useful information, too.

"The more fun you make conversations, the more language he will remember, and the greater the level of 'feel-good' hormones in his brain."

ALWAYS CURIOUS *The world is full of new discoveries for your toddler. Encourage her to tell you what she can see.*

▶ **Use past, present, and future** – your child now has a much better sense of time, but may still get confused about the difference between today, yesterday, and tomorrow. By including his own experiences in your narrative and your questions, he will pick up the idea more quickly. "If you like, we can go to the park again tomorrow; or we can go swimming with Peter, like we did last week. Which would you prefer? Going to the park or swimming with Peter?"

▶ **Mention relationships** – your toddler knows that he has a mummy, a daddy, and possibly some siblings and grandparents, but talking about how you are all related to each other, and how aunts, uncles, and cousins fit in too, will help to cement his understanding of "family" and his sense of belonging. "We can take your cousins George and Michael, too, if you like. I think Auntie Mary can take us in their car."

▶ **Help him understand his feelings** – give him the words he needs to describe the way he feels. "You sound very happy, Kyle, and very excited. Are those nice feelings? I think so, too."

▶ **Keep conversations simple** – limit each exchange to one or two pieces of information. Any more and your toddler will not remember and may become confused. Don't expect him to give a logical response to every question.

WHO'S LEADING THE CONVERSATION?

Child-led conversation, like child-led play, will help to increase your toddler's self-confidence because he will feel valued and truly listened to. Parent-led conversation, on the other hand, tends to control or instruct. The child's motive becomes the need to please the adult rather than exploring and learning for himself. There is a time and a place for both styles of conversation, but the following examples show two very different approaches and outcomes during play –

Maggie is playing with her Auntie Linda, who is showing her how to do a jigsaw puzzle:

"Now then, let's find all the pieces of the outside edge first. No, that's not edge, that's the middle. Here you are, Maggie, try this piece... No, no, other way up. No, no, the straight line has to match, do you see? Here – let me show you. There. Now then, can you see a piece with sky on it? Yes, it's a lovely sunflower, darling, but no, that piece won't fit. We need sky first... Careful, careful – you're knocking the pieces on the floor. Where are you going, sweetheart? Yes, Mummy is in the other room..."

Maggie toddles off as she can do nothing right and the fun has gone out of her jigsaw. Auntie Linda hardly notices, as she has become so intent on getting the outside edge of the puzzle in place.

Later, Maggie sits down with her Uncle Keith to do the same task, but he lets her lead the way:

"I hope you're not expecting me to do anything, Pumpkin! I don't know how to do jigsaws. You're going to have to show me. Now then, what's this funny shape? A piece of jigsaw, you say? Oh, is it? How exciting. What's this piece of yellow? Oh, a sunflower, I see. Now where would you like me to put it? Just here. OK. Now then, what happens next? Yes, that's a pretty piece, too. What are the colours on it? Oh yes – I see, that has some yellow on it, too – aha, and a green stalk – you're right. What are these funny knobbly bits for? I don't understand – will you show me? Ah! You are clever, you've fitted the pieces together and you've got a whole sunflower now. Well done, Maggie."

Maggie is feeling very happy to have her Uncle Keith's attention and she has completed her favourite piece of the puzzle. Her uncle's approach has worked most effectively because he has helped her to direct her own play, while also having fun.

Your toddler's wider world

Your two-year-old is just beginning to understand that the world extends beyond his immediate family. Grandparents, aunts, uncles, cousins, and friends are starting to play more of a part, too. He will also become more aware of the differences between being a boy and being a girl.

Understanding that there are other people in his world helps your toddler develop social skills, and enables him to develop self-awareness and an understanding of the existence of and meaning of relationships.

Getting along with others

As well as having siblings and burgeoning friendships, your toddler may also have cousins as playmates. In some families these relationships are amongst the strongest that children develop through life. How well the children bond will depend to some extent on how relaxed the relationship is between the parents. Even though two adults have been brought up by the same parents, they may have radically different views on the "correct" way to bring up their own children, and toddlers can easily pick up on any tensions and differences.

A simple way to get round differences of adult opinion on the "best" approach to parenting is to agree to respect the house rules of the home you are in. Children are happiest when their parents are happy. If the adults agree to compromise – so can they.

Practising sharing and role-play

All relationships offer toddlers the opportunity to understand how to share and take turns. You can help your toddler to develop self-awareness and to remember what is expected of him by modelling the kind of behaviour that you expect, and by describing to him what you would like him to do. For example, "Tommy, here is Martha. Martha is your cousin [explains relationship] and she would like to play with you [explains expectation]. Would you like to play with Martha [gives him control]?" When Tommy nods, his mother continues. "Good boy, Tommy [gives him praise]! I will come and help you [allows him to feel safe]." Had Tommy said "No," then rather than force the issue his mother might have suggested that she would play with Martha and that Tommy could come and watch.

Children will begin to get more of a sense of their own gender at this age, through pretend play and role-playing with other children, and also through observing adult behaviour. There is a tendency for girls to begin to model themselves on their mothers at this age. Boys, on the other hand, tend to seek out practical role models such as builders, firemen, soldiers, or perhaps members of their father's profession. It tends to be role-play during pretend play that reinforces our idea of our own gender, along with the messages we receive from those around us. This will become more sharply focused once your child starts school.

In praise of grandparents

The decision to return to work while your child is still a toddler is often a necessity rather than a choice for modern parents. For those who feel that it is too soon for their child to attend pre-school, having him cared for by grandparents is often the obvious answer. The situation allows grandparent and grandchild to bond closely, and the chances are that the approach to caring will be fairly similar to at least one of the parents.

"Yasmin's grandparents are important in her life. She has a special relationship with them, which is wonderful for us to see."

Jon, aged 41

Top tips for grandparents

While you may enjoy looking after your grandchildren, bear in mind that it might not always be easy.

▶ Agree some ground rules. Toddlers are highly intuitive and will soon discover that they can divide and rule. Find out from your son or daughter which home rules are absolutes, and which are more flexible, and do your best to stick to the agreement.

▶ Caring for your grandchild doesn't mean you need to be exhausted by him. Let him do the racing about. Don't feel you have to join in. Your encouragement and love are enough.

▶ Speak up if you feel you are being taken advantage of. Loving your grandchild doesn't mean you always have to agree to look after him.

▶ Try not to criticize the parents. Raise concerns about your grandchild's behaviour rather than prejudging the cause or their response.

Just for parents

As you have probably already realized by now, one of the greatest challenges of being a parent is juggling all your roles and responsibilities. It probably seems like there are never enough hours in a day and it can be a challenge to manage your mood at the same time as managing your toddler.

"The only way for me to get everything done is to involve the children in what I'm doing. Fortunately, they love it!"

Meera, aged 40

Balancing the never-ending round of household tasks with the art of child-rearing is a challenge for even the most well-supported adult, but it can be a source of major stress for sole carers or parents of large families. The creative answer is to try to turn household tasks into a time of fun and early learning.

Turn hard work into child's play

A young child does not recognize the difference between work and play, provided it is fun, and will find great pleasure and interest in the simplest of household tasks. However, I am not suggesting child exploitation here! Your little one is too young to be given responsibility for undertaking tasks himself, and his safety should always be a priority.

Is he a mini me? Getting chores done when you have a toddler in tow is a challenge. Make the most of his enjoyment of imitation by encouraging him to copy what you are doing (within reason) in miniature. If you are washing the car, he can wash his toy truck; if you are folding sheets, he can fold his teddy's blanket; if you are cooking, he can prepare some food, too. This is a great way for your child to learn new skills and anything you can do to keep him interested will encourage his smiles instead of tantrums.

De-stress with mess Take the stress out of your own day by turning gathering clothes and tidying up into a game with rewards. This introduces the opportunity for your toddler to copy what you do, and to add some fun to the process. You might want to take some time to look at the colours and shapes of the items around your home; you could go on a search for cobwebs and spiders (provided you are not fearful yourself), or invent a special "sorting" song. Encouraging children to put dirty clothes into the laundry basket and clean ones away in a drawer can become a game, helping them to learn colours and the name of different items of clothing, and introducing the idea of large and small sizes. Try to put the focus on enjoying colours and shapes rather than being fastidious about everything having to be neat and tidy and in the right place.

Mixing and tasting Baking cakes is a favourite way to play. Most toddlers love making a mess and will get immense enjoyment out of mixing and "helping" with their fingers, elbows, and anything else that finds its way into the mix! The enjoyment that your toddler gets from being able to eat the result of his labours will guarantee you some help with preparing food in the future. But remember not to let him near the hot oven until he is old enough to fully understand the dangers.

How does your garden grow? Growing things is exciting for small children, whether simply watching the progress of a carrot top sprouting in a saucer of water, or helping to weed a garden or grow some seeds. The changes and growth in the plant are usually a source of wonder and excitement – and offer the ideal opportunity to explain how things grow. Try to resist the temptation to introduce the true science until your little one is older. A simple explanation about seeds needing water and sunshine will be enough. Any more detail and he may appear to be listening, but he is far too young to understand what you are saying.

A word about anger

Children are often the barometers that indicate what is really going on in a household. They are intuitive and will have learned to read you in subtle ways. When adults are distressed or in conflict, children can take it personally. If you are upset, they are upset – and the chances are that they will assume it is their fault on some level (and sometimes it may be). Unable to separate your emotions from their own experience, a toddler who witnesses his parents arguing may feel fearful and be overwhelmed. He won't be able to take in or process anything else because he feels unsafe. In extreme situations, where conflict is ongoing, he may regress to an earlier stage of development. However, arguing is normal and you can't protect your child from life's unpleasantness altogether, nor would that be healthy. It is how you manage the conflict that will have the greater long-term impact. Your toddler needs to know that he can trust you to keep him safe, and help him manage his feelings by comforting him. This way he discovers that even though upsets happen, he is still loved and secure.

Coping with toddler overload

When you are tired, you may find yourself acting like your toddler. You might say "No" for the sake of it; throw an adult tantrum if you feel out of control or disregarded; occasionally feel negative and want to be left alone. This is only human and feeling fed up is your right – sometimes! However, if you are feeling low and increasingly negative towards your child, you need to ask yourself if you are stressed, exhausted, not getting support, or simply need a break. Take some time to consider what might help you to respond to your toddler and to others in a more calm and consistent way.

Do you feel as if you're always saying "No" or "Don't"? There is no one correct way to be as a parent, but trying to make sure you balance negative comments with at least an equal number of positives is the ideal. If you are in the habit of responding negatively, you are probably feeling stressed or tired. Try to consciously turn the negatives into positives next time you are playing with your child – and plan for some time off, too.

Are you exhausted by all his questions? Ignoring unwanted behaviour is an effective technique for controlling "bad" behaviour in children, but is not the ideal response if your child is being inquisitive. Children need many of their questions answered so that they learn and can begin to reason simply for themselves. If your toddler is wearing you out and you have "had enough" for one day, explain to him that "that is enough

Managing adult disagreements

Parents are human, too. Just as -you are trying to help your child to manage his frustrations, so too you may need to consciously learn how to control your own.

▶ Agree a cooling-off period before you discuss the cause of your anger.

▶ Be honest with one another about how the other person's action makes you feel.

▶ Comment on the action, but avoid criticizing the person. Adults, like children, need to know it is their behaviour you are rejecting rather than them as a person.

▶ If your child overhears your argument and is upset, explain that "Mummy was upset with Daddy [or whoever is appropriate], but we're not upset or angry with you."

▶ Offer your toddler reassuring cuddles, but don't explain the details. A child doesn't need to be burdened with adult issues.

▶ Never be tempted to encourage a child to take sides, or to act as a go-between in some way.

▶ If you find you are constantly arguing, do consider seeking help from a couples counsellor or similar.

CHILD'S PLAY *It is possible to rediscover the enjoyment of tasks such as cooking by involving your children. Instead of rushing and being stressed, you will have no choice but to take your time, and tune into the task.*

questions for one day. Daddy is tired now" so that he understands the reason for your non-response.

Are you tired of telling him off? Your toddler needs boundaries. However, constant criticism may stop him experimenting, may make him passive because he is afraid of your negative reaction, or overly accepting of his "bad" label. He is now old enough for a short and simple explanation of "No" – or to be shown why something might be dangerous.

Is he always interrupting? Your toddler can begin to understand that he sometimes has to wait for your attention. Children of this age can start to learn that you cannot always be child-focused.

Does he tend to do the opposite of what you tell him? Telling a child he can't do something is often a good way to get him to do it. Try using a paradoxical statement such as, "Bet you can't get all those toys in the box before I count to 10!" This approach can be very effective! It helps to encourage positive behaviour, too.

Are you always showing him what to do? Modelling behaviour is an ideal way to show a child what to expect, but this needs to be balanced by allowing him to make mistakes. Trial and error helps him to find his own way, without you jumping in to show him the "right" way – unless, of course, he seems unsafe or out of control.

"You are an individual as well as a parent. Make time for your own interests – you will be happier and your child will benefit, too."

Making time for you

Schedule in regular time to do something completely unrelated to anything involving children and family. Allocate time in your diary – once you have written your plans down, you are more likely to follow them through. The moment you feel you have no time for anything other than work and chores is the very moment to stop… and make a conscious decision to do something for you, now, this week.

That goes for your partner, too. If you look out for one another and make sure you are equally well supported there will be less room for tension, resentment, or exhaustion. The more relaxed and fulfilled you are, the less conflict and upset there will be.

Make good use of your support network. Have you got friends that you can call on for a chat or to relax and unwind with? Do you make good use of your health visitor, GP, and any local baby and toddler groups? It is the ideal stage for your child to start to make new friends, too.

Dear Tanya...

▶ **I feel guilty because I get so bored with playing games with my two-year-old daughter for longer than 10 minutes at a time.**

You are by no means alone in your feelings. Many parents find it extremely hard to remain consciously engaged as their son or daughter insists on playing something "Again!" The reality is that 10 minutes at a time is probably all your toddler can cope with, too. The rest of the time she is just enjoying your company.

This phase of development will pass all too quickly, so it may help to remind yourself that within six months she will be much more comfortable playing with other children and will not need to rely on you quite as much.

Use your time with her to encourage her to practise sharing and taking turns, so the adjustment to co-operative play with other toddlers will come more easily. Focusing on her, rather than the game, will stimulate your interest. Watch how she is looking, listening, and learning with every activity she takes part in – and congratulate yourself for your active part in

bringing up your happy and healthy little girl. Although child-led play is the ideal scenario, if you are getting impatient, why not involve her in something you would rather be doing – in a playful way?

▶ **I want to stop breastfeeding my two-year-old daughter, but I'm worried she will become distressed by this.**

The question of breastfeeding is a highly personal one. The reality is that by the age of 24–36 months your toddler no longer needs your breast milk for nutritional reasons. She has the ability to self-feed now, and the quality of your breast milk will no longer be as nutrient-rich as it was when she was a baby.

Therefore, the main reason for continuing to breastfeed at this age is for comfort, both yours and hers. It may be hard for both of you to adjust initially because your daughter associates breastfeeding with being loved and nurtured. But there are other ways to show her affection and she will adjust quite quickly if you begin to offer other options, such as a cup of milk while she snuggles close to you. This

replaces one association of comfort (your breast) with another (the cup). In fact, she may "let go" more easily than you.

It may be easier to stop breastfeeding when you are away from home in a different environment. By the time you return home, breastfeeding will, hopefully, be a distant memory for your daughter.

▶ **Our three-year-old son will smile at, and hug, almost everyone he meets. How can I keep him safe from strangers, while not scaring him?**

News stories may make us fearful that every child is in constant danger from strangers, but the statistical reality is that children are more at risk from traffic accidents than abduction. If they are harmed, it is more likely to be by someone they know than a stranger. However, it is important to teach your child who it is okay to hug and speak to, and to tell him not to accept gifts from strangers. There is no need for a detailed explanation. Just praise appropriate behaviour and say, "No" to inappropriate behaviour.

LIFE SKILLS *A well-trained and tolerant family pet can make the perfect playmate and companion for a young child, as well as helping him learn how to be gentle and care for others.*

5 points to remember

1 You are your toddler's anchor and his safe haven. He needs you to help him manage, understand, and direct his feelings in a way that makes him feel comfortable and that he is in control.

2 Pushing your child too fast will not lead to faster development; conversely, it may cause anxiety and lead him to give up because he cannot achieve the necessary results.

3 During difficult times you may question your parenting ability and wonder whether you are doing something wrong. When this happens try to see the situation in context. Remind yourself that it is normal for all toddlers to misbehave sometimes.

4 Help your child to rehearse a co-operative style of play, in the safety of his relationship with you, where he can avoid the power struggles that will inevitably happen with his playmates.

5 Many parents believe that their toddler is being wilfully naughty or is scheming. In fact, at this age they do not have the moral reasoning skills to do either.

LET HER HELP *Include her in activities, such as gardening. It is a great way to give her your attention but still get on with your own tasks, and she will be learning all the time.*

3–4 YEARS

YOUR INDEPENDENT CHILD

12   18   24   30   **36**   **42**   **48**

MONTHS

WANTING TO ACHIEVE YOU MAY NOTICE YOUR TODDLER HAS A NEW DETERMINATION TO TRY AND SUCCEED – GIVE HIM THE FREEDOM TO LEARN, AND PRAISE ALL HIS EFFORTS

SELF-SUFFICIENT HE'S MORE INDEPENDENT AND CAN DO MORE PRECISE TASKS, BUT ACCEPT THAT THERE MIGHT BE SOME SPILLAGES!

UNDERSTANDING OTHERS THE EMPHASIS IS MOVING AWAY FROM "ME, ME, ME" AND HE WILL BEGIN TO UNDERSTAND THE FEELINGS AND NEEDS OF OTHERS, ESPECIALLY YOURS

"He's growing up, but however independent he may seem, he needs you now more than ever."

Your toddler's development

Months 36–48 may be more peaceful than the previous year, as your child gradually leaves toddlerhood behind. During the months ahead, she will start to want to please you more, rather than just wanting to meet her own needs, but the year will present its own distinct challenges.

Your relationship with your toddler will change significantly during the year ahead, in ways that are both lovely and fascinating. Her imagination is developing rapidly now. She will be able to disappear into a of fantasy that will help her to explore different roles and behaviour. This is also the time when fears (see page 260) begin to develop and nightmares (see page 264) may make an appearance.

  With her new reasoning power comes the realization that she is separate from and different to you; she will start to understand that her actions have consequences which means she will also begin to understand the difference between "right" and "wrong". She will have an ever-increasing number of questions as she tries to make sense of the world.

"There is nothing like having a three-year-old for improving your own manners, behaviour, and attitudes. Every time I hear my daughter announce, 'My Daddy says...' my nerves jangle!" Brian, aged 38

Your toddler will now have a far better understanding of the guidelines that you give her and will be able to remember them more easily. She will still need you to remind her of what is needed, though, as she can't hold too much information in mind at any one time. She is not only aware of you as being separate from her; she is also much more in tune with your emotions and needs. Toddlers from age three and onwards are much more motivated to please their parents because they want to make them happy.

It is at this age that your toddler will start to look up to you as a role model and will start to insist that "Mummy says" or "Daddy says".

You will notice that your toddler will now look to you far more frequently for guidance on how she should act and behave and she will echo your words and phrases more than ever. These early years play an important part in developing your child's attitudes and beliefs about how the world, the self, and other people act. For that reason, it is important to try to hold a balanced view of the world and to hold back on unfair criticism of others on the basis of looks, creed, race, or gender. Each time you set an example that your child follows, remember that you are giving her a message for life.

The months ahead will also see a change in your child's self-regard. She will start to respond more and seek out your praise and appreciation, and will also begin to praise herself. This is the ideal age to begin to encourage her to help to make simple choices for herself: encourage her to make decisions by giving her two equally feasible choices. Her budding sense of achievement is crucially important for the development of her self-esteem (see page 259) and confidence.

This growing self-awareness is partnered with the beginnings of an understanding of both the consequences of her behaviour and reasons why certain behaviour might not be acceptable. She still won't be able to cope if you give her lengthy reasons for why she shouldn't do something, but short explanations will be fine. This increase in understanding and reasoning really kick-starts the development of her moral ideas and beliefs.

Moral development

Our moral awareness develops as we begin to reflect on what we hear and learn, observe the behaviour of others, and weigh up the "rights and wrongs" of a situation as we perceive it. Until now, your toddler has had very little understanding of right and wrong. Behaviour-shaping has been less about explanation and more about diversion and distraction. From about 36–42 months onwards, however, you will begin to notice a subtle change in your toddler's abilities.

As your child's reasoning skills improve, not only does she begin to understand that her behaviour has an effect, she also learns about the consequences of that effect on others and develops empathy. This ability to see and feel things from another person's point of view is crucial to her emerging understanding of the difference between "right" and "wrong". There are differing views about the age at which children develop a sense of guilt or a sense of justice about behaviour (see page 261). Your child shows signs of understanding what is "fair" by the time she is four.

Modelling behaviour

Alongside the development of moral beliefs and understanding, it is important for children to learn how to behave according to these beliefs. That is, there is a difference between a child's belief – knowing how she should behave – and her behaviour – choosing to act the "right" way. In childhood, as in life, it can be hard to choose to be "good".

Behaviour is learned, not inherited, so your child is very reliant upon you to model correct behaviour during these years. Preferred social niceties and good manners, such as saying "please" and "thank you", can be encouraged and also modelled by you. Children learn more from being shown – consistently and repetitively, and being encouraged to try (and reap the benefits!), than they do from being told. By the time your child is four she may be capable of making some moral judgements for herself (such as "it is wrong to hurt someone"), but will not come to these conclusions unless you have modelled and talked about appropriate behaviour. The earlier you model your expectations for your child by your own behaviour, the sooner the message will get through that this is important information for her to learn.

A parenting style that is sympathetic, warm, and supportive tends to help children to develop positive social skills and regulate their own emotions, as well as developing more sophisticated moral reasoning at an early age. Peers, too, are very powerful models and therefore have an influence on the development of moral behaviour, although they will have more of an impact when your child is a little older and at school.

Developing values

Children absorb information like a sponge absorbs water: quickly and indiscriminately. This is the time in your child's development when you need to be most careful about the views, fears, and prejudices you voice because her ears are like radio antennae: they will tune in and remember all sorts of

PLAYGROUPS AND LEARNING *Playgroups offer a new range of experiences and role models for your child and she may pick up new skills and behaviour from her peers.*

things that you say, and often the very thing you wish you hadn't said. We are not born with a set of values. We are born only with the ability to develop beliefs and learn the rules that guide behaviour. Values result from our personal experiences and the influences we are exposed to. They are learned from our parents, and other carers and teachers, and they develop over time. Your toddler will not be able to make up her own mind or hold an independent opinion until she is approximately seven years old. Until that time, her judgements and beliefs will be based solely on what you tell her, what she learns, and, importantly, what she sees you do.

She has not yet developed independent thinking skills and although she can be empathetic and may challenge you if your wishes conflict with her wants, she is not ready to question your authority. Therefore, at this age, she will absorb the beliefs that you hold and express unquestioningly.

Bending the truth

Your three-year-old has got a lot to take on board at once. In the past, she only had to worry about what she wanted; now she has to consider what is expected of her, too. This can result in inner confusion. How can she manage to give you what you want and gain your approval at the same time as doing what she wants? The answer is to tell a lie. However, she doesn't know it is a lie, and she isn't being consciously deceptive.

At this age, lying can be seen as a sign of her developing reasoning ability; she is testing out her ideas about reality and fantasy and this is not a cause for concern. However, it is important that your toddler does not learn that lying works, otherwise she may start to rely on it. If you know

The impact of violent images

There is a growing consensus amongst researchers that children who are exposed frequently to violent images on TV or in computer games are likely to become desensitized and may become more aggressive than those children who are not. This is especially true if children are not monitored while they are watching or playing, because they have no way of interpreting the rights and wrongs of the situation they are watching.

Violent programmes and games do not encourage reasoning; therefore for the child who is watching them there is no understanding of the true consequences of violence.

your toddler has told a lie, tackle the situation straight away, but don't get cross, and do make it easy for her to tell you the truth. You might ask her to help you figure the answer out: "I wonder how teddy got up there to break the vase?" Alternatively, you can speak to her more directly: "I think it may have been you, not teddy – is that right?"

Explain that it is important to say what really happened and that it is called "telling the truth". Tell her that you would only be cross if she didn't tell you the truth. Keep your explanation calm and simple so that she understands, and has no fear that you may get angry.

Skills development

By the end of this year you will be looking forward to your child's school years. She will probably be able to dress and undress by herself, but buttons are still a challenge; you will have a good idea of whether she is right- or left-handed, and she will be able to wash herself, clean her teeth, and brush her hair (to some extent!). Her language skills will also be improving daily. She will be able to speak in sentences of five or six words and her vocabulary will have rocketed to several hundred words. This is the perfect age to start to introduce her to letters and numbers in a light and playful way. Your child's memory and reasoning skills have now developed to a point where she will enjoy learning about sounds and words, but there is no need to rush this process.

Reading and writing

Children learn best if they are given tools that stimulate more than one sense simultaneously. That is why, when showing your toddler her A,B,Cs it is useful not only to show her what the letter A looks like, but also to reinforce the message with an image that relates to the sound (such as an Apple). Make the sound and encourage her to repeat it, so she gets used to relating the sound of the letter to the associated image and to the letter itself. This first stage is called "phonics".

In phonics, letters are identified by the sounds that they represent, not the name of the letter. (For example, A = *a*pple, rather than *a*pron.) Learning the names of letters can follow later, but research shows that children need to learn phonics first in order to develop reading skills. Any activity that helps your child to familiarize herself with letters, whether

DRAWING SKILLS *She will progress from scribbling and drawing simple shapes to creating more recognizable pictures. Comment on her drawings to encourage her.*

alphabet charts, rhymes, or matching games, will help her later reading and writing skills. She has a large enough vocabulary now to be able to look at picture books with you and pick out words that have similar sounds. Try looking for words that start with the sound "p" for example, as in "postman, picnic, parrot". Use gentle repetition, but don't pressure her to learn. There may still be some sounds that she struggles with, however. Common toddlerisms include using "r" instead of "w" ("it's waining", instead of "it's raining") or using "d" for "th" ("dis is de one" instead of "this is the one"). Adjusting her mouth and tongue to pronounce the sounds for "b", "p", "m", "w", and "h" can take months to get right. Word games and rhymes can be a useful way to help her practise.

Your toddler is too young to be able to spell words but, now that her finger skills and muscle control have improved, she can copy or trace a few letters and may be able to copy simple words, including her name, by 48 months. Start off with a single letter at a time and link it to its sound. See whether she can copy or trace it and colour it in. Before too long she will learn to recognize her name when it is written down.

Number skills

Your child may be able to learn her numbers by rote, (for example, count up to five or even 10 by the age of four), but their order and what they represent will have very little meaning until she is older. At this age, it is good to concentrate on matching numbers to the right quantity of objects. Once she has got used to the idea that numbers are symbols that represent something else, you can then go on to show her that the quantity is the same no matter what the item is. For example, 1 teddy = 1 orange; 2 eggs = 2 apples; 3 apples = 3 crayons, and so on. These are difficult concepts for children at this age, so don't overdo the "training". She is still too young to grasp the idea of changing quantities by adding and subtracting and will not master this until the age of five-and-a-half. Activities such as measuring and pouring will help her to learn the basics of counting.

Signs that development is on track

All children will develop at their own pace (see page 48). The following is an approximate guide to how your child's new skills will develop in the coming months.

By the end of months 36–39, your child:

- Can hold a conversation of 2–3 sentences.
- Is beginning to use adjectives.
- Can balance on each foot for a few seconds.
- Will be starting to dress without help.

By the end of months 40–42, your child:

- Can pedal a tricycle.
- Can walk around objects without bumping into them.
- Can kick a ball.
- Can walk on tiptoe, jump, walk backwards, and sideways.

By the end of months 43–46, your child:

- May be able to draw a head, with arms and legs but no body.
- Can use a fork and spoon.
- Can climb stairs using one foot on each step.
- Can match primary colours red and yellow, but may mix blue and green.

By the end of months 47–48, your child:

- Can remember the words and tunes of favourite songs and rhymes.
- Can use "I", "me", and "you".
- Knows that she is a girl and he is a boy.
- May know her age.

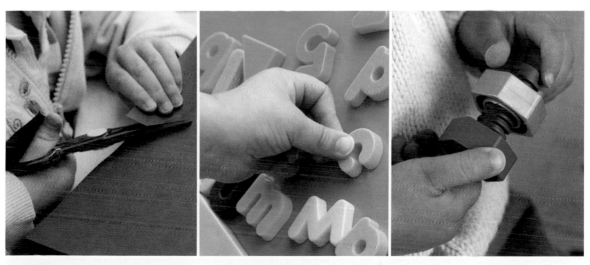

PRECISE PLAY *At this age, your child will be increasingly dextrous and will be comfortable holding child's scissors and cutting paper, and she will play with smaller toys and objects more skilfully.*

Your toddler's brain

The brain development that enabled reasoning skills to evolve during months 24–36 (see page 165) continues this year. As well as learning how to be flexible and developing memory skills, your toddler also becomes more empathetic and starts to understand that not everyone sees things the way she does.

"As her imagination begins to develop, she is able to get a sense of how others are thinking and feeling."

Only from the age of two onwards is the brain sufficiently developed to be able to remember and recall information and these skills continue to develop over the next 12 months. Even then, not all information will be remembered easily. We remember things by recognizing them, and by recalling information about them.

Your child has been able to recognize many of the important people in her world since she was two. This skill develops further now. Recognition is a less complex process than recalling information and develops much earlier. For example, Paula, aged three, can recognize her cousin Hannah when she can see her, but will find it harder to remember and recall anything about her when she is not there. Recognition happens via a fast process of comparisons: "Here is a girl. I will compare her against all my stored memories of girls. Aha! The girl matches my memory of Hannah." Accurate recall depends not only on your child's reasoning skills ("I know I like playing with Hannah,") but also on her being able to remember the

Learning and flexibility

Doing or thinking about more than one thing at a time is a challenge for toddlers, who tend to be quite fixed and rigid in their approach. For example, Annie isn't able to consider that her red crayon can easily replace her blue crayon. She might even get upset if anyone suggests it. In time, and with encouragement, Annie will be able to become more flexible and will learn to choose an alternative option. "I want the blue one, and I want it now!" will gradually become, "I wanted the blue one, but it's not here, so the red one will do just as well for now." The thinking and reasoning part of her brain allows this more flexible approach.

context of the information ("because we had fun playing on the swings.") The frontal lobes (see page 164) play a vital role in tagging memories with this kind of reminder. These memory "cues" help our recall. (In this case, Hannah is not with her, but Paula can recall her because the sight of a swing has triggered a visual memory.) The brain tags and stores information while making sure that the most useful memories can be retrieved easily when needed.

Social and emotional skills

By the age of three, your toddler will be starting to discover that other people may think and feel differently to the way she does. ("Mummy does not always know what I want. Sometimes I have to tell her.")

This development shows in a toddler's impulse to comfort another child who is upset. Over the next year, reasoning skills will develop so that, for example, Cara will not only understand that her friend Tommy "is upset, don't cry" but that "Tommy is upset because..." and she will start to modify her behaviour accordingly. This ability to empathize is vital in being able to recognize and respond sensitively to the reactions and behaviour of others.

However, the ability to feel empathy cannot develop fully until the frontal lobes have begun to mature. Your child will gradually become more consistently understanding and you will notice that she begins to play more co-operatively, showing that she has expanded her emotional range and understanding. This early breakthrough shows she is well on her way towards developing rewarding relationships in later life.

All the functions of the frontal brain develop together and each is dependent on another; so your toddler won't be able to understand her friend's feelings or be able to see life from her perspective, until she can pay attention for long enough to read her reactions and be able to recall and understand them. As memory builds over time, so will your child's sensitivity and understanding of the wider world and the people in it.

Development is rarely a steady line of forward progress. Under stress (having a tantrum, being asked to share a toy, a new sibling being born) it is possible that a child will revert back to being more egocentric and will abandon some of her compassionate skills. It is usual for skills to fluctuate in this way as they develop and become more established.

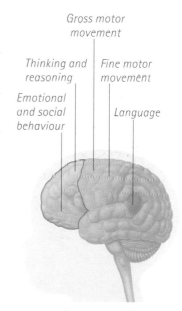

Gross motor movement

Thinking and reasoning

Fine motor movement

Emotional and social behaviour

Language

SOCIAL AND EMOTIONAL UNDERSTANDING *As the frontal lobes mature, individual personality and social behaviour develop alongside more sophisticated thinking and reasoning skills.*

Learning about gender

Until now, your toddler was almost unaware of whether she was a girl or a boy. She may have been told she was a "girl", but would not have understood what it meant, and may not have been able to recognize the differences between boys and girls.

Between the ages of 3–4, your child will become more aware of the differences between being male and female from her experiences at home, her broader environment, and via other children. Now that traditional male and female roles have become blurred, children have a more flexible interpretation of mummies' and daddies' roles, but this does not appear to affect their understanding of what it is to be a boy or a girl.

or prejudge the situation if you find your son loves dressing up or playing with dolls, or your daughter is most at home "playing soldiers".

Children tend to be attracted to the toys and games that offer the most excitement or that have the most sparkle and glitter. Some boys will prefer to play more gentle games and some girls will prefer to play rough, but this is just a part of who they are, and they will be influenced

colour you painted your baby's room and what colour clothes you bought.

Some of the messages we give our children are subtle and sub-conscious, and start very young (for example, "pink for a girl and blue for a boy"). Others are more obvious and may come out through play: "Let's play tea parties with your dollies, Jessica," versus "Let's play football in the park, Rob." Often these messages reinforce the innate differences between the

"Knowing that 'I am a boy' or 'I am a girl' helps a child to develop a sense of identity and understand where he or she fits in with the world. These differences help children learn how to behave."

The differences between girls and boys are surprisingly small during the toddler years. Hormonal differences and differences in brain development may explain the tendency for some boys to enjoy more aggressive and active play and some girls to be more chatty and "girly".

Generally speaking, however, childhood roles are fairly inter-changeable. There is no need to worry

by what Mummy or Daddy enjoy when they are relaxing and playing, too.

HOW DIFFERENCES DEVELOP

Social influences play the most important part in helping children learn male and female roles in life. Parents, carers, and other children will reinforce male and female roles and behaviour. The process starts from the moment children are born with what

sexes. For example, we offer boys more active toys and more rough-and-tumble play, while social play and chatting may be the domain of girls. This will be due to a combination of feedback from your child – doing what he or she likes doing, and what you most value – what you think little boys and little girls should be doing. There is nothing wrong with this. Boys and girls are different (although there are

WE'RE DIFFERENT *Children begin to realize some playmates are boys and some girls, and may begin to ask direct questions about their differences.*

shades of male and female characteristics in all individuals). Our ideas about gender and behaviour are influenced by our culture. Society's norms affect the way we behave, our beliefs, and how we organize our lives.

EXPLORING DIFFERENCES

During this year children may start to show a preference for gender-related toys and have more interest in friends of the same sex. They may start to judge each other: "boys, yuk" or "girls, silly", and do some personal exploring. "Show me yours and I'll show you mine," is a normal and healthy part of development and a way for your child to explore boy-girl differences.

Do what you can to allow your child to lead in her choices and try not to prejudge. Comments such as "Big boys don't cry"/"Tom, help Daddy in the garage"/"Mary, help Mummy get the lunch" will reinforce traditional roles.

There is a tendency to talk more to girls about feelings and more to boys about how to figure things out. The healthy approach is to give both genders the same toys and opportunities whilst acknowledging that differences between boys and girls do exist.

REAL LIFE

Hanif is closest in age to his sister Rana, who loves all things pink and fluffy. As a result, Hanif has learnt to enjoy "girly" games and is just as happy wearing his sister's princess costume as he is playing with his toy cars or learning to climb. "We don't worry," says his Dad, Raj. "They are just having fun! He has a fabulous imagination and they both enjoy play-acting. It will be interesting to see how their tastes change and develop as they get older and when Hanif meets new playmates at school."

Playing and learning

Your toddler is much more independent now and enjoys the company of other children. The transition from parallel play to co-operative play is happening steadily, although she will still need your help to manage her feelings when there is a disagreement with another child.

"At this age, play is a wonderful time of make-believe and role-play. The boundaries between fantasy and reality are blurred."

The biggest change you will notice during the forthcoming year is the dominance of imagination and make-believe in your toddler's style of play. Her brain has now developed to the stage where she has the ability to hold more than one perspective or point of view in mind, which means that co-operative play with other children (and with you) becomes much easier for her to maintain.

Her imagination is developing, as is her understanding and exploration of the difference between fantasy and reality. "Symbolic" or pretend play increases, too: she no longer needs a real car to make her think she's in a car or a real phone to play at telephones. Three-year-olds have the ability to turn the most mundane items into exciting possibilities for play.

There is no need to force your child to see reality during this period. It is a magical time when stories come alive; and cartoon characters, Father Christmas, fairies, and other mythical characters really do exist in her mind. Let her fantasies continue where they are enjoyable, but be aware that it can be hard for a toddler to know what is real. Sometimes she will become so engrossed in what she is doing or watching that the lines between

Real life

I was tearing around the house one day trying to tidy up before my in-laws arrived. Mark, who's nearly four, had been playing with some cardboard boxes, but had long since abandoned them for an exciting game with his brother. I had just finished crushing them when I heard the wail, "Where's my rocket gone? Mummy, mummy! Rocket GONE!" It seems it wasn't just a stack of cardboard after all...

IMAGINATIVE PLAY *Children get great enjoyment from creating and playing out imaginary scenes from everyday life, as well as building on scenes they have seen in films, cartoons, or picture books.*

NEW "FRIENDS" *Listen when she tells you about her imaginary friends – don't dismiss them. But, equally, don't allow her to use them to encourage you to give her what she wants.*

fantasy and reality blur. She may find it hard to distinguish between them because she finds it hard to hold more than one view in her mind at a time. For example, if someone is dressed up as a lion, she may think it *is* a lion. Your toddler has begun to realize that not everyone sees the world the same way that she does. She has started to be able to see the world from another person's perspective, but has difficulty holding both perspectives in her mind at the same time and so may shift between the two. What something looks like is what it is.

As well as imagining positive fantasy characters, your child will also be able to imagine frightening images. The difficulty with living with an active imagination is that it can lead to fears and phobias. This is why it is vital that you supervise her television viewing (see page 238) and try to limit exposure to inappropriate or disturbing images.

Your toddler may enjoy being slightly scared by mild surprises when playing "Boo" or reading books about monsters, but some televised cartoons, film animations, and special effects can be very scary. Even a film that is designated as suitable for a seven-year-old can be totally inappropriate for your pre-schooler.

Imaginary friends

Children find different ways to cope with, or show, their fears and anxieties, one of which is through the invention of an imaginary friend. This is nothing to be concerned about. The age of 3–4 is the time when imaginary friends may typically become a part of your child's life. They may sometimes be an indicator of a child feeling anxious and seeking comfort, but this is by no means always the case.

An imaginary friend has many advantages. He, she, or it, is always there to play with and is always co-operative. An imaginary friend will absorb your child's blame or anger as well as any destructive feelings your toddler may have because she can talk to her imaginary friend and stay in control. In times of fear, her imaginary friend can keep her safe from monsters, shadow faces on the walls, unexplained noises, and fears about new experiences such as going to the doctor. This is a healthy part of development so do not worry or try to stop the companionship. Equally, the friend can be a playmate or companion in adventure. Your child's imaginary friend will leave when your child doesn't need her any more.

One word of caution: imaginary friends can also be used as master negotiators on occasion! No matter how charming it may seem, resist the temptation to play along if your child uses her imaginary friend to try to dictate routine or avoid the consequences of unacceptable behaviour. On the other hand, appreciation of her imaginary friend when he or she is pleasant (for example, helping to set the table or kissing you goodnight) will do no harm and may help your toddler cope with learning to do new things. Imaginary friends should not become a substitute for real friends, however. It is important that your toddler has plenty of opportunities to mix with and get used to her non-imaginary peers.

Top tips for understanding imaginary friends:

■ Accept that having imaginary friends is a natural part of childhood and accept them if they make an appearance.

■ Don't be dismissive or critical, or deny the friend exists. This phase of imagination won't last forever. Let your child enjoy it while she can.

■ Don't be tempted to direct or "adopt" the imaginary friend yourself – let your toddler take the lead.

■ If your toddler seems to be using the imaginary friend to cope with negative feelings, encourage her to talk to you instead.

"As many as two out of three children have one or more imaginary friends who 'drop in' from time to time. They usually leave permanently by the time your child is five or six."

Jokes and laughter

Children love to giggle and laugh, and by the age of three can understand context and have enough memories to begin to get a joke. This will transform into a sense of humour and later an understanding of sarcasm. At age 3–4, children often have a great sense of silliness and enjoy slapstick-style humour. They like to see or hear the same funny events repeatedly, and can be very giggly. At this age, too, toddlers may laugh at inappropriate things – and may join in laughter without truly understanding what was funny. Through this year you may start to notice your child developing her own jokes about words that sound funny, or bodily functions. Toilet humour is guaranteed to get some kind of reaction from adults!

■ Do listen to how your child talks to her friend and watch how she plays with her. The relationship may give you a lot of insight into your child's thoughts and feelings.

Lying and cheating

Small lies are a natural part of mental development (see page 238) and show that thinking and reasoning skills are maturing. This doesn't mean that a lie should go unchallenged, but you needn't worry that it is an indicator that your child will make it a habit. Working out the rules of the world and recognizing moral boundaries are skills we apply throughout life. As your child gets older, she will remember the boundaries you have taught her and make judgements that take your stance into account.

"All children need opportunities to achieve and to feel good about themselves, so it is okay to let your child win sometimes. Don't make a habit of it, though, as she will notice and feel cheated."

The important factor at this age is not the lie itself, but the reason for the lie. Bear in mind that your child is keen to "get things right" and to impress and please you, and so may lie to avoid the consequences of your displeasure. Go over the incident and explain to your child why she should not lie. Children are still very egocentric at this age and so may not relate to your feelings of being upset; so your explanation needs to be clear and simple. She will learn over time, with some repetition on your part. Do also praise truth-telling and be honest with yourself about your own traits. If your child notices you aren't truthful, she may follow your lead.

Cheating at games

Age 3–4 is the time when children first encounter the urge to cheat. This is similar to lying, in that they know they will get praise and attention if they win. However, it is an interesting developmental milestone as well, in that a child cannot cheat unless she understands what is going to happen in a game. It shows her reasoning skills and intelligence are developing. She has learnt that the act of winning makes her feel good; it builds her self-esteem.

A toddler who is losing a game has several options to vent her frustration: she can end the game by destroying it; she can try to change the rules to suit her needs; or she can cheat. Your child is now old enough to understand a basic explanation of why she should not cheat. Start by explaining why rules are important; explain why fairness is important; and explain that rules apply to everyone (even Mummy and Daddy). If she keeps forgetting what the rules are, have the patience to remind her regularly.

If your child or another toddler destroys the game and ruins the fun for other people, explain why it is unacceptable to behave that way. If necessary, use "time out" techniques (see page 270) to help your child calm herself down and put some distance between her mood and her actions. The consequence of losing out on the fun of the game should help her learn that her actions do not reap rewards and hence make such behaviour less likely in the future.

However, although the recalcitrant toddler should be no longer allowed to play the game, continue it with the other children, if possible, so that they do not lose out on the satisfaction of being co-operative and remaining part of the game.

PLAYING BY THE RULES
It can be tempting to let your child cheat, but try not to as he needs to learn to tolerate the sense of frustration that losing causes.

Rough-and-tumble play

Play-fighting, and very physical, active play, will increase during years 3–4. A lot of boys and some girls will go through this development phase, which is completely normal and does not mean your child is "violent".

Rough-and-tumble play helps children to learn their physical limits as well as gaining hands-on experience of handling aggression, managing mood, enjoying competition, falling out, and making up. It is an early form of negotiation. However, some basic ground rules are necessary so that children do not hurt each other maliciously. No pinching, punching, biting, kicking, or other form of inflicting harm is appropriate.

DEVELOPING SOCIAL SKILLS *Children are ready to become more sociable by this age and enjoy having friends and playmates. It will help them adjust if they learn some early social skills before starting school, too.*

"It has been amazing to watch Oliver develop since starting nursery. He is less clingy, more sociable, and increasingly confident." Helen, aged 27

Playtime and play dates

Now that your toddler is a little older, she is ready to develop her social skills – and you are ready to enjoy the company of other adults who are experiencing the same challenges as you. There is no better way to address these two needs than to arrange for your toddler to go on "play dates", where your child goes to play with another child at his or her house, or vice versa. You may find that girls want to play with girls and boys want to play with boys at this age. Don't discourage this as it is all part of children learning about their own gender and their differences. It is a good idea to encourage a mixture of friends from both sexes and across different cultures, though, so that your toddler gets used to, and is comfortable with, diversity from a young age.

If your child already attends a pre-school or toddler group, she will be reasonably used to the company of other children by now. Not all children have had that experience, however, and for those who have spent more time solely with their family, play dates can be an ideal way of helping your child to make friends.

The basic guidelines for successful play dates are planning ahead, supervision (even in the background), co-operation (with the other parent), expecting the unexpected, and being relaxed.

Dealing with silliness

As your child's reasoning skills develop, so does her sense of humour. Your child will enjoy making you happy and laugh. This is a good skill to have but toddlers can get carried away with their sense of silliness, and so need to understand when to be sensible, too. It is a different kind of self-regulation. For some children, playing the clown can become the way they gain self-confidence and integrate with others. This will not always be welcome – especially in the classroom – so your toddler will need to learn to understand when joking is appropriate and when it isn't. He will usually learn this from you.

Playtime ideas and games

ACTION GAMES WITH OTHERS

Games that involve actions encourage children to listen carefully and to follow instructions. These games also encourage an element of competition that will enable children to learn skills from each other. Try:

▸ *Grandmother's Footsteps.*
▸ *What's the time, Mr Wolf?*
▸ *Pass the Parcel.*
▸ *Hide and Seek.*
▸ *Simon Says.*

MAKE-BELIEVE GAMES

There is scope for make-believe in almost anything at this age. Favourite play includes:

▸ **Role-play** Playing "classrooms" can be a helpful way to get your child used to the idea of going to school. "Going shopping" will get her used to swapping money for goods, rather than just taking what she wants.

Playing "house" will often include pretending to do chores like mummy and daddy. Gender differences often show markedly in this game.

▸ **Characters** She might want to be a farmer, fireman, doctor, soldier, dancer, singer, or nurse – and you might have to be a character, too!

GAMES WITH RULES

Toddlers of 3–4 years old will have a limited ability to understand, remember, and stick to rules. Games with only one or two simple rules such as *Tag* or *Stick in the Mud* are a good place to start. In a mixed age group, it can be useful to team a younger child with an older child or adult so that they can learn by observation to begin with and don't become overwhelmed by fast play.

SIMPLE CARD AND BOARD GAMES

These games encourage children's observation skills and help them to learn to take turns. Early experiences of winning and losing – as well as cheating – can be learned from card and board games.

An early competitive streak may appear. Learning to lose without becoming upset takes a lot of effort and it is a good idea to praise your child if she handles defeat well.

▸ **Dominoes** Teach children about numbers and matching.
▸ **Snakes and ladders** Help children to get used to counting as well as the concepts of "up" and "down".
▸ **Snap** Offers a lively way to speed up observational skills and to learn

about matching. It is a good idea to adjust the speed of play depending on the mix of ages.

ARTS AND CRAFTS

Children are much more dextrous at this age and many develop a natural enjoyment for drawing, sticking, and other messy delights. All kinds of household items from cardboard boxes to string, pasta shapes, buttons, and pulses offer scope for making things (but do be careful that your toddler doesn't put anything in her mouth). Activities that she needs your help with include:

▸ **Making simple hand puppets** – then acting out a story.
▸ **Simple science** – such as creating a worm farm or growing seeds.
▸ **Cutting and sticking.**
▸ **Cooking together and measuring.**
▸ **Creating a treasure hunt** for playing at "pirates".
▸ **Making a scrapbook.**

OUTDOOR GAMES

All children benefit from playing outside and will enjoy activities such as flying kites, cycling, going to the playground, or just walking in the park with you.

MULTI-TALENTED *Children aged 3–4 will be much more capable in all areas of play, and they will love to entertain and show others – especially their parents – what they have learned.*

What toddlers want and need

Thankfully, year 3–4 can sometimes feel like the calm after the storm for parents. Your toddler will still be having tantrums and testing boundaries, but with her newfound understanding of what's right and what's not, she will be keen to do things correctly in order to win your approval.

"Rebecca is developing a very loving nature and shows great concern if anyone is upset."

Fiona, aged 31

Your child enjoys more structured play and activities now and will be much more achievement-orientated because she craves your approval. Your positive regard will, in turn, help her to develop self-esteem.

Tuning in to others

Now that your child can empathize with others, she will also start to develop her ability to understand that someone else may see things differently to her. This is an important and necessary part of learning to develop friendships and later social relationships. Psychologists call it "theory of mind". It is the skill that enables us to learn to empathize with, understand, and predict the behaviour of others.

Your child starts to understand that she is a separate person with separate thoughts when she develops the ability to share attention with another person; for example, when she understands that someone else is sharing her interest by looking in the same direction and pointing (see page 217). This leads to her developing a more sophisticated understanding of the mental state (thoughts and feelings) of others, which coincides with her becoming more concerned with the feelings of others and more aware of her own behaviour.

She may begin to ask lots of "Why?" questions as she tries to make sense of the world. During year 3–4, she will progress from being able to hold two different perspectives, but only one at a time, to being able to hold in mind two (or more) perspectives simultaneously. This skill is encouraged each time you help your child to share with others and explain

AN AWARENESS OF OTHERS *Your child will now understand how his behaviour affects the people around him, and he will generally be more settled in the company of others.*

why people act or feel a certain way. Your child will become much more aware and observant of how other people behave at this age. Help her to learn by giving clear and concise answers when she asks "Why?" questions about other people's needs and feelings.

A sense of identity

Your child's sense of identity began to develop during her first year, when she recognized, for example, that her hand belonged to her. Gradually, through her daily experiences and interaction with other people, she is increasing her sense of self.

By the age of 3–4, she knows:

■ The difference between her physical self ("I am brown-haired, I am dark-skinned, and I have brown eyes"), and...

■ Her psychological self ("I am funny/clever/cheeky").

■ How she relates to other people and what she can do ("I am my mother's daughter and I can run fast").

Your child is unlikely to describe herself in terms of her personality at this age, but she is starting to learn that there is a difference between her private self and herself as others see her: her public self. She is too young to hold beliefs or personal ideals about self-image or identity. Views about how she should ideally behave or act will develop later, when she becomes

Your toddler's view of the world

Here's an insight into what your toddler might be thinking...

▶ "I am not a boy! I am a girl, and sometimes I am a fairytale princess."

▶ "I try to be good because that makes Mummy and Daddy happy and I get an extra story at bedtime."

▶ "When Mummy and Daddy go to work I go to Granny's. I love my Granny and I dress up in her party dress and hat. I know Mummy will come and get me after I've had my tea. They say they will come at 7 o'clock, but I can't tell the time."

▶ "Sometimes I see monsters in my bedroom, but they go away when Mummy puts the light on. Daddy says they are called 'shadows'."

▶ "I have a friend called 'Tina' who goes everywhere with me. We have pretend adventures and then she is a princess, too. Sometimes Mummy and Daddy talk to her, and I tell them Tina did things which I actually did so I don't get in trouble."

▶ "Sometimes I clean my teeth if Mummy's with me, but I only like the toothpaste, really."

▶ "I like dressing myself now. I use the big toilet now, too."

an adolescent. At this age self-identity is developed in the following ways:

Other people's reactions Your reaction to your child tells her what your expectations are of her behaviour, her achievements, and her beliefs. You are the mirror through which your child views herself. The more judgemental you are towards her, the harsher she will be on herself.

Comparing self with others Comparing who we are and what we have with others begins at quite a young age. Children tend to make comparisons based on physical attributes and belongings. They can be quite jealous of others (and harsh on themselves). Your child needs you to help keep comparisons in perspective and teach her the qualities that you and others value.

Imitation Children naturally identify with significant others in their life and use them as role models. Role-play is an important part of development at this age, although encouraging your child to have confidence in her views and choices can help her to begin to think for herself and not always "follow the pack".

SELF-AWARENESS

She now recognizes herself as a complete individual and begins to understand that she – and her behaviour – is sometimes judged by others, especially you.

Development of self-esteem

Self-esteem is drawn from a sense of "fitting in" and understanding society's rules and expectations, and is linked to a sense of self-awareness of gender and personal expectations of life. People with high self-esteem tend not to reflect everything that happens back on themselves. They do not consider external events to be their "fault" and have some belief in their ability to influence or control the outcome of events.

If you can foster these skills in your child from a young age, she is more likely to grow up with a strong sense of self-esteem. Children with high self-esteem have high expectations of themselves and are therefore more likely to achieve more highly; this in turn feeds self-esteem. You can foster self-esteem by encouraging your child to make her own decisions, praising when praise is due, and ensuring you allow her to make things up to you if you have needed to criticize her behaviour.

PLAYFUL BEHAVIOUR
Cheekiness and developing humour are a positive and essential part of your child's individuality. Don't confuse this with "naughtiness".

Managing behaviour

In many ways the task of helping your toddler to manage her behaviour should become easier during year 3–4. Now that she has more ability to understand and reason, you will be able to explain, rather than simply state, that she should or shouldn't behave in a certain way.

Your toddler wants to please you and enjoys being rewarded, so she has more incentive to conform to your needs. The corollary of this is that she can now ask "Why?" – often repeatedly – when you ask her to do something. She may also have very strong opinions as to why she would rather not do as you say – and can be very fast on her feet if she chooses to "go" rather than "come" when you call.

You will know and love your child's unique personality and she will know yours, too. The techniques outlined in previous chapters remain the bedrock of behaviour management during these months, with one addition. Now that your toddler is older she is more able to reason and remember, and will start to understand *why* her behaviour has consequences – both good and bad (see box, opposite).

This chapter outlines effective ways to offer rewards and incentives to your child for "good" behaviour – as well as the consequences of constant or extreme disruption. The main principle of behaviour management at this age is to put space between your child and her inappropriate behaviour to give her time for reflection and "cooling down". The aim is not to label your child as "naughty" when she behaves badly, so much as to help her to see that she could have chosen to respond differently – so she learns that different behaviour can achieve different outcomes.

Fear and phobias

You are likely to notice that your child is becoming more fearful. This tendency is linked to the development of her imagination (see page 246) and is a normal stage in her development. The level of fears and phobias experienced by young children usually peaks between the ages of 3–6.

Her world can be disrupted by fears relating to:

■ Fantasy creatures, such as monsters or ghosts.

■ Real threats, such as dogs or intruders.

■ Natural disasters, such as floods or earthquakes.

■ Separation anxiety (see page 91) – this can peak again in early childhood and children may have fears related to the death or loss of a parent.

By the time your child is three or four, she will be exposed to things that might trigger fears more often. Although her reasoning ability and memory are developing fast, she does not yet have enough life experience to distinguish between real and imaginary fears. The messages from her brain may tell her there is something to be afraid of, but she does not have the ability to consider the probability of whether that fear is real or imaginary. The distinction between reality and fantasy remains blurred.

Managing your child's fears

Childhood fears can be overwhelming in their magnitude and often the only person who can truly help them disappear will be a parent or other adult carer. Offer reassurance calmly, but without buying into the fear.

Lawrence Kohlberg

Lawrence Kohlberg (1927–1987), an American psychologist, showed that young children are capable of feeling shame and guilt. He devised five stages of moral reasoning that demonstrate how children's development progresses.

Stages 1 and 2 are usually evident in very young children. Stages 3 and 4 are more likely to develop during adolescence. Not everyone develops the traits listed at level 5.

▶ **Stage 1** A child's behaviour is governed by adults who tell her what is "right" and what is "wrong". She has no ability to consider the needs and feelings of others, so actions are determined by her own needs and feelings or by what adults say is the right thing to do.

▶ **Stage 2** She becomes more aware of others' feelings and needs, but this influences behaviour only when it links with her own needs and wants.

▶ **Stage 3** She knows what it means to be "good" and becomes more concerned with how others view her. She feels guilt or shame if she does something that others might disapprove of.

▶ **Stage 4** She develops an understanding that rules and laws govern society's behaviour. How she acts depends upon how her views fit in with these common goals.

▶ **Stage 5** She understands human rights and social welfare and uses ethical judgement and behaviour.

Your own anxiety can trigger your toddler's anxiety because she will suddenly feel vulnerable, with no-one to teach her the situation is safe and okay. At this young age, you are the rock that keeps her safe from harm. If you have beliefs that the world is unsafe, or that people are out to get you, you are likely to pass your beliefs on to your toddler and she will become more susceptible to anxiety.

Top tips for managing your child's fears:

■ Calming her fears, for example by checking that there is no "monster" under the bed, can help her feel safe. Be creative – perhaps give her a special "magic monster zapper" to reassure her she is in control, and let her keep it close by to help her curb her fears.

■ Be aware that your child's imagination will distort all kinds of sounds and images. Evening light on a large cobweb, the pattern on a curtain or wallpaper, extreme weather: all can fire up your child's imagination.

■ Never be tempted to threaten your child with imaginary creatures if she misbehaves. Telling her that "the plug hole monster will get you" if she doesn't get out of the bath may alarm her into submission, but could haunt

"Jamie feared 'the monster' who lived next door. I soon worked out it was the decorative gargoyle my neighbour had in his garden." Philip, aged 41

her dreams later – and may well come back to haunt you, too, next time you need to get her into the bath!

■ No matter what your own beliefs about the world's dangers – from war and disaster, to paranormal experiences, death, or even spiders – try not to show your child your anxieties.

■ Aim to normalize fears when they occur. For example, explain to your toddler that it is normal to feel "fizzy in the tummy" before doing something new, but that the feeling will pass once it is over.

Adjusting to new experiences

Fears may arise at any point, but are especially likely during new stages in a child's life; for example, when acquiring a new skill (such as swimming) or making a big change (such as starting school or moving house).

REASSURING YOUR CHILD *No matter how bizarre your child's fear may seem, it is important not to belittle him or dismiss the way he is feeling. Aim to normalize the situation rather than magnify it.*

"My fear of the dentist stems back to my own childhood and I worry that I may pass my nervousness on to my children."

Sara, aged 38

If you allow your child to give into her fear, it will grow stronger and she will feel even more afraid. The answer is to continue with the activity that is causing her anxiety, but at a consistent pace and with gentle reassurance. Your child needs to know that she has a choice in the matter, and that you will not allow her to come to any harm.

The common approach used to be to encourage children to confront their fears by exposing them to the fear head on. This is now felt to be unethical and frightening for children. Exposing your child to high levels of emotion when she doesn't have the reasoning capacity to make sense of what is happening, or why you are not protecting her, could just be severely traumatic. The advisable alternative approach is gradual exposure to the fear, with support. Think of it as the difference between teaching your child to swim by throwing her into the deep end of the pool, or starting her in the shallow end and progressing gradually from paddling to swimming as she increases in confidence. Only when a child becomes happy at the lowest fear stage do you move up to the next one. The advantage of this technique is that it enables a child to learn a strategy for managing and overcoming other fears, too.

Coping with nightmares

Nightmares differ from night terrors (see page 205) in that your child may remember what she has dreamt. They usually occur in the second half of the night when dreaming is at its most intense and are usually very short, because the child wakes up. Your child is seeing and experiencing new things on a daily basis and her imagination is becoming far more active. She can't always tell the difference between fantasy and reality, especially

Real life

We had recently moved house and our youngest child, Karen, was scared of her new bedroom. The combination of a new environment and having a room to herself was proving too much. We considered asking her older sister to share with her, but that seemed unfair and was giving in to the fear. Instead, we tried to help Karen to get used to her room by having a bedroom "picnic party" and involving her in choosing how to decorate it. She got used to the new situation within a couple of weeks and now loves her room.

during the night. Bad dreams and nightmares may be triggered by something she thought was strange or scary during the day; or by an event that has upset her equilibrium, such as a house move, the arrival of a new sibling, or starting pre-school. You may also notice that bad dreams are more likely to occur if your toddler has had a big tantrum during the day. The following example shows how daytime experiences can affect a child.

Tyler was entranced by his auntie's caged parrot and, in spite of being warned not to, pushed his finger through the bars to try to touch it. Of course the parrot tried to peck his finger. When he shouted, it flapped its wings and cawed. For the next two nights, Tyler woke up screaming, terrified by dreams of an enormous flapping bird. Each time he woke, his parents let him sob and chat. They then gave him a cuddle and reassured him they were only in the next room and that he really was quite safe – and that the parrot was safely asleep at Auntie Elaine's house.

A toddler who wakes up and is still distressed by images from her dream may want to talk about it, even though she doesn't yet have the vocabulary to describe what she experienced. Let her chat if she wants to, and explain to her what she is feeling, but don't lead the conversation or deny her fears. Acknowledge that she is afraid, but offer her reassurance that it was not real. This will help her start to learn the difference between fantasy and reality. Children continue to believe in monsters until they are older, so reassuring calmly, and with imagination, is the best method at this age. (For example, "Daddy is using his magic powers to put a monster-dissolving shield around our house!")

Once she has shown signs of calming down, try to settle her in her own bed. Removing her from the room will reinforce the fear she associates with being in her own bed and risks setting up a pattern of behaviour where "nightmares" are rewarded by sleeping with Mum and Dad. As children grow older and begin to learn the difference between reality and fantasy, they will become less disturbed by nightmares, but they may recur at times of stress. Whatever your child's age, offer reassurance.

NIGHT-TIME FEARS
Nightmares are understandably distressing, but can be dealt with quickly if they're acknowledged and followed up with some love and comfort.

Behaviour and consequences

The previous chapters have explained the principles of "praise good behaviour; ignore bad behaviour". This chapter introduces "time out" as a more extreme form of "ignoring". It should only be used occasionally, but can be extremely effective. Remember, also, to keep an eye on the A,B,C, of your child's behaviour (see page 193). Look at **A**: what was happening immediately before the bad behaviour struck. Can you alter something at that point, rather than having to focus on the **B**ehaviour and the **C**onsequence every time?

When your child behaves in a certain way, you will either do something or give her something to reinforce the behaviour; or you will stop doing something or take something away that will decrease her behaviour. The ideal is to reward and reinforce good behaviour and to stop rewarding bad behaviour. Under pressure, it is easy inadvertently to do this the other way around. The difficulty is that bad behaviour often triggers your attention, which has the effect of reinforcing and encouraging the behaviour. For example, a tantrum will get your attention; or a child hitting a sibling who picks up her toy may mean that the hurt sibling is taken away, leaving the misbehaving one rewarded by not having to share.

The strategies to focus on for this age group are positive reinforcement (rewarding and praising what you want to see more of) and negative punishment (ignoring, removing attention, and taking away favoured things, as a consequence of the behaviour you don't want to see).

Positive reinforcement Giving something positive to your child means the behaviour – good or bad – will increase. (Selma's Mum is on the phone, so Selma throws her drink. Mum's focus switches to her, so Selma is more likely to do it again. By ignoring Selma, she will learn not to do this again.)

Negative reinforcement Taking away something negative leads to an increase in the behaviour. (Juan is waiting to leave the table. He says,

Real life

I can remember being smacked when we were children. Everyone was smacked in those days; it's not that our mother was being deliberately cruel. However, I can also remember the day it stopped. My brother must have been nearly four years old when he took to hitting back. Mum has said since that she realized at that moment that it was pointless. We have my brother to thank for discovering that talking was the better way forward. I have never needed to lay a hand on my children (although I have been tempted!). My brother feels even more strongly that it is never an acceptable way for an adult to treat a child.

"Most children become outwardly immune to smacking. It does not educate or modify the behaviour: all it does is increase the level of stress hormones and send the message that violence is acceptable."

"Down please." Mummy lifts him down and praises him for asking nicely. By removing the wait and Juan's frustration she has reinforced the effect of asking nicely and has made it more likely that he will ask again in future.)

Positive punishment Experiencing something unpleasant leads to a decrease in the behaviour. These experiences may include lessons that children tend to learn for themselves, even if the experience itself is not positive. (Mummy tells Tilly not to touch the barbeque because it is "hot" and "ouch". Tilly touches it anyway, and burns her hand. The painful blisters serve as a positive reminder for Tilly, who is very unlikely to touch the barbeque again in the future.)

Negative punishment Removing something positive reduces the behaviour. (Louis is playing *Snap*, but screams when he loses and tears up a card. Louis is removed from the game and the others continue without him.)

The problem with smacking

Smacking and other forms of physical abuse are very problematic as a means of behaviour control because they are not effective and they also inflict pain. Smacking tends to set up ever-escalating patterns of punishment, which lead potentially to very negative and damaging ways of adult and child interaction. Smacking represents adult frustration and most parents feel guilty afterwards. Smacking your child also sends her the message that hitting when angry is okay, and so your child will then copy you and smack, too. The message is further confused if the parent combines hitting with telling a child that she is loved.

Behaviour techniques for 3-4-year-olds

Up until now the main focus has been on distraction techniques and removing your child from a potentially volatile situation. Children from age three and upwards are better able to understand that their behaviour

ATTENTION-SEEKING
Attention positively reinforces both desirable and unwanted behaviour. Try to reinforce the desirable and ignore the unwanted.

Warnings and countdowns

Your toddler needs time to remember that there are consequences for unwanted behaviour and to make a choice about her next action. Warnings allow her to have some control over her behaviour and to make amends. For example, tell her, "I am going to count to three, and then I want you to get into bed... 1, 2, 3." Once she becomes familiar with warnings, and especially if you use them consistently, they often become sufficient in themselves to manage her behaviour, especially as she starts to develop moral reasoning skills.

will have consequences (whether good or bad). You can therefore use her awareness of those consequences to help manage her behaviour. Toddlers still have an under-developed idea of time at this age and so any consequences will need to be made clear, consistent, and immediate, otherwise they will lose their impact. There is no need for lots of words or explanations at this age. You are the adult and if you say "No" then your child needs to learn to respect that you mean it. Parents can struggle with this, as they often feel uncomfortable being so direct and bold with their child. However, clarity doesn't need to mean coldness.

Try to avoid *asking* your toddler to do something at this age as that may lead to another tussle if she refuses. Simply make a request in a positive and directive fashion and add a time limit: for example, say, "Lucy, go and kiss Grandad goodnight and then off you go to bed."

Why discipline and control are important

Behaviour management is not just for the convenience of parents; learning self-control is vital for your child's social development and personal safety. It is the first step towards teaching children about wider responsibilities and begins their moral development. Children need to learn that what you say goes, in order to keep safe and learn about danger.

Self-control is important for a contented home and social life, too, as a "difficult" child is more likely to be socially isolated or labelled, which may lead to problems in coping in the playground and a higher risk of being rejected by peers. Knowing when to be compliant and when to listen will improve your child's social skills and her ability to concentrate, as well as her self-control. This will give her a better chance of settling at school.

Positive consequences

Rewards for good behaviour do not need to be elaborate. Giving your child a cuddle, praising her, playing a game that she likes, letting her choose a book to read, or collecting beads or stickers (see page 271) is often enough. The most effective method is to reward frequently, but not necessarily for everything or every time. For example, if you are having difficulty with a particular issue, such as getting your child to sit in her car seat, give her rewards more frequently initially, and then start to phase them out as she learns and adjusts her behaviour.

Negative consequences

Introducing negative consequences for unwanted behaviour serves two main purposes. One is to create a negative association between the behaviour and its effect (for example, by removing your attention or a favourite toy). The other is to put some distance between your child and her behaviour (for example by ignoring, or using "time out"). A negative consequence does not mean that you should shout or smack, which would

SIMPLE REWARDS *Allowing your child to help with a task can be a reward for good behaviour. Being able to do anything with Mummy or Daddy will still be a big incentive at this age.*

> "'Time out' allows a cooling-off period where there is a brief separation from the difficult situation and no physical contact."

be counter-productive (see page 267). In the case of a young child, any negative consequence should be limited to a short length of time – no longer than 3–4 minutes.

The use of "time out"

"Time out" is the immediate removal of your child from a situation where she is being too disruptive or dangerous and it should only be used as a last resort. It is an extension of the ignoring procedures described earlier (see page 197) and should be used only when all other methods have failed, otherwise it will lose its effectiveness.

The basic rules of using and applying "time out" are:

■ Tell your child she is going to spend some time in "time out", now.

■ Lead her to her bedroom or another safe area (carry her there if necessary), and close the door.

■ Tell her you are going to hold the door shut for three minutes (one minute for each year of her life – no more and no less), and in that time you want her to calm down and be ready to say sorry. By holding the door she knows you are there and is aware she has not been locked in.

■ Ignore her behaviour, what she says, and everything she does for the next three minutes. Remember that she needs to realize that she is on her own and that you disapprove of her behaviour.

■ When the time is up, crouch down and look your child in the eye. Explain to her clearly and firmly why she was in "time out".

The naughty step

There has been widespread use of a variation of "time out" in recent years called "the naughty step". If the procedure is followed as for "time out", above, this too can work.

Beware, however, that in calling it the "naughty" step, you are focusing on the behaviour rather than the gap between the unwanted behaviour and the positive outcome. You are also very dependent upon the location of the step so a portable mat may be more effective. Avoid things becoming physical if you have to resort to holding your child down on the step. "Time out" should ideally be applicable anywhere it is needed, from your home to the home of a friend, to a doctor's surgery or in a supermarket. Remember, you can use "time out" when your child is in the same room as you, but do not make any eye contact or talk to him.

- Ask her to apologize to whoever deserves the apology.
- If she is not ready to calm down or apologize, repeat the process, but don't do it with anger or vindictiveness. Remember that the reason for using this technique is so that your child learns that her bad behaviour has negative consequences.
- Then follow up with a cuddle to show her that you have all moved on.

The amazing power of stickers

By the age of 3–4 your toddler will probably be able to understand a sticker chart – one of the clearest ways to introduce incentives, rewards, and consequences "on the spot" and on the move. There are different types, depending on whether you want to improve a specific behaviour, such as "Sit nicely at the table", "Stay in bed quietly", or for more general behaviour-shaping, such as curbing tantrums for a specific period of time.

A sticker chart has four very simple functions – it shows your child:

- What you want her to do.
- How you want her to behave.
- How long you want her to behave for.
- How she will be rewarded.

Children love stickers and find it easy to understand how well or badly they are doing by looking at their chart. They are a valuable way for both parent and child to see the pathway of progress and success, as well as identifying weak spots and setbacks. Collecting coloured balls or large beads can be an effective alternative to using stickers.

A sticker chart is something you create with your child. If you involve her in the process, she will consider the chart is "hers" and will care more about winning her stickers. First, decide how you are going to use the chart. Is it for improving her sleep patterns? Is it to maintain good behaviour on a long journey? Don't try to use one chart for more than one purpose at a time. The time frame for measuring behaviour needs to be short and fixed. Award a sticker every 5–10 minutes during the course of an hour as a reward for good behaviour (no sticker for bad behaviour). There should be the promise of a tangible reward at the end of the time frame if at least 75 per cent of the stickers have been earned. (You may decide that 50 per cent deserves a reward if the improvement has been significant.) You must keep to your promise if it is to work.

"The use of warnings is important as children get older as it gives them a chance to show self-control and choose to avoid the consequence."

FIRST DAY *Incredibly, your child will be ready to start school soon after her fourth birthday. This is a major milestone for both of you, but try not to let your anxieties show.*

Your toddler's wider world

Time flies when your child is a toddler and before you know it you will be planning for her first day at school. If she has been getting used to spending time with other children, you may also notice an increasing hunger to try new things or a need to be constantly stimulated by new challenges.

Toddlers on the verge of starting school can often be quite a handful because they are growing up so fast. Your child may seem clearly ready for the next step in her life. Not all schools share the same criteria for deciding when a child might be ready for school but, in general, children will start soon after their fourth birthday.

Although each school may look for different skills and levels of ability, one thing remains constant: your child needs to have competent social skills for her age, be able to sit and pay attention, be able to listen and follow instructions, and be able to share attention with other children. Generally speaking, you are likely to have been introducing these skills at home – every time she sits to have a meal, each time she listens to a story, whenever she plays with another child, and so on.

Easy first steps from home to school:

■ Visit the school with your toddler before her first day so that she knows what to expect in advance, and for your own peace of mind. The school environment will be quite different to home, although some elements will be similar to nursery and play school.

■ Use pretend play to get her used to what might happen in a classroom or in a playtime situation, and read "going to school" books together.

■ Help your child to build her confidence by encouraging her to try new activities and not give up.

■ Help her to be more independent by choosing clothes she can manage unassisted. Opt for Velcro fastenings rather than laces on her shoes.

■ Praise her ability to manage her feelings and develop self-control.

■ Encourage her to talk and to ask questions that develop empathy
with other children. ("What's wrong with Zak? Why is he sad?")
■ Arrange for your child to attend for half days only, initially.
■ Make a "going to school" scrapbook.

Your feelings and attitude

Your child's first day at school is a day that you are likely to remember for
the rest of your life. She will head off with excitement, and probably some
fear – and so will you! The impact of waving goodbye on that first day can
be quite profound for some parents. If you find yourself feeling emotional,
try to manage your feelings so that your toddler does not pick up on your
mood and does not need to worry about you.

Even if you hated school yourself, stay positive, so that your past
experiences don't impact on how you talk about your child's school or her
teachers. If you can avoid discussing any concerns you may have in front
of your child, you will avoid causing her unnecessary worry. Make time to
visit the school, get to know the teachers and other parents – most of all,
take time to share your child's excitement.

Dr Benjamin Spock

The author of the world-famous
*Common Sense Book of Baby and
Child Care*, Dr Benjamin Spock
(1903–1998), was probably the most
influential paediatrician of the 20th
century and one of the first to
propose a move towards child-
centred parenting.

He had a great interest in family
dynamics and children's needs, and
spent six years studying psycho-
analysis, which gave him a unique
perspective on childcare and
parenting. The standard advice at the
time was that picking up infants
when they cried would spoil them.
Spock's view was that cuddling
babies and showing them affection
would make them happier and more
secure. Instead of recommending
regimes for everything from
discipline to toilet training, Spock
urged parents to take a flexible
approach and to see their children as
individuals. He assured them that
they were all childcare experts.

He introduced the idea that
parenting was allowed to be fun,
and that mothers and fathers could
actually enjoy their children.

His ideas were revolutionary at
the time, and were in stark contrast
to the general advice of doctors and
other childcare professionals of the
day. Some argue that he was the
father of the permissive society. In
his lifetime, Spock's book sold more
than 50 million copies and was
translated into 39 languages.

Keeping your child safe

Now your toddler is on the move and can speak for herself, she is more independent and potentially more vulnerable. Begin to teach her about safety issues in the home and elsewhere, but emphasize the need for awareness rather than increasing fears.

All parents worry about their child's safety. It is a natural instinct and a healthy one. However, as your child gets older, she will be safer if you introduce her to dangers and teach her how to avoid them than if you try to protect her from any exposure at all. Toddlers will not fully understand the concept of danger yet because they have not encountered very much. Keep your explanations about potential threats as simple and unemotional as possible. Explain to her that the word "danger" means that something is especially threatening and could cause her "big hurt". As a general rule, think about your home and everyday environment from your child's point of view. If something looks loose, frayed, sharp, poisonous, or hazardous the chances are your toddler will find it at some point. Water, electricity, and roads are especially dangerous. Take care to lock or tidy away anything that might pose a danger and "think toddler" at all times.

ON THE MOVE

We live in a world where vehicles move faster and are quieter than ever before. It is therefore essential that your toddler understands that roads and vehicles are dangerous. She must always "stop, look, and listen" and respect that if you say "stop and wait", it is an instruction that must be obeyed. No matter how pushed you are for time, make sure that your toddler is fully belted up in her car seat or buggy before you leave the house. Explain to her that it is to stop her getting hurt. Encourage her to look left and right before crossing the road, and get her used to pushing the buttons at

INTERNET SAFETY *Choose from the wide range of products that make the Internet safe and protect children from disturbing sites and images.*

"Be prepared for accidents. Stay calm, make sure you have a well-stocked first-aid kit, and keep the phone numbers for your doctor and the emergency unit keyed into your phone."

pedestrian crossings. Ask her to tell you when she thinks it is safe to cross and praise her when she gets it right.

Children on tricycles need to wear helmets and they are so close to the ground that they are invisible to motorists. Allow them to pedal in an enclosed park or other space and never on, or near, a main road.

STRANGER DANGER

It is a sad fact of life that there is a small percentage of people in our society who pose a threat to children. Statistically the threat is extremely small, but emotionally it is likely to be a major concern.

To keep your child completely safe you would need to be with her every minute of the day. This will become increasingly impossible as she gets older and is not a healthy way forward if she is to become independent.

Teaching her to be wary of strangers without being scared of new people is a fine balance, but the traditional rules still apply. "Never accept sweets or other gifts from someone you don't know." "Don't get into a car without me." "If someone scares you, it's okay to tell."

TODDLER-PROOFING – AT HOME AND AWAY

It takes planning to keep your home a safe place for your young child.

▶ **DO** tell her that lots of things can be hot or dangerous, even if they look safe.

▶ **DO** put safety catches on cupboards and doors.

▶ **DO** add childproof covers to electrical sockets and tuck away any electrical wires.

▶ **DO** put child-proof gates at the top and bottom of stairs.

▶ **DO** keep household cleaners, medicines, paints, and other poisons well out of your child's reach.

▶ **DO** clear away uneaten pet food and other foodstuffs.

▶ **DO** keep your floors clean and free of dust and debris.

▶ **DO** turn saucepan handles away from the reach of small fingers.

▶ **DO** keep your child away from hot ovens and hotplates.

▶ **DON'T** leave hard foodstuffs and small items such as nuts, buttons, pens, matches, keys, and lighters in easy reach.

▶ **DON'T** leave your child unattended in a room where there may be hazards.

▶ **DON'T** carry or place hot foods or liquids near your child.

▶ **DON'T** leave your child on her own in a bath or anywhere near water.

Managing young toddlers in new or unfamiliar situations where there are possible hazards or dangers can be very challenging.

▶ **DO** rehearse your child. Ask her, "What did we say we must be careful about?" Possible answers include: busy roads, cars, the water, strangers, and getting lost.

▶ **DO** tell your child not to say "hello" or go up to people she doesn't know.

▶ **DO** encourage her to "Wait for Mummy or Daddy" or to hold your hand.

▶ **DO** teach her to ask for help if she is lost.

▶ **DON'T** leave her in the car with the engine running.

▶ **DON'T** leave your child unattended in a new situation.

Just for parents

As your child becomes more active it is natural to feel anxious about her safety, as you want to protect her from harm. But she needs to be allowed to explore and make a few mistakes, too. One of the hardest aspects of parenting is learning how and when to "let go" of your child.

Your toddler is now old enough to be left without you to play with another child in the company of a responsible and mature adult. How long this should be for depends on how well you and your toddler know the other parents and children. It is a nice idea to take the time to get to know your hosts well enough to be able to reach mutual agreement and understanding about "house rules" and attitudes, otherwise it can be a shock to your child to discover that "what goes" at home, is different elsewhere. Tell your host if your child has any particular likes, dislikes,

"Your child will have developed distinct personality traits by the ages of 3–4. Helping her to learn how to self-manage when she is feeling excitable or anxious will help her to adjust more easily when she is away from home."

allergies, or personality traits. For example, if she hates sardines and is suddenly confronted with a plateful, she may never want to visit again. Explaining in advance will prevent misunderstandings and help your child to enjoy her play dates and want to go again. This is as much for the ease and the benefit of the other parent as for your own peace of mind.

Find out in advance whether the other parent has any plans to do anything out of the ordinary, such as go to the seaside or a funfair, so that you can prepare your child ahead of time. Your child may become unsettled if she is faced with a new situation and you are not there – and it will also mean you can make sure she takes appropriate clothes.

If you have agreed a delivery and a pick-up time for your child, try to stick to it. Looking after other people's toddlers can be exhausting. It is good practise for future relationships between you all if you arrive when you say you will, and it will be reassuring for your child.

Try not to be over-protective of your child for the sake of it. She is more robust than you may realize, and needs your encouragement to develop a sense of independence. A change of environment and new experiences that don't involve you will be healthy for her. The most important aspect is to make sure she feels safe and is safe wherever she goes. You may want to accompany her on her first play date with a new friend so that she can familiarize herself with the environment in your company, and you can make sure that you are happy for her to play there.

Play dates at home

If children come to play with your toddler, make sure that they feel very welcome, safe, and secure. Talk about their Mummy or Daddy so that they do not feel isolated, and if they appear to be nervous or uncertain make sure they are not forced to do anything they are uncomfortable with.

Managing a visiting toddler

When hosting a play date, bear the following in mind:

▶ Don't be tempted to favour the visitor over your own child, or you may find your child will "play up" or resent her new friend. Don't make comparisons between the children.

▶ Let the children direct their own play unless they come to you for ideas and input.

▶ Minor disagreements will probably resolve themselves without your intervention. However, never leave small children unaccompanied or out of earshot.

▶ Treat your young visitor with respect and never lay a hand on someone else's child.

▶ If the other child is aggressive, explain that it is unacceptable to behave in that way in your house.

▶ Bear in mind that visiting toddlers are away from their environment and may be "playing up" because they are anxious. Make sure they are not intimidated or frightened in any way

and ask what is troubling them.

▶ If the behaviour is severe, get in touch with the parent. Do not apply ignoring techniques or "time out" (see page 270). You should never discipline another person's child. You may risk the child being scared and the anger of the other parent.

▶ If you need to reprimand, make sure you criticize the behaviour and never the child.

▶ Ideally agree strategies with the visiting child's parent beforehand.

Don't be surprised if your child's behaviour changes when she is with her friends. Her friend is her priority. She wants to be liked and accepted by her and to show independence. Small signs of rebellion are a positive sign that she is developing normally. If you apply the normal behaviour guidelines, she will soon understand that normal rules apply.

Now that your child is beginning to understand the difference between right and wrong, she is also developing a sense of social justice. A cry of, "Sam hit me!" has the built-in implication that, "You need to do something about it, Daddy!" This can be a challenge when other people's children are involved (see page 277).

The way your child thinks and assesses situations will affect her moral development: for example, a child who has difficulty regulating her own emotions will tend to blame others for her behaviour and think that aggressive action is justified. Children see things from their own viewpoint. In the scenario above, your child may have left out the fact that, "Sam hit me because I grabbed the toy he was playing with!"

Your child will want to co-operate far more with other children now, but will continue to need your help in learning how to share. Her tendency may still be to fight rather than use words. You can help her to change the way she deals with disagreements by asking her to say in words how she is feeling and what she would like to happen. Try to smooth things over or encourage the children to resolve the crisis themselves, rather than apportion blame (especially if you didn't witness what happened). For example, say, "Do you remember what sharing is? Yes? And do you remember how to take turns? That's good. Let Sam have a go first please, Sally, because he is the guest. Well done." Or, "No more hitting, or I shall have to ask Sam's Daddy to take him home."

Sibling rivalry

Siblings who are close in age are likely to behave in the ways mentioned here. Parents need to stay objective during scraps and to make sure they do not assume that one child is more to blame than the other. Likewise, if your toddler has an older brother or sister, be ready for jealousy to raise its head. Rivalry amongst children, for your affection, for toys or for attention, is completely natural. Remember that rough-and-tumble play may get quite aggressive if an older child finds a younger one very

PLAY DATES *Increasingly, as your child gets older, you will find you have responsibility for looking after his friends, too. Keep play dates to one child at a time at this age, as this will be much more manageable.*

annoying. Avoid casting your older child in the role of "childminder" when you are busy, but do let her know how much you appreciate her ability to manage her own behaviour and tolerate her smaller sibling's behaviour. Encourage each child to appreciate the other and to say "sorry" if they have fallen out.

Role models and parental preferences

As your toddler's sense of identity and self-image develops, he or she may start to treat their same sex parent as a role model (Daddy for little boys and Mummy for little girls). This, in turn, can lead to a child developing a preference for their parent of the opposite sex (Mummy for boys, Daddy for girls) because they are copying Daddy or Mummy's example. Most children show this behaviour to some extent, but the length of time it lasts and how exaggerated the behaviour is can differ greatly between children.

This happens because your child will have a sense of the special relationship between Mummy and Daddy and will want to recreate that for herself. So little girls might want to do everything with Daddy and get very jealous when he wants to spend time with Mummy. Likewise, little boys may tell Daddy to "go away" if he talks to Mummy. He or she might also talk about wanting to marry Mummy or Daddy. This is all perfectly normal and children grow out of it. It is a sign of how much they look up to you and want to be like you. Remember, it is not a rejection of you but an important part of your child's social and emotional development.

How to deal with disputes

A play date can go wrong in an instant. Children are easily bored and may sometimes resort to hitting out of frustration. To address this:
▶ Use questions, such as: "Did Sam hit you for a reason, Sally?"/"Sam, was there a reason why you hit Sally?"/"Are you hurt? No. That's

good. Do you want to keep playing this game or have you both had enough now?"
▶ Make your expectation clear: "You know that hitting is not allowed. I expect you to play together nicely. Can you do that?"
▶ Make the consequence clear:

"If this continues, you will need to stop playing this game and I may need to separate you."

Provided there is no fear or true violence involved, children forgive and forget quite quickly. At this age, the occasional fracas is to be expected.

Dear Tanya...

▶ **Should I allow my three-year-old daughter to watch television and can computer games and Internet activities cause harm?**
Television is a fact of life, and many parents use TV as an electronic "nanny" to get some peace and quiet in order to do other things. While doing that occasionally and for a short period may be convenient, there is no doubt that leaving a young child unaccompanied in front of any sort of screen is never a good idea.

Children have a short attention span and need you to help them understand what they are seeing. If you know that the quality of the programme is good and designed for toddlers, and you or another responsible adult is able to watch with your child and monitor her reactions, then in moderation it is unlikely to do her any harm.

Computers, too, may have their benefits as children as young as three learn quite quickly how to manipulate a mouse and to click on game options. However, remember that neither a TV nor a computer will develop your child's social or reasoning skills and may expose her to images and influences that may be unsuitable, disturbing, or damaging.

▶ **Since our daughter was born, my three-and-a-half-year-old son has reverted to baby language, crawling, and wants to wear a nappy. What is going on?**
This kind of regressive behaviour is not unusual when a first child has to adjust to sharing your time and attention. Having a new sibling is stressful, and your son is crying out for your attention and reassurance that you love him just as much as before. Regression is quite common anyway in children of this age. It is almost as if they feel they are growing up too quickly and want to put the brakes on temporarily. It is a phase and it will pass.

Sensitive reassurance combined with encouragement will help your son to let go and move on. Allow him to remember what it was like to be a baby. Ask him whether he is remembering what it was like and praise him for all his new skills and for being such a clever, grown-up boy. Have special time with him on his own, and consider introducing a new activity to acknowledge that he is now older, such as learning to ride a tricycle. If he seems distressed or angry encourage him to vent his feelings, and empathize with what he is going through.

▶ **How can I help my three-year-old son adjust to moving house?**
Take time to involve your son in the process. It will help him to get used to the idea of moving and make it a positive adventure. Give him the choice concerning which toys to take as he will have favourites. It can also be an idea to pack your son's room last, so that he experiences as little "strangeness" as possible. If the new house is nearby, show him where you will be moving to. If it is further away, show him a picture and point out the window of his new bedroom.

Once you've moved, be aware that it will be things like different shaped shadows on the ceiling and new sounds and smells that he will take time to adjust to. Let him help set up his room so that he feels at home. So long as your son feels safe and secure, he should adjust to his new environment quite quickly.

END OF AN ERA *You can congratulate yourself on getting him through the toddler years. The skills he has learned have nurtured his curiosity and will help him to settle at school and adapt to exciting challenges during the years ahead.*

5 points to remember

1 Your child will start to understand that her actions have consequences, which means she will also begin to understand the difference between "right" and "wrong".

2 You are your child's role model and she looks up to you. Be aware that at this age her judgements and beliefs will be based solely on what you tell her, what she learns and, importantly, what she sees you do.

3 Children with high self-esteem have positive expectations of themselves and therefore achieve more highly; this, in turn, feeds self-esteem.

4 With an increasingly active imagination, your child will probably develop some fears. No matter how absurd these may seem, it is important not to belittle your child or dismiss the way she is feeling. Aim to normalize the situation as much as possible.

5 Accept that your child is growing up and try not to be overprotective. She is more robust than you may realize, and a change of environment and new experiences that don't involve you from time to time will be healthy for her.

HAVING FUN *Let him try different experiences. Achieving new things will help to continue to develop his confidence and self-esteem.*

FAMILY LIFE

Families in transition

By the time your toddler reaches his fourth birthday he will be well aware of his place in the family, and the people within it will make up the largest part of his world. This chapter looks at some of the broader areas that may affect your toddler's upbringing and your parenting choices.

Every family is unique and has evolved as a result of the mix of personal history, cultural influences, temperaments, talents, and the experiences of those people within it. The traditional family model of parents with "2.2 children" is no longer the norm and a family may take several different forms as it alters over time. Families are anything but homogenous. Blended, multi-racial, and single-parent families are all the norm.

Handling change

Transitions occur in all families as individual family members, and the unit as a whole, pass through life stages such as the birth of a baby, the arrival of new siblings, moving house, or a child starting school. These periods, although positive, can be surprisingly challenging and stressful because the role each person holds within the family may change completely when the group as a whole enters a new phase of change. The way that children and parents have learned to get along with each other may change, too.

During periods of change, your toddler may not be able to talk about what is worrying him, but his unhappiness may show in other ways. If you notice any changes in your child's behaviour (such as sleeping difficulties, bedwetting, soiling, or clinginess) offer him reassurance and help him to express his feelings and worries. Your child is going to look to you for comfort when distressed. Try to make space for him even during times when you are facing difficulties yourself. If he is unable to get comfort and reassurance from you, it will make him increasingly anxious. When change happens, keeping routines in place can be hard, and may be at odds with the way your family is evolving. Your toddler will notice, but will adapt more quickly if your feelings and responses towards him are unchanged.

"I missed so much of my children's early years because I was working. It is a joy to spend time with my grandson now."

Niall, aged 66

KEEPING THINGS NORMAL

Whatever the changes a family may be going through, from moving house to changing schools or jobs, a familiar routine will help everyone adjust.

Coping with separation and divorce

No parent wants their relationship to break down but sadly separation and divorce are a fact of life, particularly in western cultures. In 2005, in the UK alone, over 60 per cent of all children affected by divorce were under 11 years old. The process of divorcing is a challenge; it is usually painful and often messy, but it is a transition that many families have to make. You may be separating from someone who isn't your child's birth parent, but nevertheless the change will be extremely unsettling, especially if your child has a strong bond with your partner. Whatever your issues as a couple, remember to keep considering the situation from your child's point of view and keep the lines of communication open for your child. Always think about the long-term effects of your choices and behaviour.

While it is tempting to offer your child false reassurances that "everything will be all right", don't say it will if it won't. Although the short-term will be difficult, research suggests that there are no long-lasting negative implications for the vast majority of children, provided the break-up is managed considerately. The way the parents conduct themselves is the single most important factor affecting a child's ability to adjust in the short- and long-term. The longer and more distressing the disruption, the greater the child's distress and the slower his adjustment.

When you tell your child you are parting, keep things simple. Explain what is going to happen. "Daddy (or Mummy) is not going to live with us any more. He/she will live in X instead. We will still live here and you will see him/her on such and such days. Daddy is still your daddy and Mummy is still your mummy and we both love you very much." You might need to answer tough questions such as, "Do you still love each other?" Children do not need to know all the facts even if you feel a need to talk about them. Keep the adult issues and your child's needs clearly separated. All your toddler wants to know is that you are going to be fine and that you still love him. Be clear about what will be best for him.

Managing emotions

It won't harm your child to see you upset, but it is not good for him to see you totally out of control. If you are feeling vulnerable and can't control your emotions, make use of friends or relatives to offer your child some distracting fun or quiet reassurance. You will need their emotional support, too, during this difficult time. Younger toddlers, aged 2–3, tend to show regressive behaviour whilst slightly older children, aged 3–4, may show self-blame, confusion, irritability, and increased aggression. Even when you are going through a difficult time, it is important to keep behaviour boundaries and consequences in place.

Hearing prolonged arguments or witnessing fighting on a regular basis is not good for children of any age and they may blame themselves for the problems that they are witnessing. The under-fours are unable to see the world from your perspective and think that everything that happens is because of them. They need repeated reassurance from both parents that any upset and distress is not their fault. Although a small child may not have the emotional range or the words to express how he is feeling, there is no doubt that a relationship break-up will rock his world to the core.

Accept that your toddler is going to miss Daddy or Mummy and feel sad. Let him say this and show his feelings without him having to worry about the emotional effect that this may have on you. Don't be tempted to involve your child in your decision to separate or ask him to choose who he should live with. His loyalties will be torn and he is far too young to take on such a large responsibility. It is your decision to take, not his. Avoid using your children as bargaining tools. It is unfair to them and may be damaging to your relationship with them in the longer term.

Once you have navigated your way through the maelstrom that follows a divorce or separation, you may feel ready to begin another serious relationship – and that relationship may also include children. What is most important for your child throughout this time is the knowledge that he is still central to your world.

Your toddler needs both of you

No matter what you are going through, remind yourself that your "ex" is still your child's parent. Your toddler will still expect to be the centre of your world and is ready to switch to playtime any time. Make sure he still has plenty of one-to-one time with each parent and allow him to talk about his Mum or Dad. Do not say derogatory things about your former partner in front of your child – this can have a major impact on his behaviour and be very confusing. Always have in mind the long-term effects of your behaviour.

Step-families

There are many variables involved in creating a blended or step-family. Generally speaking, if the relationship is a happy one and there is adequate time given to the needs and feelings of each of the children within the new extended family, then in time the children will adapt. For a toddler, the important things are to feel loved by you and safe with all the members of his new extended family.

Of course, in practice, there will be many mixed feelings – especially if there are a number of children involved. Meeting new partners is hard for children. Ideally there will have been a period of adjustment prior to the new relationship becoming permanent, but this may not always be the case. A toddler may find it hard to manage his feelings and, as explained earlier (see page 256), often cannot hold two different thoughts in mind at once. Jealousy, envy, fear (of loss or separation), anger (at a parent being replaced), as well as excitement, and happiness can alternate on a minute-by-minute and hour-by-hour basis; he will react to whichever thought or feeling is most prominent in his mind at any given time.

Take things slowly. Your step-children's readiness to accept you will depend on how well they know you already. Be patient and don't be tempted to try to take the place of their parent. Children's feelings cannot

"Our break-up was bitter as my husband was having an affair. It is still so painful to leave Mark with his dad and 'the other woman'. I feel venomous, but I need to hold my tongue for the sake of our son." Teresa, aged 29

be forced or bought and their emotions can often be misunderstood. For example, a toddler's apparent hostility may be his way of showing uncertainty or expressing mixed loyalties. Give him time. He needs to learn he can trust you and that you have his best interests at heart.

As a step-parent you will be tested – but not necessarily any more than you will be as a parent to your own children. If you can offer the same degree of warmth, constancy, and responsive care as would any parent, the rewards of acceptance and even love may follow. It may be harder as a step-parent to give the unconditional love that you show your own child, but compassion, kindness, and the fundamental principles of praise, reward, fairness, and respect should remain the same.

Coping with bereavement

Some children have to face the pain of loss, death, or extreme change very early in life. However, your child's understanding of what dying means in an abstract sense will be separate from the sense of grief and loss that he will experience on losing a beloved relative or a familiar pet. Children do not always understand or have the words to express how they feel; instead they may become clingy, anxious, or frustrated. This is your toddler's way of asking

for help. Don't shy away from the topic of death. Children may find it easier to talk about death than adults do; the world of the imagination is very real for children aged 3–4 so it may not seem unusual to them to imagine they are talking to a person or to a pet that has died.

The way you choose to describe death and whether or not there is an afterlife will depend on your own beliefs, but at some point it is useful to use the words "death" or "died" and to explain that the person is not coming back. Talking in euphemisms isn't helpful for a small child. For example, telling a child that "Granny has gone away" will leave him expecting her to return at some point. He needs to know the reality in order to make sense of it and adjust to it.

If your child has lost someone very close or important to him, it can be helpful to start to build a collection of photos and a book of memories to talk through and look at. Try to keep other things in life constant, such as the family routine, playing games, and so on. It can be tempting to overcompensate for his loss or to become overprotective, but he needs you to treat him like a normal child. How those around him manage their own grief and how available they are for him during this difficult time are the most influential factors in helping him to grow through his loss.

BEING THERE *It can be hard to explain loss, such as the death of a family pet, to a very young child, so your reassurance and cuddles become even more important.*

When a child has special needs

A child with special needs is a child first and foremost. As such he needs everything that has already been talked about in this book: warm, responsive, sensitive parenting with firm and consistent boundaries, as well as plenty of opportunities for play, exploration, and development.

"Special needs" is the term used to cover the requirements of children who need help and support with particular areas of learning and development. Parenting a child with special needs can have its own particular challenges.

Comparing your child's progress with that of other children is never to be recommended; and this is particularly true in the case of children with special needs. While certain patterns of development or behaviour might be expected to be linked to certain conditions, it is not inevitable. Each child is an individual, and therefore may not fit the box society chooses to put him into.

If you have concerns about your child's development, a clear diagnosis can come as a relief. At this early stage the "special needs" label is useful:

Communication challenges

Learning to communicate with a young child with learning difficulties can be particularly challenging. As early as the baby stage, parents may feel there is something "wrong" and this can have a major impact on the early parent/baby relationship. If a baby seems unresponsive, this can set up a vicious cycle where the parents interact less with their baby and he therefore receives even less stimulation. It is particularly hard if the special needs have been difficult to diagnose, in which case the parent may have felt isolated with their concerns in the early days (or may later feel guilty that they didn't notice the delayed development). If you are having difficulties, your health visitor can point you in the right direction to get support.

when identifying symptoms, when contacting parents in similar
circumstances, or when approaching appropriate support and services.
Beyond the functional use, however, labels are probably best avoided.
Just as no two children with brown hair or freckles are the same, no two
children with autism or with Down's syndrome are the same either. The
label should be reserved for the condition and not applied to the child.
Hence, it is usual these days to say, "Tom is a child with autism,"
rather than "Tom is autistic"; the same applies to children with hearing
difficulties or visual impairment. To be able to judge what your child can
and can't do and identify areas where his personal skills can dominate
instead, will help others see past the special needs and see the real person.

Special demands

While there are more similarities than differences between children with
special needs and the average toddler, it does help to be realistic and aware
of where the differences lie: the length of time it takes to do things; the
extra strain on finances for special equipment; the many specialist and
medical appointments; the necessary involvement of specialist agencies
and support, can all seem endless – to the extent that nothing about your
situation feels private or special. Don't be afraid to seek support and
advice from specialist professionals and carers.

You will need to become the expert in your child's condition so
that you can inform others how best to help you to manage and cope.
It can also be beneficial to develop a rapport and a co-operative
relationship with those who are funded to help you. It is in your child's
best interests to work together as a team.

All behaviour is a form of communication, so if your toddler is having
difficulty making himself understood he may act up. The ABC approach
(see page 193) to identify the causes of behaviour can be particularly
useful for parents of children with special needs. It can help to identify the
progression of a behaviour and focus you on its triggers (**A** cause), the way
your child shows the **B**ehaviour – such as a tantrum – and the **C**onsequence,
so it can be a very useful way of changing the outcome.

Looking after a toddler with special needs can be demanding and it is
important to become attuned to your own stress levels and triggers, and to
know when you need to take time out – for yourself. This is a very

"A child's
special needs
are as much
a part of his
individuality
as his finger-
prints."

important aspect of parenting a child with special needs, even though it can be difficult to find carers that you feel confident can manage in your absence. Equally important is to allow yourself the time to relax and enjoy your child. Fun times will help you build a stronger bond.

Developmental delay

Most children follow the same pattern of development and reach milestones in a similar sequence, even if there is a difference in timing. When children are slower to reach milestones or development plateaus across many areas (movement, cognitive skills, language, social, and emotional development) this is known as global developmental delay.

Not all children with developmental delay experience global problems; for some, development may be delayed in only one or two areas – for example, motor or language skills may be affected by certain conditions. There are many different causes linked to developmental delay, but in around 50 per cent of cases it is not possible to identify a cause. Possible contributing factors include genetic conditions (such as Down's syndrome), brain trauma during birth or as a young child, illness, and early environmental experiences.

The diagnosis (to see whether the milestones are achieved within normal age ranges) can take time. Some genetic conditions are more apparent than others and several may be tested for during pregnancy or at birth. If you suspect something is amiss during your child's early months, it is important to raise queries and concerns with your health visitor or GP.

Children who are experiencing developmental delay may need extra support. You may benefit from advice on effective ways to communicate with your child (such as signs or pictures to compliment words to help your child express himself). Managing behaviour may present extra challenges. Support groups can be particularly helpful in combating any sense of isolation that you may feel. Parenting a child with a disability has challenges and extra support is invaluable, so do seek it out.

Autistic Spectrum Disorders (ASD)

Nearly four times more boys than girls are diagnosed with an Autistic Spectrum Disorder (ASD), which may first begin to show in the toddler years. Boys, it seems, are more genetically and developmentally vulnerable

A BEAUTIFUL CHILD

A child with special needs is a child to love, respect, and celebrate as any other. Give her opportunities to succeed from an early age.

than girls. The causes of autism are still not clear, but it is now generally accepted that it stems from the way that the neurons in the brain are connected at an early stage of development. (This suggests that both genetic factors, and brain trauma may be implicated.)

ASD is a generic term for a range of conditions including classical autism and Asperger's syndrome. ASD is not the same as global developmental delay (see page 294). Some children with autism may have an average or above average IQ and may develop language at an appropriate age; others may not develop language skills at all and some will have global developmental delay or severe learning disabilities alongside ASD. It is generally accepted that children who are diagnosed with autism will, to some degree, have difficulties in the following areas:

Relating to other people Children with autism lack the ability to share attention with other people (see page 256) and appear not to understand that someone else can think or feel differently to themselves. This can lead to an apparent lack of empathy, difficulty in relating to other people, or may be seen as aloofness. These children may not want to interact with others apart from to have their own needs met. Their social behaviour may

What you can do

Here are a few ways in which you can help your toddler overcome some of the difficulties he may have:

▶ **Play with him appropriately** – for example, if your two-year-old is finding language skills a challenge, play games and activities appropriate for his own level. Echoing back his early sounds and using word and action games will give meaning to his communication. Find toys appropriate to his developmental stage rather than his chronological age.

▶ **Encourage his social skills** – help your toddler to develop social skills and interact with other people. Some children with developmental disabilities may be less responsive to adults than others. Try to notice your child's communication cues and respond to him sensitively.

▶ **Set clear behaviour boundaries** – use behaviour management strategies that are appropriate to your child's developmental level. For example, if your child is three years

old, but is developmentally on a par with a toddler of 18 months, use ignoring and distraction techniques (see page 85) rather than "time out" (page 270) and start to introduce simple consequences. Behavioural strategies, and the reasons for using them, are important for all ages and developmental levels.

▶ **Promote self-esteem** – find things that your child is good at and is able to do well and encourage him to develop them further.

be inappropriate or unusual. Some children fail to develop language skills, others may echo words but use them inappropriately, or appear to use odd turns of phrase or "set pieces". Some children have difficulties associated with understanding non-verbal language, such as interpreting body language or facial expressions.

Imagination Children who are diagnosed with autism often lack the ability to play imaginatively or to use symbolic play. Play with toys tends to be repetitive (see below) or has to be learned. They may enjoy and crave sensory stimulation – so a child may bang bricks together to make a noise rather than using them to build something. Lack of imagination relates to language development and those children who develop language skills may have a very literal understanding of the words you use. The use of metaphors and sayings, such as "Pull your socks up" or "I'm over the moon", will be taken literally and can be confusing.

Restricted routines and interests Children with autism often have a limited range of interests and may show repetitive behaviour. They may have an almost obsessive fascination with a single topic, and want to talk about it all the time or repeat an action again and again – for example, twirling string. Habits, familiar rituals, and predictability can be very comforting to those with autism; your child may need to have things done in a particular way, and everything put in its place. Change, unscheduled separation, and bereavement can be very hard for these children.

The age at which you first notice your child is having difficulties will depend upon the extent of his problems. For example, some children appear to cope socially until they start school. Depending upon where in the autism spectrum your child falls, he may manage quite well in

Early warning signs

Retrospectively parents can usually identify some differences in the timing or style of their child's social development. For example, learning to point may happen very late or not at all; there may be problems making eye contact, unusual behaviours, delayed language or play skills, a lack of interest in people generally, and extra-sensitivity to noise, textures, movement, light, or change. Early diagnosis and parental support can make a positive difference to a child with autism. Health visitor and GP support is vital, too.

mainstream school, perhaps with some extra support, or he may need specialist provision. However, even the most academically able child with autism will struggle when it comes to interacting with his peers, and will need some help so that he does not become isolated or anxious. (See pages 310–311 for useful organizations.)

Attention Deficit Hyperactivity Disorder (ADHD)

There are approximately six times more boys than girls diagnosed with this condition. A diagnosis under the age of five years old is rare because so many indicators of ADHD are similar to normal toddler behaviour, but it can usually be identified by the age of seven.

The causes of ADHD are not fully understood but are likely to be a combination of genetic and developmental factors, meaning that children with the condition find it hard to control their responses. At home, the ADHD behaviour can be hard to manage and may lead to a worsening in behaviour habits. Children find it difficult to regulate their emotions and are likely to need ongoing support with setting their own behaviour boundaries and problem-solving. At school, children who suffer with ADHD tend to be very impulsive and may have difficulty developing social skills and managing conflict. Children with ADHD may have other difficulties, too, such as behavioural disorders and specific learning difficulties, with reading or maths, for example.

Given all this, positive behaviour reinforcements are really important for a child with ADHD. Cuddle him often. Rewards for good behaviour should be frequent and immediate, routines should be clear and consistent, and the use of consequences is also beneficial in making clear to your child

"My four-year-old, Joe, finds it easier to follow my instructions if I use his name first and make eye contact at his level."

Brenda, aged 43

Identifying key issues for a child with ADHD

A child with ADHD will have three main difficulties:

▸ **Inattention** He will find it difficult to sustain attention for any length of time, be easily bored, lack persistence,

and be easily distracted by what is going on around him.

▸ **Hyperactivity** He will always be on the go, fidget, have lots of energy, and be unable to sit still.

▸ **Impulsiveness** He will show signs of risky behaviour, and say and do things without thinking so can appear to be insensitive to those around him.

what is expected from him. In some cases, medication is recommended for use in conjunction with behavioural strategies – although you are advised to discuss this route with a specialist doctor.

Parents need support, too, as children with ADHD can be a challenge. Any tension in the parent–child relationship can lead to an escalation in the unwanted behaviour, so seek support and take time out for yourself.

Dyslexia, dyspraxia, and other conditions

It is natural for parents to worry if they think that their child's development is much slower than expected in certain areas. However, conditions such as dyslexia (difficulty with letters and reading), dyscalculia (difficulty with numbers and maths), dyspraxia (problems with co-ordination), or specific language problems such as stammering, are very difficult to diagnose during the toddler years, because language skills, reasoning skills, gross, and fine motor skills (see page 48) are not yet fully developed. Not until the age of five or six will it be possible to detect these specific developmental problems accurately.

If your child seems to have continuing difficulties in specific areas after he starts school, speak to his teachers and to your GP about whether an assessment might be needed. In the meantime, bear in mind that it will take time for your child's skills to develop and for him to feel confident in using them. Try not to trigger anxiety by putting him under undue pressure to improve.

Sensory impairment

Children with sensory impairment include those with sight and hearing difficulties. Children with multiple sensory difficulties can have very complex needs and specialist support is vital for both them and their parents. Behaviour difficulties shown by children with sensory problems may be due to a variety of reasons, including personal frustration when trying to make themselves understood, difficulty in understanding what is going on around them, and as a response to parents who find it hard to set and enforce behavioural guidelines.

Whatever your concern, if you believe your child suffers from sensory impairment, talk to your health visitor and your GP who may advise referral to a specialist.

"Meeting other parents with similar difficulties means we can share our ups and downs and pool our experience."

Clement, aged 40

Sight Visual problems can vary from blindness to having a squint or wearing glasses. A child with impaired sight may not be able to pick up on visual clues such as facial expressions, and will need you to be verbally clear and to use noise cues to help him. He may turn his head to hear better rather than look in the direction of a noise. Find ways to interact using other senses (through touch, or using noises to indicate turn-taking).

Reduced vision also impacts on his self-awareness (of his own body, for example) and may delay general development. He will also find it harder than a visually able child to learn by imitation, and his ability to explore and to learn through play will be restricted. Try to adapt his environment to encourage exploration.

Hearing Signs of deafness may first show when your young toddler's babbling comes to an early halt. He stops responding because he cannot hear your verbal feedback. Children are good at compensating for a missing sense (and of course have never known life to be any different), so it is not uncommon for less severe hearing difficulties to be overlooked until your child begins school.

If your child has a hearing difficulty, concentrate on building communication via the other senses instead, such as his vision. Visual props and picture cues can be used to remind him of a routine or to back up your behaviour guidelines.

EXPLORING TOUCH
A child with hearing difficulties will enjoy using other senses in his exploration of the world; and a discreet hearing aid can help him.

A parent's needs

A child with special needs is vulnerable and so should be given every opportunity to develop a strong sense of self and self-esteem. However, families can struggle to cope and there can be tensions that stem from parents feeling anxious or sometimes guilty about their child's difficulties. Don't be afraid to ask for support – you deserve it. It will enable you to relax and enjoy your child, and give him the kind of family environment that will provide the best start and so the best chance in life. See pages 310–311 for details of useful support organizations.

Managing challenging behaviour

Toddlers usually grow out of the habits that make adults feel uncomfortable, although occasionally these may be a sign of deeper distress. This section looks at common types of behaviour that sit on the borderline between acceptable and unwanted toddler behaviour, and suggests coping strategies.

"Make sure your child has plenty of opportunities to be 'good' too, so that he does not become labelled as the 'bad' child."

Throughout this book different behaviour techniques have been recommended for different ages and stages of development. The general principle with toddlers is to reward good behaviour, to ignore unwanted behaviour, and to be consistent. Matching a behaviour strategy to the age of your child, and also to his development stage, is crucial to success.

Any habit that is unwanted by a parent could reasonably be called a "nasty" habit! However, many types of behaviour are not worth negotiating with your child until he is at least three years old and can understand your reasoning. Nose-picking is a useful example. Explain that it is dirty, but do not give it lots of attention or squeal or make it into a game, or praise him for behaving any differently. This strategy applies to most unwanted habits.

Going naked and other natural instincts

Toddlers are very physical. They will happily run around naked rather than be restricted by clothes and enjoy exploring their bodies. Along with the understanding that "my bed is here" and "my potty is there" comes an awareness that "I can poo" and "I can wee".

Both boys and girls are often fascinated by their bodily functions and by their genitals, which they will spend time touching out of interest and because it feels nice. This can often cause parents a great deal of anxiety and embarrassment as they worry about whether it is sexual behaviour, whether it might put their child at risk from predatory adults, and how to curtail or put an end to the behaviour.

First some words of reassurance: your child is not masturbating when he is exploring himself. Even though boys may have occasional erections, this is a purely biological reflex. Toddlers are far too young to have any sexual impulses; nor is there any emotional connection with the sensations they are experiencing other than it is pleasurable.

Under normal circumstances there is no need to worry. Your own level of ease or discomfort with your child's behaviour will depend on how at ease you are personally with physicality, but the usual rules of behaviour apply. Ignore the behaviour and don't be tempted to comment on the size of a boy's penis, or draw attention to a toddler's actions by making a joke of them (and make sure that any siblings don't, either). These are grown-up responses that are inappropriate for a child of this age. Your reactions will be confusing and will inadvertently reinforce the behaviour because you are paying attention to it.

Encouraging positive behaviour

A consistent approach by all carers and in all settings will help your toddler to understand that you mean what you say In time, he will manage his own behaviour more effectively and without your help.

▶ **Stay calm** You are your child's role model and he will copy your reactions and model your behaviour.

▶ **Don't argue** Don't hit. You will reinforce the negative behaviour and send the message that it is reasonable to be aggressive in order to get what you want (see page 267).

▶ **Use distraction** This is the ideal tactic, especially if combined with humour (see page 85).

▶ **Use the ABC technique** (see page 193) to work out what is triggering the behaviour.

▶ **Set boundaries** Decide on your routines and boundaries and stick to them. Familiarity and clarity are very reassuring for toddlers (see page 151).

▶ **Explain the consequences** Children aged three years and older will be able to understand that there will be a negative consequence if they break your rules (see page 268).

▶ Make sure "No" means "No"! (see page 268).

▶ **Give a warning** This allows children the chance to change and avoid being reprimanded (see page 268).

▶ **Use a reward system** Make rewards appropriate to the age and the task (see page 271).

▶ **Give praise.** Remember to praise your child more often than you criticize. You will generally get more of the behaviour that you pay the most attention to (see page 266).

▶ **Use "time out"** This technique (see page 270) is an extreme form of ignoring and must only be used in extreme circumstances for a child aged three or more. It enables both you and him to manage your emotions and calm down.

▶ **Teach him the power of "sorry"** – and move on with love and cuddles.

If you are in a situation where your child's behaviour is inappropriate, avoid focusing on the behaviour directly. Being directly disapproving or obviously cross about genital exploration could trigger the beginnings of personal inhibition and feeling ashamed of his body. Instead, use distraction techniques to encourage interest in something more exciting, such as playing *Pat-a-Cake*, or going for a walk, or say "Show me how you can put your clothes on now."

It is more usual for a toddler to put his hands down his trousers or nappies when he is out and about, rather than to strip off, which he is more likely to do at home – so distraction techniques tend to work best. Give him things to play with, or teach him socially appropriate behaviour (as in the examples above). Alternatively, simply pick your toddler up and sweep him off to a different location. Be reassured that your toddler will grow out of this phase and will benefit from your encouragement to be relaxed about his body.

Head-banging

Watching a baby or toddler bang his head can be extremely distressing, no matter how often you are told that your little one will not do himself any harm. A toddler who frequently bangs his head may feel overwhelmed by his feelings, may be self-soothing, or alternatively, may be looking for a reaction from you. Try to work out which trigger is the cause. If it is a habitual behaviour, you may be able to see the visual cues that develop before he starts to head-bang. Encourage him to find other ways to express his anger and frustration, such as running around to burn off his excess energy.

Head-banging is best ignored, as responding to the behaviour may reinforce it as an effective way to get your attention. Children do have a self-regulatory mechanism that will prevent them from doing serious damage. Use ignoring techniques and, if necessary, the firm hold (see page 200). You can take strength from the knowledge that most children

"Lucy will bang her head mid-tantrum to get our attention – especially if we have said 'No' to something. I find it so upsetting and very hard to ignore." Rick, aged 31

tend to grow out of this behaviour by the age of 2–3 as they learn other ways to soothe themselves. As language develops they will find alternative ways to let you know how they feel.

Toileting problems

By the end of their third year, the majority of children will be partly or wholly potty trained during the day (see page 128), but night-time dryness may take a little longer to achieve. If your toddler has managed to stay dry for several nights in a row, start to put him to bed without wearing a nappy. Do not cut out fluids during the day. Not only are they important for his health, but he also needs his bladder to be full so that he knows when to wee. Sudden spells of bedwetting can indicate your child is upset about something, so enquire sensitively. Ongoing bedwetting in older children can be managed using an enuresis alarm. Give him praise when he gets it right, but make no fuss when there are accidents. Alternating more than one layer of plastic and cotton sheets can save a lot of time if there is an accident in the night. Night-time soiling may take longer to overcome.

NIGHT-TIME DRYNESS *In time, and with gentle encouragement from you, she will learn how to stay dry at night. Don't expect this to happen instantly and avoid pressuring her.*

Changes in your toddler's toilet habits (once he has been toilet trained) can be a sign of physical or emotional difficulties. It is always wise to go to your doctor and ask for your toddler to have a physical check-up, as constipation and other bowel problems can mean a child has difficulties with controlling bowel movements and may be in pain. A medical check-up is needed in order to rule this out.

If your family is going through a period of change and your child is finding this difficult or stressful, his feelings may be reflected in changes in his toileting behaviour. Talk to other people involved with caring for your child, at nursery for example, to try and work out what might be causing difficulties. Don't show your child your concerns; instead, offer him reassurance and return to an earlier stage of toilet training.

If your child seems to be soiling longer than expected, for example, beyond five years of age, seek medical advice. A doctor will check that your toddler's nerves are sending messages appropriately or whether he may need help in learning a new toileting system or routine. Persistent soiling (particularly if he previously had control) may be a sign of tension or difficulties in your child's life. If you are struggling to understand his behaviour or how to manage it, then your GP is the first port of call for advice or referral to a specialist service for help (see pages 310–311).

Some children may smear their poo with their fingers, which can be a sign of distress or indicative of a medical problem. Speak to your doctor if this happens more than once. In a child with special needs, such as developmental delay or autism (see page 294), there are other

> "See all types of your child's behaviour as manageable with thought and, if necessary, with additional support. Try not to let your anxiety inadvertently make the problems worse."

considerations: for example, could he be benefiting from the sensation in some way, or asking for your attention?

Whatever the toileting problem, avoid paying attention to the behaviour and do not make it a negative experience. Even a young child may find bedwetting, soiling, or smearing quite shameful, so avoid reinforcing any negative feelings.

Why problems occur

Severe behaviour problems in young children can be understood in two main ways: as indicative of unclear parenting messages and poor behavioural boundaries, or as an indication of unhappiness or anxiety. Sometimes behaviour problems exist for both these reasons.

Because a child's communication skills are still developing, actions are more effective than words for this age group, so all behaviours need to be considered in the context of what they mean, as well as how to solve them. Most importantly, despite how anxious and frustrated they might also make you feel – the most effective parents are those who are calm, consistent, and clear in their responses.

Recognizing child abuse

The subject of child abuse is a very difficult one to read about and harder still to acknowledge if it occurs within your own family. However, the reality is that in the vast majority of cases, child abuse is carried out by someone who is already known to the abused child.

Toddlers have limited skills of expression and little world experience, so it is not always easy for them to let us know what is causing them distress or concern, or even for them to be aware that there is anything "wrong". Dramatic changes in behaviour that start suddenly may be a clue that something different is going on in your child's life that is causing distress.

One possible cause of this behaviour is abuse, but there are many others. However, it is a sad reality that for a very small minority of children abuse does happen, and so it is important for every parent to be aware of it – and the warning signs (see page 307).

Children's fundamental rights

Every child has basic rights: to develop attachments; to have a permanent home; the right to education; and importantly, the right to remain mentally and physically safe, and as healthy as possible. The Children's Act (1989) states that if children are at risk of "significant harm" there is a legal right to compulsory intervention (led by Child and Family Services) in a child's

Support for abused children

Children who are abused are victims of the mental, emotional, and behavioural problems of the adults abusing them. They are not responsible for what is happening to them, but are often made to feel that they are. They need gentle and compassionate support to process their experiences (via play, talking, or family therapies), often over an extended period. Given time, care, and plenty of specialist support, there is no reason why these children should not grow up to be strong, positive, and non-abusive adults.

life in order to keep the child safe. This concept covers ill treatment, impairment of physical or mental health or development, and includes the four different kinds of abuse: physical abuse, sexual abuse, abuse through neglect, and emotional abuse.

Physical abuse This is a common style of abuse. Approximately one-third of all child abuse is physical: hitting, shaking, throwing, and causing any harm harsh enough to leave a mark is considered physical abuse. Children who demonstrate difficult behaviour or behaviour that challenges parents to their limits are more likely to be physically abused.

Children under five, and those with special needs, are considered most at risk. Parents who suffer from a range of stress factors such as low income, marital conflict, lone parenting, poor social support, or poor mental health, can sometimes be more vulnerable to the tendency to abuse (though this is by no means inevitable).

Be aware also: if a child is thought of as difficult, manipulative, or negative; if the parent has unrealistic developmental expectations; or if a parent is emotionally distant, the risk of physical abuse increases. Self-awareness, a sensitivity to your own stress points, and having a good support network are all useful in ensuring you don't overstep the mark when you are feeling tired, tense, or fed up with your vulnerable toddler. Try to develop social networks that will help you to feel supported to avoid overload and exhaustion.

Sexual abuse Forcing or enticing a young person to watch or take part in sexual activities, whether or not the child is aware of what is happening, is classified as sexual abuse. It includes physical sexual contact as well as non-contact (for example, exposing a child to pornographic images and sex acts between others, or encouraging sexually inappropriate behaviour). The effects are destructive and it is a misuse of adult power.

"Children are vulnerable and need adults to protect their interests. If a child acts or speaks in a way that makes you suspect abuse, it is essential to show that you believe him and will take action to stop it."

Sexual abuse accounts for as much as one-fifth of all child abuse in the UK and with the increasing use of the Internet, children are increasingly vulnerable to exploitation.

Abuse through neglect The persistent failure to meet a child's basic physical, psychological, and emotional needs is likely to lead to the serious deterioration of a child's physical and mental health and development. While this category of abuse is more difficult to assess and measure – it is also more subjective – it nevertheless accounts for nearly one-half of all child abuse cases.

Emotional abuse The persistent, emotional ill-treatment of a child will have long-term, severe, and adverse side-effects. Emotional abuse cannot be seen except through how a child behaves. Giving a child the persistent message that he is unwanted, worthless, unloved, inadequate, and not valued can make him feel deeply insecure, frightened, and in danger. Emotional abuse may also occur alongside with the other types of abuse – sexual abuse, physical abuse, or abuse through neglect – but also occurs on its own. The long-term impact of emotional abuse on a child's self-esteem is seriously damaging.

Warning signs of possible abuse

It is important to emphasize that there are many other reasons why one or more of these signs might appear on its own, either temporarily or over time. However, if all or most of the warning signs seem to be in evidence for much of the time, then it is worth investigating whether there is something amiss with a child's development and treatment:

▶ The child shows sexualized behaviour and play, talks about sex acts, and uses words that are developmentally inappropriate.

▶ The child appears uncared for, dirty, and dishevelled.

▶ The child has unexplained or unusual marks or bruises.

▶ There are sudden changes in a child's behaviour: he starts to destroy things, becomes very clingy, starts soiling, or becomes very afraid of certain places and people.

▶ There are sudden changes in a child's emotional behaviour: for example, he becomes very anxious, scared, or angry.

▶ The child shows persistently aggressive and destructive behaviour.

▶ The child has chronic low self-esteem and a lack of confidence with a tendency to make very negative comments about himself.

Child protection is everyone's responsibility, so if you suspect a child is unsafe then you have a responsibility to report the matter to Child and Family Services for investigation.

Family time

Seeing you relax will allow your children to get to know you as a whole person, rather than simply the person who comes home from work and takes care of his every need. However, in reality, the needs of adults who want to unwind don't always mix smoothly with the needs of toddlers.

There is no reason why there can't be something for everyone on a family holiday. Each parent can take it in turns to have time alone; or you may choose to go away with another family with children so that you can all share responsibilities. Young children are able to cope with cultural activities in short bursts, and anywhere that focuses on sporting events and outdoor activities is bound to have a children's play area, too.

Holidaying with toddlers

Bear in mind that young children do not need expensive holidays in luxury hotels. All they want is your company and to have the freedom to explore and play. Even though you are away from home, your toddler still needs his routine. If you can anchor his days in a familiar pattern of sleep, eat, and play, then he is more likely to adapt to the new places and experiences that he is being exposed to – and less likely to become fretful.

Pay attention to new risks when you are away from home. Don't leave your child unattended; always use a child's car seat and make sure he is safely strapped in; encourage him to be aware of common dangers, and tell him what to do if he is lost. For example, "Never go off with a stranger. Stay where you are and wait for Mummy. I will come and find you."

Special occasions

Whatever the occasion – whether a birthday party, a wedding reception, a religious festival, or simply a family dinner invitation – the idea of attending a smart occasion with your unpredictable toddler can be quite daunting. The answer to preventing any problems and making events stress-free is to plan ahead.

Ideas for managing special events:

■ Give your toddler a choice of two or three toys and books that he can take with him on the day. Having something absorbing and familiar to occupy or distract him will make your life much easier.

■ If your toddler is old enough, explain that you would like him to behave well for the occasion and that, if he does he, will have a special treat.

■ If it is to be a formal occasion, play games of make-believe to help your toddler get used to saying "Hello", "Please", and "Thank you".

■ If you are likely to be away from home beyond his normal bedtime, don't be shy about taking pyjamas and wash things with you. Transporting him home in his pyjamas will reduce the upheaval when you get back.

■ If he plays up on the day, make allowances. Simply remove him from the room and go somewhere quiet. Normal behaviour management rules apply (see page 301); but bear in mind that a new place, new faces, and lots of noise can be overwhelming for a small child. His only form of defence is to challenge you so that he knows you have remembered he is there.

The future

Whatever your hopes, plans, and expectations of parenthood, your experience of being a parent will be different from the one you expected: more joyous, more delightful, more extraordinary – and also more tiring, rewarding, and unpredictable than you would ever have believed possible!

Parenting is an instinctive process that builds upon a number of emotions: love, wonderment, fear, guilt, but, above all, pleasure. My heartfelt wish has been to provide parents with honest and objective advice and choices that put Mum or Dad back where he or she belongs – at the centre of their child's life. Every one of us is responsible for the future care and welfare of our children but, at home, and especially during the toddler years, the most important person in your child's life is you.

"The true measure of a nation's standing is how well it attends to its children... their sense of being loved, valued, and included in the families and societies into which they are born." UNICEF report 2007

Useful addresses

Afasic
A parent-led organization for those
with speech and language
impairment.
Tel: 08453 55 55 77
Web: www.afasic.org.uk

**Attention Deficit Disorder
Information and Support Service
(ADDISS)**
Provides support and information,
for parents and sufferers.
Tel: 020 8952 2800
Web: www.addiss.co.uk

**Association of Breastfeeding
Mothers**
A charity run by mothers,
for all women wishing to
breastfeed.
Tel: 0844 4 122 949
Web: www.abm.me.uk

**Association of Child
Psychotherapists**
Holds a directory of accredited
child psychotherapists.
Tel: 020 8458 1609
Web: www.acp.uk.net

**Australian Breastfeeding
Association**
1818–1811 Malvern Road
East Malvern
Victoria 3145
Provides breastfeeding information
and support.
Tel: (03) 9885 0855
Web: www.breastfeeding.asn.au

**British Association for Adoption &
Fostering**
Provides for children separated
from their families of origin.
Tel: 020 7421 2600
Web: www.baaf.org.uk

**British Association for Counselling
and Psychotherapy**
Provides details of local counsellors
and psychotherapists.
Tel: 0870 443 5252
Web: www.counselling.co.uk

The British Dyslexia Association
Offers support and promotes early
identification in schools.
Tel: 0118 966 8271
Web: www.bdadyslexia.org.uk

British Stammering Association
The national organization for adults
and children who stammer.
Tel: 020 8983 1003
Web: www.stammering.org

**Child Accident Prevention
Foundation of Australia**
Dedicated to preventing
unintentional childhood injuries.
Tel: Regional offices
Web: www.kidsafe.com.au

The Child Bereavement Trust
Support for parents and children
who've suffered a bereavement.
Tel: 0845 357 1000
Web: www.childbereavement.org.uk

Child Support Agency
Is concerned with child support
maintenance.
Tel: 08457 133 133
Web: www.csa.gov.uk

Childcare Access Hotline
Australian telephone service to help
choose childcare.
Tel: 1800 670 305

Contact a Family
Support for parents of children with
special needs and disabilities.
Tel: 0808 808 3555
Text: 0808 808 3556
Web: www.cafamily.org.uk

Council for Disabled Children
Provides information on disabilities
and special educational needs.
Tel: 020 7843 6000
Web: www.ncb.org.uk

Cry-sis
Helpline for parents with crying and
sleepless children.
Tel: 08451 228 669
Web: www.cry-sis.org.uk

Daycare Trust
Provides information to parents,
employers, policy-makers, and
providers.
Tel: 020 7840 3350
Web: www.daycaretrust.org.uk

**Department for Children, Schools
and Families**
Government department committed
to children and young people.
Tel: 0870 000 2288
Web: www.dfes.gov.uk

Disabled Parents Network
For disabled people who are parents
or who hope to become parents.
Tel: 08702 410 450
Web: www.disabledparentsnetwork.
org.uk

Down's Syndrome Association
Helps people with Down's
syndrome to live full lives.
Tel: 0845 230 0372
Web: www.downs-syndrome.org.uk

Dyspraxia Foundation
Increases understanding and offers
help with the condition.
Tel: 01462 454 986
Web: www.dyspraxiafoundation.
org.uk

Eric
Education and resources for
improving childhood continence.
Tel: 0845 370 8008
Web: www.enuresis.org.uk

4Children
The national organization for
out-of-school care.
Tel: 020 7512 2100
Web: www.4children.org.uk

The Family Fund
Provides grants to families with
severely disabled children.
Tel: 0845 130 4542
Web: www.familyfund.org.uk

Family Mediators Association
Supports couples who are

considering separation or divorce.
Tel: 0808 200 0033
Web: www.thefma.co.uk

Gingerbread
Self-help organization for lone-parent families.
Tel: 0800 018 5026
Web: www.gingerbread.org.uk

Grandparents' Association
Information for grandparents.
Tel: 0845 434 9585
Web: www.grandparents-association.org.uk

Home-Start
Provides support and friendship to parents of under-fives.
Tel: 0800 068 6368
Web: www.home-start.org.uk

Karitane
24-hour parent counselling – Australia.
Tel: 1300 227 464
Web: www.karitane.com.au

Kidscape
Aims to keep children safe from bullying, harm or abuse.
Tel: 08451 205 204
Web: www.kidscape.org.uk

Mencap National Centre
For people with learning difficulties, their families and carers.
Tel: 0808 808 1111
Web: www.mencap.org.uk

National Association of Citizens Advice Bureaux
Free advice on issues including work and pregnancy.
Tel: local numbers only
Web: www.citizensadvice.org.uk

The National Autistic Society
Helping those with autism to receive quality services.
Tel: 0845 070 4004
Web: www.nas.org.uk

NCT (National Childbirth Trust)
Offering guidance on pregnancy, birth, and parenting.
Tel: 0870 444 8708
Web: www.nct.org.uk

National Childminding Association of England and Wales
Promotes quality, registered childminding.
Tel: 0800 169 4486
Web: www.ncma.org.uk

National Council of Voluntary Child Care Organisations (NCVCCO)
The umbrella organization for voluntary child care organizations.
Tel: 020 7833 3319
Web: www.ncvcco.org

The National Deaf Children's Society
Supports deaf children, their families, and professionals.
Tel: 0808 800 8880
Web: www.ndcs.org.uk

NHS Direct
National helpline that offers medical guidance.
Tel: 0845 4647
Web: www.nhsdirect.org.uk

NSPCC (National Society for the Prevention of Cruelty to Children)
Specializes in child protection and the prevention of cruelty.
Tel: 0808 800 5000
Web: www.nspcc.org.uk

Parentline Plus
Provides information and support to families.
Tel: 0808 800 2222
Web: www.parentlineplus.org.uk

Relate
Provides couple counselling for those with relationship problems.
Tel: 0845 456 1310
Web: www.relate.org.uk

RNIB (Royal National Institute of the Blind)
Offers information, support, and advice to people with sight loss.
Tel: 0845 766 9999
Web: www.rnib.org.uk

Sense
For those children who are deafblind or have associated disabilities.
Tel: 0845 127 0060
Web: www.sense.org.uk

Talking Point
A website about speech and language development.
Tel: 020 7674 2799
Web: www.ican.org.uk

TAMBA (The Twin and Multiple Birth Association)
Provides support for families of twins, triplets, and more.
Tel: 0800 138 0509
Web: www.tamba.org.uk

Winston's Wish
Helps bereaved children and young people rebuild their lives.
Tel: 08452 03 04 05
Web: www.winstonswish.org.uk

Young Minds
Is concerned with the mental health of children and young people.
Tel: 0800 018 2138
Web: www.youngminds.org.uk

Useful web resources

BBC Lifestyle
Parenting information online.
Web: www.bbc.co.uk/parenting/your_kids

Mumsnet
Offers a useful, fun, and supportive community for parents on the web.
Web: www.mumsnet.com

Parents Online
For parents by parents. Covers all aspects of parenting.
Web: www.parents.org.uk

Raising Children Network
An Australian parenting website.
Web: www.raisingchildren.net.au

Raising Kids
Offers support to anyone who is raising children of any age.
Web: www.raisingkids.co.uk

Zero to Three
An information resource that focuses on children aged 0–3 years.
Web: www.zerotothree.org

Index

"The most important thing is to find what sits with your own beliefs and what works for you and your child."

Acknowledgments

Tanya Byron's acknowledgments

My hugest thanks go to my best friend and business partner, Sam Richards, who made this book happen in many significant and spectacular ways.

Great thanks also to the fabulous Stephanie Jackson for bringing me into the DK stable and to the lovely Corinne Roberts who has steered this book so expertly, with her talented team – Emma Forge and Dawn Bates.

Especial thanks to the amazing Sarah Sutton who I enjoy working with each and every time and look forward to there being many more. Additionally a special thank you to Clinical Psychologist, Dr Sarah Gregory, who has provided invaluable research to enrich the text.

And, finally, my love and thanks for being the best to my husband Bruce and our gorgeous Lily and incredible Jack.

Publisher's acknowledgments

Production design **Tom Forge**
Proofreader **Andi Sisodia**
Indexer **Sue Bosanko**
Picture researcher **Myriam Megharbi and Romaine Werblow**
Photographer's assistants **Fanny Du Pont and Kate Malone**
Shoot assistant **Laura Green**
Medical and scientific illustrator **Philip Wilson**
Author photo page 9 © Jim Marks www.marks.co.uk

With special thanks to:

Esther Ripley and Dawn Bates for their expert editorial skills and Emma Forge for her expert design skills; KK; Katherine Howard of KHP; Emma Mauger; Jane Stanton; the parents who were willing to share their stories; and also to Doris Vivienne. Also to teachers, parents, and children of the Nursery Class at Collis Primary School, Middlesex, www.collis.richmond.sch.uk; and Kate at Kindertots, www.lekinderclub.com

Further reading

Ainsworth, M.D.S., Blehar, M.C., Waters, E. and Wall, S. (1978) *Patterns of Attachment: A psychological study of the strange situation,* Hillsdale NJ: Lawrence Erlbaum
Biddulph, Steve (2003) *Raising Boys,* London: Thorsons
Britton, Lesley (1992) *Montessori Play and Learn,* London: Vermilion
Byron, Dr Tanya (2005) *The House of Tiny Tearaways,* London: BBC Books
Byron, Dr Tanya (2007) *Your Child…Your Way,* London: Michael Joseph
Byron, Dr Tanya and Baveystock, Sacha (2003) *Little Angels,* London: BBC Books

Chess, Stella and Thomas, Alexander (1996) *Temperament: Theory and Practice,* New York: Brunner/Mazel
Einon, Dorothy (1998) *Child Behaviour,* London: Penguin Books
Faber, Adele and Mazlish, Elaine (2001) *How to Talk so Kids will Listen, and Listen so Kids will Talk,* London: Piccadilly Press
Flanagan, C. (1996) *Applying Psychology to Early Child Development,* London: Hodder and Stoughton
Gerhardt, Sue (2004) *Why Love Matters,* Hove: Routledge
Green, Dr Christopher (2006) *New Toddler Taming,* London: Vermilion
Parker, Jan and Stimson, Jan (1999) *Raising Happy Children,* London: Hodder & Stoughton
Reichlin, Gail and Winkler, Caroline (2001) *The Pocket Parent,* New York: Workman
Seldin, Tim (2007) *How to Raise an Amazing Child,* London: Dorling Kindersley
Siegel, D. (1999) *The Developing Mind,* New York: Siegel Press
Slater, Alan and Bremner, Gavin (2003) *An Introduction to Developmental Psychology,* Oxford: Blackwell Publishing
Smith, Peter K., Cowie, Helen and Blades, Mark (2003) *Understanding Children's Development* (4th edition), Oxford: Blackwell Publishing
Stoppard, Dr Miriam (2002) *Dr Miriam Stoppard's Family Health Guide,* London: Dorling Kindersley
Sunderland, Margot (2006) *The Science of Parenting,* London: Dorling Kindersley

Picture credits

The publisher would like to thank the following for their kind permission to reproduce their photographs:
(Key: a-above; b-below/bottom; c-centre; l-left; r-right; t-top)

40 Getty Images: Barros & Barros. **60 Getty Images:** Camille Tokerud. **90 Getty Images:** Erin Patrice O'Brien. **95 Bubbles. 100 Getty Images:** Gary Bryan. **126 Alamy Images:** Photofusion Picture Library (b). **196 Getty Images:** Seiya Kawamoto. **202 Getty Images:** Tara Moore. **207 Getty Images:** Maria Spann. **211 Getty Images:** Bill Sykes Images. **220 Alamy Images:** Leblond. **255 Getty Images:** Reggie Casagrande (t). **259 Alamy Images:** Felipe Rodriguez. **265 The Wellcome Institute Library, London:** Anthea Sieveking. **274 Getty Images:** Erik Soh. **294 John Birdsall Photo Library:** John Birdsall. **299 John Birdsall Photo Library:** John Birdsall. **303 Mother & Baby Picture Library:** Ian Hooton. **308 Getty Images:** Macduff Everton

Jacket images: *Front:* **Bubbles:** (main image); **jupiterimages:** Claudia Rehm br; author photo © Jim Marks www.marks.co.uk

All other images © Dorling Kindersley
For further information see: www.dkimages.com